'Mesmeris   ...
intelligent ...   n
from his si..., ...   in
insanity for the rest of his life are unforgettable.' *Telegraph*

'Des... the sad, upsetting nature of Nijinsky's story, Moore's
enjoy... e biography does a fine job of explaining not only who
Nijin... was, but – once you peel away the glitter – why he really
matte... d.' *Scotsman*

'C... lling, well-researched, timely and hugely enjoyable' *Spectator*

'Exce... nt' *The Times*

'She... er loses sight of why Nijinsky's art was so great. The result is
a ca... ting biography.' *Financial Times*

'Moc... a historian with a novelist's relish for human foibles.'
Sunda... mes

'His f... curtain was cruel, and Moore lowers the darkness with great
tender... s.' *Guardian*

'Highl... telligent, lucidly presented and consistently absorbing ...
a clear... objective picture of a tragically wounded genius.' Rupert
Christi... en, *Literary Review*

'Lucid... se ... The colour and the pain of an extraordinary life come
across... ily.' *BBC Music Magazine*

'Highl... idable and absorbing' *Lady*

LUCY ...ORE is a writer and broadcaster whose books include the best-
selling *Maharanis*. Her most recent book, *Anything Goes: A Biography of the
Roaring Twenties* was described by the *Sunday Times* as 'dazzling'.

ALSO BY LUCY MOORE

*The Thieves' Opera: The Remarkable Lives and Deaths of Jonathan Wild,
Thief-Taker, and Jack Sheppard, House-Breaker*

Con Men and Cutpurses: Scenes from the Hogarthian Underworld

Amphibious Thing: The Life of Lord Hervey

Maharanis: The Lives and Times of Three Generations of Indian Princesses

Liberty: The Lives and Times of Six Women in Revolutionary France

Anything Goes: A Biography of the Roaring Twenties

NIJINSKY

LUCY MOORE

PROFILE BOOKS

This paperback edition published in 2014

First published in Great Britain in 2013 by
Profile Books Ltd
3A Exmouth House
Pine Street
Exmouth Market
London EC1R 0JH
www.profilebooks.com

1 3 5 7 9 10 8 6 4 2

A CIP catalogue record for this book is available from the British Library.

ISBN: 978 1 84668 619 1
eISBN: 978 1 84765 828 9

Typeset in Iowan by MacGuru Ltd
info@macguru.org.uk

Printed and bound in Great Britain by
CPI Group (UK) Ltd, Croydon CR0 4YY

for Otto

'... yes, in spite of all,
Some shape of beauty moves away the pall
From our dark spirits.'

John Keats, *Endymion*, Book I

Contents

Author's note

MY SPELLING OF RUSSIAN PROPER NAMES is – I hope – an acceptable mixture of common usage (for example, Tchaikovsky or Massine) and a standard transliteration. At the turn of the twentieth century, a rouble was worth sixteen pence or seventy-six cents.

I have not included descriptions of every ballet in which Nijinsky appeared because I thought it would interrupt the narrative to have too many long technical passages; I only used those that seemed to me to have been important biographically as well as artistically. However, Nijinsky's first biographer, Richard Buckle, was scrupulous about this, so any reader who wants to learn about the more minor roles would enjoy his detailed account of Nijinsky's career.

There are some small controversies (for example, the issue of exactly who was present at the dinner and carriage ride after the premiere of *Le Sacre du printemps*) into which, again for the sake of the narrative, I have not delved too deeply, preferring instead to present what I think is the most likely version of events. In these cases the sources I used (or did not use) and notes for further reading appear in the footnotes.

Sketch of Nijinsky as the Rose by Valentine Hugo, *c.*1912.

The Premiere of *Le Sacre du printemps*

29 May 1913, Théâtre des Champs-Elysées, Paris

FOR ONCE ON A FIRST NIGHT he was backstage in his practice clothes, rather than in his dressing room trying to ignore the throng of admirers while he put on his costume and made up his face. He wore a full white crêpe de Chine shirt and narrow black trousers, buttoned down the calves. It was the first interval and the audience was restive, shifting and murmuring. *Les Sylphides*, their opening piece, had received the usual rapturous applause.

The dancers moved loosely around him, some warming up, some pretending nonchalance, a few grouped together, whispering. He avoided eye contact with them, but then he usually preferred not to look directly at people. Their brightly coloured costumes were heavy and unwieldy and the men had complained about their false beards. Some crossed themselves, lips moving silently. Like all experienced performers, he recognised how important the backstage mood would be for the success of his debut. On a first night, doubts in the wings, as his sister would observe, can lead to catastrophe. If only she were dancing the role he had conceived for her.

Most of them, he knew, disliked the ballet he had created, could not understand what he was asking of them or what he wanted to achieve. That was partly his fault: movement was his medium of communication, not words. The dancers resented being ordered brusquely to move exactly as he instructed them, without any opportunity for interpreting their roles at all. The shuffling steps, flat-footed jumps, clenched hands, hunched shoulders and unsynchronised, deliberately primitive choreography seemed to them ugly and painful. He knew they asked themselves what ballet was for, if beauty and grace had been removed. It was a question he asked himself.

At least the theatre was packed, despite the fact that they had charged double the normal ticket price. For the past four years, all Paris had been obsessed by the Ballets Russes and by him, its star, Nijinsky – the young savage. Tonight, an unseasonably warm evening at the end of May, they were to premiere a daring new ballet billed as being created by three poets: Igor Stravinsky, its thoroughly modern composer; Nicholas Roerich, a distinguished student of pre-historical, pagan Russia, its set designer; and Nijinsky, its brilliant twenty-four-year-old choreographer. Although it was rumoured that their charming but ruthless impresario, Sergey Diaghilev, was not above giving away tickets to ensure a full house, the thought of empty seats on such a night was inconceivable.

Through the peephole in the curtain he could see his mother in the front row (her usual seat; her one evening dress), and then all around her the city's cultural and social elite. The diamonds on the bosoms and the bare, white arms of chic ladies from the grand *arrondissements* – the sort whose parties dapper little Monsieur Proust (his *Du côté de chez Swann* would come out in six months' time) schemed to get invited to – glittered alongside the soft jackets worn by self-proclaimed aesthetes, writers and artists, who scorned formal evening wear as bourgeois trappings of an outdated society, considering themselves guardians of the new wave. Igor in his element, four rows from the front, nervously anticipating the applause; glamorous Misia Sert, fanning herself against the heat, waiting for Diaghilev to join her in the box she had booked for every night of their season. Many of them were friends and acquaintances, here to defend their bold new work. The grandees, he knew, were here to be shocked by it.

Aware that some of the audience might find the new material

disturbing, Sergey Pavlovich had constructed the rest of the programme to pander to potential critics. The show had opened with the moon-lit elegance of Chopin and tulle skirts and would progress, after their premiere, to the ethereal romance of *Le Spectre de la Rose* – his virtuoso role, the one that made audiences gasp, and the only part he would be dancing tonight – before concluding with the wild, warlike Tatar dances from the opera *Prince Igor*. Only *Le Sacre du printemps* could possibly be seen as controversial.

This was the Ballets Russes' third performance at the brand-new Théâtre des Champs-Elysées and he should have been encouraged by the knowledge that it was his image, alongside that of Isadora Duncan, that had inspired the decorative bas-reliefs on the exterior, almost leaping out of the marble into the air. All things considered, the dress rehearsal had gone well (as it ought to have done, after the nearly one hundred expensive practice sessions he had insisted upon) and that morning an early notice in *Le Figaro* had raved about the ballet's dazzling modernity. His sister Bronia thought he was calm, waiting to be judged but confident his art would not be found wanting.

But the nerves would not be silenced. Relentlessly they bubbled up into his throat. *L'Après-midi d'un faune*, his first composition, premiered the previous year, in which he played the faun, had caused such a scandal that the onanistic ending had to be altered for subsequent performances. Only two weeks earlier at the Théâtre des Champs-Elysées' grand opening, *Jeux*, the second ballet he had choreographed, had been greeted with hisses and derisive laughter. Despite its score by Debussy, the setting by Léon Bakst of a garden at dusk, and Nijinsky himself in the lead role, its slight premise – two girls and a boy in modern tennis clothes flirting with one another – had not impressed. *Jeux* had been dismissed as immature and ugly. Beneath his arms, the thin silk of his shirt was already wet through.

He knew that, in private, Sergey had begun to lose faith, to doubt the wisdom of entrusting all the Ballets Russes' choreography to his young protégé. Of late all he could see when he looked at him was dyed hair, false teeth and an oily smile. Their arguments were a measure of the stresses under which their relationship – professionally and personally – was labouring. Over the past few months, Sergey had insisted more and more vehemently that although a painting or a piece of music might be misunderstood at first, even remain unappreciated for many years, and yet still be considered a true work of art, a ballet must be well received by the public or it would be doomed to obscurity: it must sell tickets. This was his first major work. It had to succeed.

But why shouldn't it? Igor was, perhaps, no stranger to controversy, but he was acclaimed as the greatest young composer of the twentieth century. *L'Oiseau de feu* and *Petrushka* were dazzling ballets, even without him dancing them. Roerich – he had nicknamed him the Professor – had created a wild and primitive world in which their sacred mystery would be enacted, a tree-studded hill on a lush, green plain. Most importantly, Sergey had trusted them with this work, placing his faith and experience in their united talents. Between them they were creating a revolutionary, entirely modern form of ballet, stripped of the tinselled artifice of previous generations.

And, as he told himself, he was the greatest dancer of his age – the greatest dancer and, God willing, the greatest choreographer. An artist, as well as a performer. Over and again the public had proclaimed him the god of the dance; Sergey had annointed him the prophet of ballet's future. One day, perhaps even tonight, with this ballet, the power and beauty of his work would prove all the critics wrong.

The *chef de la scène* banged his stick hard on the floor three times, a signal for all non-performers to clear the stage. That girl was here again, her blue eyes soaking everything up from behind the Baron de Günzburg's shoulder, looking – he knew – for him. He would not think about that now. Reluctantly – or was he imagining it? – the dancers moved to their places, their make-up already softening beneath the hot lights.

He saw Diaghilev standing in his usual spot, solemn and magnificent, his expression revealing nothing, scanning the stage to ensure everyone was in the correct position before he gave the sign for the curtain to be raised. He had given orders that whatever happened they must not stop dancing. The white streak in his brilliantine hair echoed the starched white shirt-front standing out against his black tailcoat; the almond-blossom scent of his hair-wax hung in the air, an overpowering waft of stale aftershave.

Outside in the pit, he knew, the conductor would be standing before the orchestra with his still arms upraised. Vaslav Nijinsky, possibly the greatest genius of twentieth-century dance, drew in a deep breath, closed his eyes, and waited for the music to begin.

CHAPTER I

Yaponchik
1889–1905

ONE LOST NIGHT IN PARIS in the mid-1920s, Alabama Knight, the discontented heroine of Zelda Fitzgerald's autobiographical novel *Save Me the Waltz*, finds herself at the Théâtre du Châtelet where Diaghilev's Ballets Russes are playing. After the performance, spellbound, she is introduced to 'a woman with a shaved head and the big ears of a gargoyle ... [parading] a Mexican hairless [Chihuahua] through the lobby'. This woman, she is told, had once been a ballerina.

'How did you get in the ballet?' Alabama asks breathlessly, her heart suddenly set on becoming a dancer. The woman seems almost confused by the question: the answer is so simple. One has to imagine a gravelly émigré accent and a sense of surprised finality about her reply. 'But I was born in the ballet.'

This was the case with the majority of Russian dancers at the start of the twentieth century and of no one could it be said with more accuracy than Vaslav Fomich Nijinsky,* acclaimed as the *dieu de la danse*, whose parents were both gifted professional dancers and whose childhood

---

* 'Vaslav' is pronounced 'Vatslav', hence his family nickname Vatsa; Fomich is his patronymic, indicating that he is the son of Foma, or Thomas. The Polish spelling of his name is Wacław Nizynski.

was largely spent in and around theatres. He may not actually have been born in a dressing room, like his venerable ballet master, Enrico Cecchetti, or during a performance, like his sister (their mother went into labour while dancing a polonaise at the Opera Theatre in Minsk, dashed off to a nearby hospital after arranging for an extra to take her place on stage and gave birth to Bronislava before the final curtain fell), but he might as well have been.

As Bronislava, or Bronia, would write of their early years, 'We were born artists of the dance. We accepted without question our birthright from our parents – our dancing bodies. The theatre and the dance were a natural way of life for us from birth. It was as if, in the theatre, we were in our natural element, where everything responded in our souls.'

Neither of the Nijinsky parents – Foma (Thomas) and Eleonora, née Bereda – came from theatrical families. Foma was born in Warsaw in 1862. His grandfather, father and brother were activists, devoted to the cause of liberating Poland from Russian rule, but although he was a proud patriot Foma knew from childhood that his fate did not lie in politics. At eight he began attending the Wielki Theatre School at the Warsaw State Theatre.

In 1870, when Foma began his career there, fourteen-year-old Eleonora Bereda had already left the Wielki School. Her father, a Warsaw cabinet-maker, had died when she was seven, after his compulsive gambling bankrupted their family – and her mother had died days later. She and her nine-year-old sister Stephanie began attending classes in secret at the Theatre School and, defying the disapproval of their elder siblings who thought a career on the stage was not respectable, were soon contributing to the household expenses by performing in ballets and operas. At fourteen Eleonora, chaperoned by her two elder sisters, had been working for two years as part of the *corps de ballet* of a small company touring provincial Russia's thriving theatres.

Like Eleonora, Foma worked as a migrant dancer after leaving the Wielki School. Higher wages compensated for the insecurity and questionable status of this type of work, for despite his talents as dancer and choreographer, headstrong Foma recognised that he lacked the patience and diplomacy to progress steadily through the *corps* of the great state-funded theatres of Moscow or St Petersburg, as a civil servant in the Tsar's employ, to the coveted ranks of *premier danseur* and, ultimately, ballet-master.

The two young dancers met and fell in love in Odessa in 1882. Eleonora was five years older than Foma and at first she was reluctant to commit to him. After two years' passionate courtship she relented and they were married in Baku on the Caspian Sea, the capital of modern Azerbaijan. Two years later their first child, Stanislas, was born on a return trip to the Caucasus; Vaslav followed on 12 March 1889 in Kiev; and Bronia made her dramatic entrance in Minsk in 1891.

Although Eleonora had not planned to have so many children, nor so quickly (a family made a carefree, itinerant life with Foma and, indeed, her own career, increasingly untenable), according to Bronia the first years of her parents' marriage were happy ones, united by love and a shared devotion to their art. Certainly they were picturesque. In her memoirs, Bronia describes travelling the length and breadth of Russia, galloping through the Caucasus along the Georgian Military Highway from Vladikavkaz to Tbilisi as fast as possible to avoid being ambushed by brigands in the narrow passes between the mountains, or steaming down the Volga at dusk, lulled to sleep in violet light by sailors singing along to the music of balalaikas playing on the banks and the gentle splashing of the river against the sides of the boat. Bronia remembered her father one afternoon bringing home Caucasian-style Turkish delight, stuffed with almonds and delicately flower-scented; try though she might, for the rest of her life, nothing else ever tasted as good. For a long time her bed was the family's travelling trunk filled with blankets, its top wedged open.

Dance and the theatre were at the centre of the Nijinsky family's life. In 1893, when Vaslav was four, they lived in a *dacha* beside Kiev's Summer Theatre, where Foma and Eleonora were engaged for the season, on Trukhanov Island, across the Dnieper from the city. The children's nanny would sometimes take them out secretly after bedtime, while Foma and Eleonora performed, and they would tiptoe to the theatre through illuminated gardens, where the muffled strains of the orchestra could be heard, and into the stage door. Bronia would always remember being dazzled by the 'fairy-tale lights' and Vaslav told her, years later, 'of his delight in that mysterious night walk and how he used to run in front of everyone to see the lights of the many coloured paper lanterns, hanging on so many chains in so many directions'.

In an interview given in 1912, Vaslav couldn't recall when his formal dance training began – 'My parents considered it as natural to teach me to dance as to walk and talk. Even my mother who, of course, could recall my first tooth, couldn't say just exactly when my first lesson was' – but he and his elder brother Stanislas, or Stassik, joined in the classes both his parents gave society children in ballroom-dancing – waltzes, polkas, quadrilles and Russian country dances – and also in the informal ballet lessons Foma gave the children of other artists.

Other performers, friends of the family, were happy to share their knowledge, too. Three-year-old Bronia and five-year-old Vaslav persuaded Jackson and Johnson, two young African-American music-hall artists who performed to a ragtime soundtrack in top hats and white satin tailcoats with black lapels, to teach them to tap-dance – something absolutely forbidden in the tradition of classical dance because it was thought to weaken the knees and ankles. And there was much to be learned just by watching Foma rehearse his small company or befriending the gypsies in their jangling, colourful costumes, who passed by every now and then leading strings of gleaming ponies, singing and dancing along the way. Years later, Vaslav would thrill his family by imitating these 'wild, fierce, savage' gypsy girls, 'trembling all over from the tips of his fingers to his toes, shaking his shoulders as if they were independent of the rest of his body'.

Vaslav performed in public for the first time in Odessa at Easter 1894, when he was just five. He and Stassik danced the *hopak*, a Cossack dance, with Stassik, wearing blue pantaloons, a loose white blouse and a broad red sash, playing the boy, and Vaslav, in an embroidered Ukrainian dress and a garland of poppies, cornflowers and ribbons on his head, the girl. Both wore knee-high boots of soft red leather and a touch of rouge, applied by Eleonora with her hare's foot. 'With his slightly dark skin, big brown eyes, and long fluffy eyelashes, it was impossible to tell that he was a boy,' recalled Bronia. The audience loved their performance with its jumps, whirling turns, low squats and high leg lifts. 'To the shouts of "Bravo" and "Bis," they had to repeat their performance once, and then again.'

By the time Vaslav performed again, at Christmas the same year, Foma had begun regularly teaching the boys the positions and first steps of classical ballet as well as rehearsing them in folk dances like the Cossack *hopak* and the *mazurka*. For this performance Vaslav was elevated to dancing the *hopak* as a solo, wearing Stassik's outfit from six months earlier. 'How high he jumped, throwing his legs from side to side and touching the heels of his boots with his hands, striking his heels together, crouching down to dance the *prisyadka* [literally translated as 'squat', the most famous element in Russian folk dancing], flinging his legs forward faster and faster, and finishing by whirling around in a spinning *prisyatka* close to the ground! Father was so pleased with Vatsa. He said later that not every adult dancer could manage all those difficult stunts of the *hopak*.'

The three young Nijinskys then performed a sailor dance and finally, along with some other children, a Chinese dance (though Bronia commented that it only remotely resembled anything Chinese). Vaslav, as a comical old man, stole the show, taking several curtain calls on his own. It was this that Vaslav would remember with pride as his 'first appearance in public'.

Despite Vaslav's early theatrical triumphs, life on the road could be hard and Foma and Eleonora struggled to hold their young family together. Tsar Alexander III's death in October 1894 closed every Russian theatre for a period of official mourning and even private dancing lessons, usually a lucrative source of income, were seen as improper while the nation grieved. 'Throughout our childhood this would happen,' wrote Bronia, 'one day prosperity, the next anxiety.' Increasingly, over the coming years, anxiety would predominate.

Accidents and ill-health – the constant nearness of death – were one source of this anxiety. Eleonora had been orphaned at seven; she was always afraid for her children and with reason. When Stassik was two and a half, he climbed up onto the window ledge of their rented Moscow apartment to watch a military band pass by and fell three storeys onto the cobbled street below. He was unconscious for three days and, although he recovered physically, gradually it became clear that his mental development had ceased after the accident.

A few years later, Vaslav contracted scarlet fever and diphtheria simultaneously and the doctors feared he would not survive; in 1897 Bronia and Stassik made miraculous recoveries from typhoid. Five years later, sixteen-year-old Stassik, who had never recovered from his fall as a toddler, was placed in a psychiatric hospital because Eleonora could no longer control his rages at home. Nineteenth-century mental institutions were not known for treating their inmates with compassion and the knowledge of where Stassik was and what had happened to him left its scars on Eleonora, Bronia and Vaslav, too.

Financially there were always worries. One month Foma and Eleonora could afford a clean, comfortable apartment with a nanny to look after the children while they danced in a glittering *belle époque* theatre; weeks later and thousands of miles away they would be forced to leave the children alone in cold rooms bleakly lit by paraffin lamps to perform alongside clowns and trained animals to make enough money to feed the family. Jobs could be cancelled at a moment's notice and injury was a constant threat. When Foma broke his leg, no money came in until he could dance again. There was never any possibility of saving for the future; survival was their only concern. The Nijinskys were by no means unusual in coping with such grave anxieties – these were the ordinary trials of the late nineteenth century, the dull hum of despair that throbbed beneath daily life for the vast majority of people – but they touched Vaslav's childhood with a sense of struggle against an uncaring universe that would linger with him for the rest of his life.

When times were good, Foma and Eleonora worked with the greatest dancers of their day – Maria Giuri, Virginia Zucchi, Carlotta Brianza, Enrico Cecchetti – and, although they were never employed by the legendary Imperial Theatre in St Petersburg, they did perform at the theatre attached to the tsar's summer palace in Krasnoye Selo, just outside St Petersburg. When times were bad, they took roles wherever they could – as dancers in light opera and musicals, in *café-chantants* and, most frequently, as part of circuses.

Though being a circus performer was very far from being a *premier danseur*, the highest rank at the Imperial Theatres, the work had its attractions. Foma liked theatre-circuses like the one in Nizhny Novgorod because they allowed him to stage spectacular pantomime ballets on a grander scale than in an ordinary theatre; the children liked the clowns. Watching them, Vaslav quickly learned to juggle, turn cartwheels and walk on his hands. In 1896, Foma accepted a summer engagement in Vilno with Salamonsky's Circus and Vaslav and Bronia were taken on as performers in one of the animal acts. Vaslav played a heroic chimney sweep, who assisted an animal fire brigade in rescuing more animals from a small burning house. He and Bronia were overjoyed at being 'artists' in their own right and Bronia noticed that every evening after his performance, Vatsa, as she called him, would be unusually quiet, thinking about what he could improve upon the next day.

In his wonderful 1975 album of Nijinsky images, *Nijinsky Dancing*, Lincoln Kirstein emphasises the importance of Vaslav's early exposure to the circus, arguing that it gave him a broader vocabulary of mime and mimicry than the limited repertoire taught in the traditions of classical ballet, as well as fostering in him a powerful sense of sympathy for the underdog and a love of the surreal, the satirical and the absurd. Like Charlie Chaplin, who grew up in the parallel world of the music hall, the adult Nijinsky was a master at the art of communicating pretension and status – and sending them up – with the smallest of gestures.

As a man Vaslav would make no secret of his unwillingness to perform alongside circus acts and remembered feeling physical pain at the idea of his mother having to degrade herself by taking circus work, but the very strength of his later feeling shows the power of its early impact on him, positive as well as negative. For all his later successes, he, like Chaplin, never stopped seeing himself as an outsider: a shivering little boy with his nose pressed up against a window-pane, looking in at a world of warmth and security of which he could never feel a part.

As the years went by, one argument recurred over and again, prompted by Eleonora's desire to settle in one place so that the children could begin their schooling and Foma's competing urge to keep moving and resentment of the family that tied him to jobs he didn't want to take. By the mid-1890s he had fallen in love with another young dancer in their company. During their engagement at the summer theatres outside St Petersburg in 1897, after many anguished nights of discussion inevitably overheard by their frightened children, Foma and Eleonora decided to separate. They agreed that when the season ended, Eleonora would take Stassik, Vaslav and Bronia, then aged eleven, eight and five, to live in St Petersburg, while Foma accepted an engagement in Moscow, where he would live with his mistress.

Each of the children, Bronia recalled, was deeply affected by the impending separation from their father, but Vaslav reacted to it differently from his brother and sister, defending his mother violently and behaving with stormy recklessness and disobedience towards Foma. As the day of their parting drew near, Vaslav could hardly bear even to look at him. 'It was as if he were throwing him out of his heart.'

Eleonora had never lived in St Petersburg and she had no family and few friends there but she had chosen it for a single reason that eclipsed every other concern: the Imperial Theatre School. Each year, the school received thousands of written applications for fewer than twenty places on offer. Acceptance into the school meant the one thing Eleonora longed to give her children: an assured future. From the age of eleven onwards, the state – or rather the Tsar – assumed responsibility for all the students' expenses. When they graduated in their late teens they were almost certain to become Artists of the Imperial Theatres with a place in the *corps de ballet* of the Mariinsky Theatre, a government position which was equivalent to that of a junior civil servant, and they would be obliged to remain with the Mariinsky for five years after graduation. If the young dancer demonstrated enough special talent to become a soloist, greater rewards were guaranteed: recognised status in society and, on retirement, a generous pension.

The reigning *prima ballerina assoluta* of the day, Mathilde Kshesin-skaya, epitomised the *demi-mondaine* heights a dancer could scale: she had seduced the young Nicholas II before he ascended the throne and then become the richly rewarded mistress of two of the Tsar's cousins, bearing a son who was never quite sure which of the imposing Grand Dukes who visited his mother was his father. Isadora Duncan disin-genuously described Kshesinskaya as 'a charming little lady, wrapped in sables, with diamonds hanging from her ears and her neck circled in pearls'; in fact the dazzling jewels only served to emphasise her steely ambition and hunger for the spotlight.

In August 1898, Vaslav was one of the three hundred nine-year-olds – one hundred boys and two hundred girls – invited to the school to audition for entry that September. Just ensuring his presence at the audition had required Eleonora to pull every string she could, but her connections were impeccable: she had worked with Enrico Cecchetti, head of the Girls' School, and his Polish assistant, Stanislav Gillert, was a friend. Gillert had told Sergey Legat, one of the Boys' School instruc-tors, about Vaslav. And though neither Eleonora nor Foma had per-formed at the Imperial Theatres, their careers would have been known to their peers. At least one or two of the twenty-five examiners would have been looking out for Foma and Eleonora Nijinsky's son.

The Imperial Theatre School was housed in a magnificent ochre-plastered, marble-pilastered building that extended over an entire block abutting the Alexandrinsky Theatre where the students of its drama sec-tion would one day go on to perform. Eleonora had dressed Vaslav as if for a wedding in an expensive blue sailor suit, black patent pumps and a hat – of which Vaslav was inordinately proud – with the word 'RUS-SIA' spelled out in gold letters on a dark blue ribbon. Bronia, with the prospect of her own audition for the school two years ahead of her, was the most eager and enthusiastic of audiences.

'Before leaving the house, Vatsa had to show Mama one more time how he would bow to everyone at the examination, as she had taught him: "Draw your feet together, then, without bending your back, bow your head low and hold your arms in line with the seams of your trousers. Smile so you will look pleasant. And don't you dare play any pranks there."

'We all looked at Vaslav, and I thought he was the most handsome boy with his dark brown hair … his long, thick, black eyelashes … his high cheekbones. His face was radiant, his expressive, slanted, dark brown eyes sparkled with excitement, and his almond-shaped teeth flashed in spontaneous smiles. Then Mama crossed herself and blessed Vaslav, and we were ready to go.'

Eleonora and Bronia waited in one of the ballet school's large, light practice rooms while Vaslav went off with the other boys for his examination. The candidates were watched closely while they walked, ran and jumped for the assembled instructors, artists and directors. Even in this pressurised environment Vaslav shone; he reported back to his mother and Bronia that when they saw him jump, the inspectors 'praised me very much'. Next, the boys' insteps and the turn-out of their hips and legs were inspected. Successful applicants would be handsome and well built, obviously, but other specialised qualities were considered essential for potential classical dancers: straight knees, arched feet, flexible, open hips and shoulder blades that lay flat against the back.

Most were dismissed at this stage, and then in the infirmary the few remaining boys stripped while doctors examined their hearts, lungs and joints. Finally their eyesight and hearing were tested: the instructors whispered to them through a closed door, an approximation of the stage whispers they would have to learn to decipher. Three more applicants were dropped as unsuitable, but Vaslav's was one of the names read out as having received a place for a preliminary trial year at the school. If the chosen boys showed progress in Dance and General Subjects they would be formally enrolled as students the following year.

In May 1899, at the end of this first year, Vaslav was officially admitted to the Imperial Theatre School and the following year, aged eleven, he became one of six boarding students in his year, winning a prestigious Didelot Scholarship which would fund his academic career. Although life at the school was austere and rigorous in its total dedication to ballet, the students were considered an elite and treated as such. Every boy was given six sets of linen underwear, practice clothes and shoes and a blue woollen dress suit with a high velvet collar embroidered with silver lyres, the school's insignia. Outside the school they wore military-style peaked caps and, in winter, double-breasted coats with astrakhan collars, silver buttons and scarlet silk linings. The female students wore brown cashmere day dresses – with pink dresses given out as coveted marks of distinction for the juniors and white for seniors.

Inside the school's vast, temple-like premises, the future stars of the Mariinsky Theatre, fewer than twenty boys and girls in each year, lived in almost total seclusion in a world centred around realising their potential for the delight of the Imperial family and the court. No expense was spared in funding this lavish enterprise: the state spent two million gold roubles a year to ensure its brilliance. The ground floor of the school housed the Mariinsky's make-up, wardrobe, set and administrative departments. On the first and second floors, vast practice rooms with sloping floors that replicated the slant of the Mariinsky's stage were lined with mirrors and windows and punctuated by portraits of ballet-loving tsars and tsarinas. Inside the compound were separate dormitories, classrooms and infirmaries for the boys and girls, a bathhouse, even a church. Naturally, the students had their own chiropodist.

At half past seven every morning the boys were woken by a brass bell and the heavy green curtains of their dormitory window were drawn back by a servant. After washing with cold water, they breakfasted on bread and tea before walking around the block as a warm-up and then beginning their ballet lesson, the focal point of the day. Lunch was at twelve, followed by academic classes (never Nijinsky's strong point; he was always behind in his lessons), dinner at five, more classes – this time in specialised areas like music, ballroom dancing, character dance, fencing and gymnastics – supper at nine and then bed. Once a week they filed through a series of ever-smaller courtyards to a tiny wooden bathhouse which, lit up on winter evenings, looked as though it belonged in a forest in a fairy tale, and lay inside it on wooden benches with steam billowing around them while they were scrubbed until they were pink.

The teachers at the Imperial Theatre School – dancers, actors and choreographers – were the best in the world: the octogenarian Frenchman Marius Petipa, celebrated for his good taste and the elegance of his style; Pavel Gerdt, the great character dancer; tall, lean Christian Johansson, who always carried a violin under one arm and led what was known as 'the class of perfection', which aimed to transform the senior students from dancers into artists. His line of teaching stretched directly back through the Bournonvilles *père et fils*, Maximilien Gardel and Auguste Vestris to Jean-Georges Noverre, Marie Antoinette's *maître des ballets*. Enrico Cecchetti represented the newer Italian style of ballet, athletic and highly technical, which had produced the most celebrated dancers of the late nineteenth century.

From his first year at the school, Vaslav attracted his teachers' attention. He was a particular favourite of Sergey Legat, the younger of two brothers who were both soloists at the Mariinsky and instructors at the school, as well as the lover of Marius Petipa's fiery daughter Marie (this was a very small world); and of Mikhail Obukhov, who early on singled him out for individual lessons and throughout his years at the school gently encouraged him to realise his potential. 'The little devil never comes down [from a jump] with the music,' Obukhov said to Tamara Karsavina, the first time she watched Nijinsky in a class.

Despite these mentors, Vaslav's introduction to the school was not easy. Not until the summer holidays after his first year did he confess to Bronia that he was being bullied. He told her his classmates pushed him and provoked him, and said things like, 'Are you a girl, to dance so well?'. But according to one of his fellow students, the reality was much worse. As a Pole, with a strong accent, and notably poorer than the others, he was despised by his peers, ignored in all the school games and 'made to feel inferior at every turn'. They ordered him about, scorned him and sneered at him; no one would sit at his desk or share their lunch with him. To these insults Vaslav – or *Yaponchik* (Little Jap), as they called him, because of his slanted, Tatar eyes – responded with dogged perseverance.

Most galling for his tormentors was his quite evidently exceptional talent. Throughout their schooling, his rivals bubbled with 'anger and jealousy' about Vaslav and in their first year as boarders engineered a trick that very nearly killed him. Three boys challenged Vaslav, who could jump further than any of them – over seven benches – to prove how high he could leap, and they set up a tall, solid music stand in the centre of the room for him to jump over. While Vaslav wasn't looking they raised it even higher and then rubbed soap on the floor in front of it, where he would take off. Going full pelt, he slipped and crashed into the stand and collapsed onto the floor; the boys who had been egging him on fled the room, leaving him lying there alone and unconscious. He lay in a coma for five days – later he remembered seeing death while he was in hospital – and even when he came to, the great fear of internal bleeding, remained. Without X-rays there was nothing to be done but wait. Gradually he recovered his strength and rejoined his class after recuperating over the long summer break.

After this his classmates, chastened by what they had done, seem to have begun treating him better. Vaslav learned that their admiration could be gained through naughtiness ('I played a lot of pranks, and the boys liked me for it'), and because he was strong, a good fighter and had perfect aim he was always getting himself into trouble – for example, being the only one blamed when all the boys went through a craze of lashing each other with leather belts after lights out.

Although Vaslav excelled in Dance, Music and Drawing he couldn't be bothered with academic subjects. None of his classmates thought French would ever be any use to them – according to a student a few years ahead of Nijinsky, they all considered it an 'unnecessary torment' – and Vaslav only managed to pass because the other boys would whisper the answers to him and the teacher preferred to let him scrape through rather than expose his own shortcomings as an instructor. In vain did the school provide him with private elocution lessons to soften his Polish accent.

One of the responsibilities and privileges of being a student at the Imperial Theatre School was playing small parts in productions at the

Mariinsky (ballet and opera) and Alexandrinsky (drama) Theatres. The young artists were taken to the theatre in a coach and paid 60 kopeks for an evening's work but, although Vaslav was saving up for a mandolin from the wages he received for playing a mouse in *The Nutcracker* and a page in *Swan Lake*, the real importance of these appearances was far greater than the excitement of staying up late and receiving a salary. The school's daily training sessions were physically gruelling and often relentlessly boring, involving hours of repetitions; they were something to be endured rather than enjoyed. These performances kept the students inspired, giving them the chance to see at close hand what they were working so hard to achieve. When he was barely in his teens, Vaslav found himself on stage beside the most celebrated artists of his day: the great bass, Fyodor Chaliapin; the *prima ballerina assoluta*, Mathilde Kshesinskaya; and gracefully etiolated Anna Pavlova, the Imperial Ballet's unconventional rising star.

The theatre exerts its own special magic – the 'red and gold disease' to which Jean Cocteau famously described himself succumbing. All his life Alexandre Benois, whose maternal grandfather had designed the Mariinsky, would remember the intoxicating smell of the gas-lamps as he entered its foyer. Prince Peter Lieven described driving up to the theatre as a child with the carriage wheels crunching over the snow, seeing the attendant in gold braid and white stockings waiting to help him out of the coach, and then the special 'hot-house' smell inside. The three main state-funded theatres in St Petersburg blazed white and gold, with blue brocade on the Mariinsky walls, egg-yolk yellow on the Alexandrinsky's and crimson in the Mikhailovsky.

But while audiences experience the public face of a theatre – the crystal and gilt opulence of the vast public spaces, the luxury of the red velvet seats and the buzzing, glittering crowd all around them – performers are in thrall to quite a different spell. When the young Rudolf Nureyev's sister was studying theatre, she sometimes used to bring home costumes for him to look at. 'That to me was heaven,' Nureyev remembered. 'I would spread them out on the bed and gaze at them – gaze at them so intensely that I could feel myself actually inside them.

I would fondle them for hours, smooth them and smell them. There is no other word for it – I was like a dope addict.'

As a student Tamara Karsavina, who entered the Girls' School four years before Vaslav, learned to love rehearsing out of hours, when the theatre was dark and empty, the chandeliers shrouded in dust sheets and brown holland covers over the seats. 'The theatre in its unguarded moments, curtain up, stage abandoned, and lights lowered, has a strange poignancy,' she wrote. 'The faint ghostliness of it touches a vulnerable spot of incurable sentimentality, a professional disease of those bred in the artificial emotions of the footlights.'

Karsavina was one of several of Vaslav's contemporaries who came from a similarly theatrical background. Her grandfather had been a provincial actor and playwright and her father, Platon Karsavin, had been a great dancer and a teacher at the Imperial Theatre School; Pavel Gerdt, a legendary character dancer and one of the teachers at the school, was her godfather. Kshesinskaya's father and brother were dancers in the Imperial Theatre. Léonide Massine, six years Nijinsky's junior, was the son of a French horn-player in Moscow's Bolshoy Orchestra. Lydia Lopokova's father was a lowly usher at the Alexandrinsky – perhaps the very man the young Prince Lieven remembered waiting to assist him up the stairs – but he got four of his five children into the Imperial Theatre School and Fyodor, Lydia's brother, went on to become *maître de ballet* at the Mariinsky. The theatre was in their blood.

In 1903 Vaslav narrowly avoided being expelled from the school. Since his accident three years earlier he had learned to get along with the boys in his class but they still encouraged him to perform wildly dangerous pranks. One day he and some others were on their way to the theatre for a matinee performance, covertly hitting lampposts and trees with their slingshots out of the carriage window. As they turned into St Isaac's Square, one of their darts hit (but did not knock off) a top hat on a passing gentleman's head. It was unfortunate for Vaslav that this gentleman was a government official. He went to the school's Director and demanded that the guilty boy be expelled.

It was hard to determine who the guilty boy was – there had been two carriages filled with boys, most of them carrying slingshots – but his classmates encouraged Vaslav to confess on the grounds that he was such a good dancer they would never expel him. Questioning revealed that Vaslav was considered the best shot at school and his past years of poor academic work, bad conduct, regular disciplining and warnings sent home to Eleonora sealed his fate. Initially he was expelled but, after hearing arguments from Eleonora, Vaslav's tutors and the offended official, whom Eleonora had persuaded to relent, the school's Director agreed to suspend him for two weeks and then allow him back as a non-resident, returning all the clothes and books with which the school had supplied him – a terrible humiliation and a heavy burden on Eleonora, who would have to pay to outfit Vaslav herself. This was granted only on condition that while he was at home Eleonora would birch him, which she forced herself to do. It was a turning point. From the moment he was reinstated as a boarder a month later, having 'felt a great pain in my soul' to have caused his mother such distress and jeopardised his future, Vaslav devoted himself to achieving his potential.

After the annual examinations that took place the following spring, Bronia, by then a student at the school herself, first heard her fifteen-year-old brother being talked about as a future star. Mikhail Fokine, one of the instructors at the Girls' School, rushed into class late, coming straight up to Bronia where she stood at the bar in her blue serge practice dress. 'You have such a brother that I must congratulate you!' It was almost unheard of for a teacher to talk about a student in front of other students, but Fokine could not control his raptures. 'For Nijinsky today we should have come up with a new grade. If anybody had suggested it, I would have given a 20 or even a 30 [the highest mark was 12]. He surpassed anything we have seen.' Fokine said that Vaslav had danced as part of a group and was then asked to dance his role alone. When he had finished, the examining board (comprising the Director, Vladimir Telyakovsky, and all the instructors) had burst into spontaneous applause. 'I'm late because we could not leave right away; we were all talking about Nijinsky. A great future awaits your brother.'

Nikolay Legat, another teacher present that day, agreed with Fokine's assessment. Vaslav possessed a rare otherworldly quality. While remaining totally natural, he was somehow transformed when he danced: 'exalted, vibrant, free and so ecstatic'. Far more than mere technical brilliance – that marvellous jump, during which he appeared to be suspended in the air – even at school Nijinsky seemed to belong 'to a plane above ours' which he could only make his audience understand through dance. This elusive quality, possessed so abundantly by Nijinsky, lies at the core of what makes dance, and ballet in particular, so powerful. In their desire to fly, 'above all to ascend', dancers become, like angels, a 'link binding man and god, heaven and earth'. Even as a boy it was these celestial heights that Nijinsky strove to inhabit.

Although the Imperial Ballet School was a place of 'convent-like seclusion', very occasionally events from the outside world intruded into its rarified atmosphere. One such moment occurred in the winter of 1904–1905 and continued on through 1905, when Russia was shaken by the first powerful stirrings against the Tsar and the old regime.

The Imperial Theatres – with their rigid traditions and hierarchy, political in-fighting and insistence upon the strictest obedience to their decisions – replicated in miniature the Tsar's entire unwieldy and unpopular administration. As a reminder of the extent of their dependence on the monarch, every year the season opened on the first Sunday in September with a performance of Glinka's *A Life for the Tsar*. Debentures were handed down from generation to generation. Balletomanes, as they were known, followed the objects of their adoration from performance to performance, if necessary from city to city. When Kshesinskaya went to perform at the Bolshoy in Moscow, the front row of stalls at the Mariinsky would be empty: her fans were all in Moscow. As the favourite of the Tsar and his cousins, she had her pick of roles, even though in 1905 she was several years over the age of thirty; younger dancers, with arguably more talent, found their careers at a standstill because she still reigned absolute.

As if to underline the younger dancers' artistic grievances, Isadora Duncan came to St Petersburg in December 1904. The Russian ballet world turned out to greet her: she dined with an assortment of creative grandees-in-training, including the then artists Alexandre Benois and Léon Bakst and the then curator and editor, Sergey Diaghilev, watched Anna Pavlova's daily practice with Marius Petipa (reflecting with relief, when she saw the sparse lunch Pavlova permitted herself after three hours' training, that she was not a classical ballet dancer), and observed the classes at the Imperial Ballet School which she thought seemed a 'torture chamber'. Even Kshesinskaya invited her to come and see her perform.

Her own performances at the Mariinsky had an immediate impact. Duncan's style could not have been further from the traditions the Imperial Theatres held so dear; it was, in fact, an explicit reproach to them. She danced alone, barefoot, wearing what she described as a 'tunic of cobweb' (and almost nothing in the way of underwear, at a time when Russian ballerinas still danced in boned corsets), in front of a plain blue velvet curtain, to music that was not considered 'ballet music'. She was self-taught and relied on not technical virtuosity but feeling and emotion, often improvised, to communicate with her audience. 'Like eager springtime', this pink-cheeked girl 'distilled joy and vividness'.

Despite her lack of training, she was by all accounts an extraordinarily powerful performer. As Mikhail Fokine, a Mariinsky dancer who was just beginning his choreographic career when he saw Duncan perform, would write, she 'reminded us: *Do not forget that beauty and expressiveness are of the greatest importance.*' Although he went on to qualify his praise – 'the new Russian ballet answered: *Do not forget that a rich technique will create natural grace and expressiveness, through the really great art form*' – everything he would compose in the future would be touched by Isadora's influence.

Radical politics were an important and, given that ballet had always been associated with royal courts, highly unusual element of Duncan's work. She was a socialist (despite her fondness for champagne) and she was appalled by the misery she saw on St Petersburg's streets in contrast to the wealth in which the audiences at the Mariinsky luxuriated. Her sense of drama blurred her memory; she claimed in her memoirs to have arrived in Russia later than she actually did, in January 1905, 'remembering' driving to her hotel through a deserted city past a procession of coffins – the coffins of the protestors shot on Bloody Sunday at the Winter Palace by the Tsar's troops. When she danced in St Petersburg (and this may well have been true, though she would already have been there for a few weeks by the time Bloody Sunday happened) her 'soul wept with righteous anger, thinking of the martyrs of that funeral procession of the dawn'.

The Mariinsky's younger dancers – Anna Pavlova, Tamara Karsavina, Valsav's adored teacher Sergey Legat and others – were as appalled as Duncan by the massacre of unarmed, peaceful demonstrators in front of the Winter Palace; Mikhail Fokine in particular had well-established connections with émigré dissidents and was influenced by anarchist writers like Mikhail Bakunin and Pyotr Kropotkin. But they also had their own issues about which to protest. The Imperial Theatres were intimate, interbred places where former lovers worked together for years after their relationships had ended, members of the same family taught and danced alongside one another, and throughout their careers artists were constantly working in direct competition with their peers. Getting out of the Imperial Theatres was almost as hard as getting into them because the artists had essentially handed their careers over to the Tsar in return for their training. In the autumn of 1905 they led a strike against the management, demanding better working conditions and greater autonomy for the artists, and proposing an elected committee which would have a say in artistic questions as well as salaries and appointments.

When Sergey Legat, under intense pressure from the governing board, signed a declaration of loyalty to the Theatres and then, overcome by having betrayed his friends (and possibly unhappy because of his tumultuous affair with Marie Petipa, twenty years his senior, whom he apparently suspected of infidelity and who also, apparently, had persuaded him to sign the declaration), slit his own throat,* the dancers

---

* Marie Petipa's father, Marius, wrote in his diary that Legat 'went mad, biting Marie, then, he killed himself' (L. Garafola, *Legacies of Twentieth Century Dance*, 2005, p. 26).

had their own revolutionary martyr. Sergey Diaghilev, who had served a short, frustrating stint in the administration of the Imperial Theatres three years earlier, published an article eleven days after Legat's suicide, blaming his death on Vladimir Telyakovsky, the theatre's Director, and privately echoed the dissatisfied dancers' complaints that careers at the theatre were determined not 'by talent but by toadying, tattling and malicious gossip'.

Telyakovsky managed to bring the striking dancers round by promising them amnesty. He admonished them not with anger, according to Karsavina, but with mild fatherliness and she attested to the fact that not one of the rebels later suffered professionally from their involvement in the protest. The world of the theatre was dearer to her than ever after this upheaval, she wrote, surrendering to the perennial argument of established power: everything that had happened had served only to remind her that she ought to be thankful for the opportunities she had been given, rather than ungratefully demanding change.

The students at the Imperial Theatre School were sheltered from these storms but they too had their 'revolutionary demands': better instruction in theatrical make-up and permission for the older students (boys only) to smoke, and to wear their own shoes, collars and cuffs rather than the school's regulation ones. Though he was not a smoker, Vaslav supported these demands, reporting back to Bronia about the meetings he attended. The death of Legat, whom Vaslav had worshipped, was a terrible blow; to add insult to injury his students were not permitted to attend his funeral.

He also found himself, inadvertently, in the front line. A large group of railway workers were protesting on Nevsky Prospekt during the Bloody Sunday riots when Vaslav, on his way home to visit Eleonora, got swept up along with them. Cossack cavalrymen were riding through the demonstrators to scatter them while rows of foot soldiers fired on the panicking crowds. Taking Vaslav for a protestor, a Cossack slashed at him with his whip, cutting through his overcoat and the top part of his boot as if with a sabre. He narrowly avoided falling beneath the hooves of his attacker's galloping horse. Anatole Bourman also described (in an unsubstantiated anecdote) how the next day he, Nijinsky and their classmates searched through the mutilated, waxen corpses on marble slabs in the morgues and hospitals of St Petersburg, desperately looking for their friend Grigory Babich's beautiful sister, who had gone missing and was never found.

But while the avenues of open protest were closed to the young dissidents at the Mariinsky after the theatre's governing board regained control in late 1905, a powerful means of expressing their ideas still remained to them: their work. Just as the actors of pre-revolutionary France led by the great François-Joseph Talma strove for a new authenticity on stage to reflect the political debates taking place around them, so too did Fokine and his favourite dancers learn to express their liberal ideology through their performances.

The twenty-something ballets Fokine would go on to choreograph between 1906 and 1909, in the majority of which Nijinsky would dance, rejected the established traditions of the Mariinsky and, by extension, the traditions of the Tsar's regime. Where once a ballet representing an Egyptian dance would have demonstrated its 'Egyptian-ness' merely by adding a row of hieroglyphic motifs to the edging of a traditional short, stiff tutu (the kind Kshesinskaya favoured, because they showed off her sturdy legs to perfection), Fokine put his dancers in tunics (à la Isadora), kohled their eyes and darkened their skin with make-up, and included in his choreography profile positions gleaned from studying Egyptian culture. This ethnographic method, as the historian Lynn Garafola explains, was an implicit criticism of Russia's stridently jingoistic politics.

'Complete unity of expression' was paramount and his method of working was collaborative. He would take the dancers into his confidence and encourage them 'to participate in the creation' of their roles. He was less interested in having the *corps de ballet* dance in perfect, rigid unison than, in crowd scenes, allowing the dancers to express their roles individually, creating an overall atmosphere that evoked the story or era he was describing instead of demonstrating the company's superlatively disciplined training.

Fokine was particularly opposed to the focus on the individual ballerina at the expense of the ballet as a whole. He saw a *prima ballerina* as first among equals, rather than a star around whom everything revolved as if by divine decree. The Imperial Theatres, though, were organised to celebrate stars. When Kshesinskaya danced, her make-up, hairstyle and costume were chosen to set her off to her best advantage, rather than to create a character or enhance the narrative, and she was always emblazoned with her own fabulous jewels whether she was playing a swan or a peasant-girl. After every solo, which had been tailored to show off her athleticism and technical virtuosity, Kshesinskaya would come to the front of the stage to receive the audience's applause, interrupting the company's performance and the atmosphere they had collectively created on stage. Fokine deplored these traditions.

One artist who instinctively understood Fokine's desire to stop dancers performing 'for the audience's pleasure, exhibiting himself as if saying, "Look how good I am"' was the young Nijinsky. Fokine never needed to explain to him 'this new meaning of the dance'. Nijinsky may not have been 'an articulate conversationalist, but who could so quickly and thoroughly understand what I tried to convey about the dances?' recalled Fokine of working with him in his early career. 'Who could catch each detail of the movement to interpret the style of the dance? He grasped quickly and exactly, and retained what he had learned all his dancing career, never forgetting the slightest detail.'

In the spring of 1905 Fokine cast Nijinsky as a Faun in a student-only revival of *Acis and Galatea*, his first work commissioned by the Marinsky and the first time that Nijinsky, still two years from graduating, would dance a solo and a *pas de deux* in public. *Acis and Galatea* contained many of the Duncanesque traits that would become hallmark Fokine: it was inspired by his study of Pompeian frescos and he urged the dancers to form asymmetrical groups on stage and to relax when they weren't dancing to create an air of naturalness. He was, however, unable to persuade the authorities to allow his nymphs to dance in sandals rather than pointe shoes.

On the night of the performance, Nijinsky overshadowed everyone else on stage. Eleonora sat proudly in the audience – she later said that watching Vaslav perform at the Mariinsky was like going to church on Sunday – and Bronia, watching from backstage, said she had never seen Vaslav dance so brilliantly. Years later she would remember this image of her brother as if she could still see him. 'As he extends upwards, a barely perceptible quiver runs through his body; his left hand close to his face, he seems to be listening to sounds, only heard by him, which fill all his being. He radiates an inner force that by its very radiance envelops the theatre, establishing a complete rapport with the audience.' When Vaslav came to the front of the stage, he acknowledged the applause 'like a bashful schoolboy'; he was, after all, only sixteen. The next day, the critics – who attended student performances like this precisely because they were looking for the next big thing – singled him out as the most distinguished of the young debutantes.

CHAPTER 2

The Favourite Slave
1906–1909

ALTHOUGH THE IMPERIAL THEATRE SCHOOL suggested to Vaslav that he graduate in the spring of 1906, his mother insisted that he remain at the school until the following year so that he would be eighteen when he officially became an Artist of the Imperial Theatres. Even so, following his 1905 debut at the Mariinsky, he began to behave (as only a younger sister could phrase it, half proud and half teasing) as if he were already an Artist, wearing an immaculate white collar and cuffs, his hair smoothly brushed, and holding his head slightly thrown back. When his mother urged him to pay attention to his lessons, he responded grandly that he was studying 'not merely to be a *premier danseur* but to become an Artist of the Dance'.

He began performing regularly at the Mariinsky, partnering Anna Pavlova for the first time in January 1906. Bronia recalled the senior girls as well as her classmates starting to say to her, 'Bronia, tell Vaslav that I adore him,' and 'Nijinsky, what a nice fellow … he is a *doushka* [darling].' In his turn, Vaslav developed crushes on friends of Bronia's and girls he partnered on stage. These romances never turned into anything more than innocent flirtations, with shy smiles exchanged and notes passed in the school's halls, partly because Vaslav, adoring his mother and sister, was devoutly respectful towards women, but also because Eleonora, mindful of Foma's thwarted career, insisted that for the sake of his art a young dancer must not fall in love and tie himself down too soon.

Foma reappeared in Vaslav's life in his final years at the school. He came to St Petersburg to see some of Vaslav's performances, but his comments were usually critical, forcing Vaslav onto the defensive: if he thought Vaslav was being praised for his elevation, he would remind him that he needed to work to become a dancer, not a jumper; when Vaslav partnered a ballerina well he would derisively call him a *porteur*. Jealous of Vaslav's talent and potential, he made a great show of demonstrating his own dances to his children, and though Bronia was impressed – and struck continually by the physical similarities between her, Vaslav and Foma, from the musculature of their legs and feet to the almond shapes of their nails – Vaslav dismissed them as acrobatics. When he left after his first visit, Bronia cried, but Vaslav was glad to see him go. He had not forgiven him.

In 1907, the year he graduated, Foma gave Vaslav a hundred roubles as a graduation present and invited him to visit him in Nizhny Novgorod. The plan was to stay for a week but on the first night his father took Vaslav to a restaurant and told him that now he was a man it was time for him to meet Foma's mistress and the mother of his ten-year-old daughter: Rumyantseva, the woman for whom he had left Eleonora and the children a decade earlier. In response, Vaslav poured out all the pain he had endured over the years as, powerless, he had watched his mother struggle to bring them up alone, taking in boarders, unable to pay her bills, making sacrifice after sacrifice to give her children a roof over their heads and pay for firewood and even food. As Rumyantseva approached their table, Vaslav got up and left the restaurant, setting off for St Petersburg that night. Foma never contacted Vaslav or Bronia again.

As an Artist of the Imperial Theatres, Vaslav was now distinguished with the rank of *coryphé*, one step below soloist, with an annual salary of 780 roubles, 180 more than a member of the *corps de ballet*. This was starting out, as Tamara Karsavina, who had begun her career as a *coryphée* five years earlier, put it, 'amongst the chosen'. Vaslav danced at the Tsar's summer theatre in Krasnoye Selo that summer and returned to St Petersburg – after his disastrous trip to Nizhny Novgorod – in the autumn for his first season as an Artist at the Mariinsky.

Very quickly Mathilde Kshesinskaya singled out Nijinsky, choosing him to partner her first in one of her favourite ballets, *La Fille Mal Gardée*, in November 1907 and then as a regular partner. She found Vaslav 'a charming boy, friendly and very modest'; perhaps their shared Polish roots further predisposed her to favour him. His modesty was also crucial, for Kshesinskaya did not care to share the spotlight. She had this trait in common with her rival, Anna Pavlova, though at least Kshesinskaya, from the lofty height of her connections with the Tsar and her years as undisputed *prima ballerina assoluta*, was willing to help younger dancers – especially if, like Vaslav, they made her look good. Tamara Karsavina remembered her teaching all the younger girls which forks to use at the gala dinners they had to attend, where ten baffling pieces of cutlery might await them. Pavlova also danced with Vaslav, but from the day she heard the audience shout his name louder than hers she was wary of him. Bronia recorded her repeated questions about the 'secret' of Vaslav's jump. Half-jokingly, she would take off Bronia's shoes to examine her feet after class to see 'what secrets Nijinsky shares with his sister'.

Tall and slender to the point of frailty, 'like some exotic and fastidious bird', Anna Pavlova did not fit the image of an ideal ballerina. Until she became a star, the perfect ballerina's body was thought to be compact and muscular, like Kshesinskaya's. In fact it was Pavlova's attenuated physique which led Kshesinskaya to underestimate her as a rival: she allowed Pavlova, then in her second season at the Mariinsky, to take over her roles while she was pregnant in 1901–2, unable to believe that Pavlova could really compete with her. When Pavlova was at the Imperial Theatre School the governesses had tried unsuccessfully to feed her up with cod liver oil and her classmates teased her by calling her 'The Broom', but as a ballerina Pavlova converted what was apparently a flaw into a great and unique asset. Her on-stage fragility, the effect she created of floating ethereally across the stage, was the essence of her phenomenal success.

Off-stage she was a far more powerful creature, whose glamour was electric and whose relentless focus and ambition were sometimes, in the words of Serge Lifar, 'unworthy of her genius'. The actress Sarah Bernhardt, who could hardly be described as retiring, told Pavlova that she 'sought more success' than there was in the world. Even though she liked Lydia Lopokova, a dancer in her own company, Pavlova would send her flowers on the nights she danced badly. Karsavina, whom she saw as direct competition, recalled the venom with which Pavlova tried to scupper her career, refusing to help Karsavina learn 'her' role of Giselle and, pretending concern, falsely telling the Mariinsky's Director that he shouldn't burden Karsavina with too much work because she was consumptive. Kshesinskaya was happy to set Director Telyakovsky straight on Karsavina's behalf.

Pavlova's creed was simple: great art required the greatest of sacrifices. 'If a dancer, yielding to temptation, ceases to exercise over herself the strictest control, she will find it impossible to continue dancing,' she wrote. 'She must sacrifice herself to her art. Her reward will be the power to help those who come to see her forget awhile the sadnesses and monotony of life.' Normality was impossible: the discipline and commitment required to produce his or her art meant the *premier danseur* or ballerina could not seek and should not mourn the consolations of everyday life, contentment with a partner and children, 'the quiet joys of the fireside,' as Pavlova put it.

Many years later, Rudolf Nureyev would echo her ideas. Domesticity, he wrote, 'shows onstage. You watch and you can see, he or she has a family, children, a cottage in the country and goes there every Friday. Dancing can't be a job, like going to the office. It means everything.'

Vaslav would learn to what lengths ambitious dancers were willing to go for their careers when, at about this time, he fell in love with the beautiful Maria Gorshkova, whom he had met in the summer at Krasnoye Selo. He visited her regularly, bringing her flowers and chocolates, until his mother found out and warned him off her, speculating that she might be using him to further her career. Vaslav turned pale at her words, but later told Eleonora that she had been right. 'I had my arms around her and was about to kiss her when she coyly whispered, "Vatsa, promise me that you will insist on dancing a *pas de deux* with me ..." Now I am cured of love.'

Love and sex, sex and love. In his diary, Vaslav remembered masturbating furiously at school after lights out – nothing unusual in a teenage boy, except for the overpowering sense of wrong-doing he felt, leading him to believe that when he masturbated a lot his dancing deteriorated, as well as being afraid that his teeth would rot and his hair fall out. At fifteen, for his mother's sake, he forced himself to give it up. This was when, according to his diary, 'I started to dance like God' – a direct association between sexual self-control and success on stage. He may have meant that he literally danced like a god but his phrase is just as likely to mean that this was the time people started to take notice of his talents, because as a famous dancer he was often called the God of the Dance. 'Everyone started talking about me.'

Although he tried to control his masturbation, Vaslav allowed his so-called friend Anatole Bourman to persuade him to lose his virginity with a prostitute. She gave him a serious case of gonorrhoea which took five months to treat (the doctor applied leeches to his swollen testicles as Vaslav looked on, horrified). Between her and the calculating Maria Gorshkova, Vaslav began to distrust women. Perhaps he, like Pavlova, was learning that artists were exempt from the pleasures of ordinary relationships.

The kind of relationships a dancer could have – though of course Pavlova would never have put it like this – were with rich patrons. By the time she was twenty in 1901, after two years in the Imperial Theatres, Pavlova, whose mother was a laundress (she never knew her father), lived in a flat of her own with a maid and a large private studio where every day Enrico Cecchetti came to give her several hours of private tuition, although she was still a *coryphée* on the same salary level as Nijinsky. Her lovers are reputed to have included a general, a prince and, usefully, a nephew of the Mariinsky's Director, Vladimir Telyakovsky, as well as the influential critic Valerian Svetlov. Baron Victor Dandré, who became her manager and with whom she lived for years (and may have married, though she was always ambiguous about this), was a well-connected man of property in St Petersburg.

Subservience on one side and exploitation on the other had traditionally been part of a Russian dancer's experience. The first dancers and actors in Russia had been serfs, trained by their owners to perform in private theatres on their estates. Although many were talented artists, well educated and cultured, they were still considered chattels – which in practice meant concubines. Prince Nikolay Yusupov, owner of a private theatre and Director of the Imperial Theatres in the 1790s, required his female serfs to undress on stage at the end of their performances. Though the serfs had long been freed by Nijinsky's time, in most cases artists had simply exchanged one kind of master for another. Attitudes of entitlement and submission endured. It was this aspect of the ballet world that gave it a bad name. When Mikhail Fokine asked a group of friends if they thought ballet needed to be reformed, one replied, 'Ballet is pornography, plain and simple.'

There are several accounts – not entirely mutually contradictory – of how Vaslav, still smarting over the incident with Gorshkova, met his first serious lover, Prince Pavel Lvov. The basic version has the thirty-five-year-old prince sending a note backstage to Nijinsky, inviting him to dinner in a private room at Cubat, one of St Petersburg's fashionable restaurants. Another account has Lvov using the services of a pander, a well-connected fellow dancer who was the illegitimate son of a nobleman, to introduce him to Nijinsky for a fee of 1,000 roubles. Between them they apparently concocted a story about a mysterious princess who admired Nijinsky from afar and had asked Lvov to act as her go-between. They met for the first time at a restaurant and the next day Nijinsky received a note asking him to go to Fabergé, where he was fitted with a diamond and platinum ring, ostensibly from the princess. Gradually the imaginary princess receded into the background and Lvov and Nijinsky became lovers. 'He loved me as a man does a boy,' wrote Vaslav, years later. 'I loved him because I knew he wished me well.'

Pavel Lvov was a handsome playboy with charming manners, a sports enthusiast and one of the first people in St Petersburg to own a motor car. He was the type of man, according to Bourman, who handed out 100-rouble notes at parties – the same sum Foma Nijinsky had given Vaslav for his graduation: it was a different world. The life to which he introduced the unsophisticated eighteen-year-old was one of fabulous luxury and, in the word of the day, decadence.

A month after meeting Vaslav, Lvov invited him, Bronia and Eleonora to dinner to celebrate Bronia's birthday. She was overwhelmed by his mansion, with its thick carpets, silk-draped windows and the footmen in yellow-braided tailcoats who waited on them, piling their gold plates high with caviar and sturgeon and making the huge fires blaze merrily. In the centre of the table were arranged branches of hothouse fruit trees, with the fruit still on them, and at each place-setting stood a little vase containing mimosa and violets so that although it was December everything smelt 'marvellously' like spring. Vaslav seemed 'completely relaxed and at ease' in Lvov's splendid house, though Bronia wondered whether he had felt as 'stupefied'as her when he first saw it.

One day Vaslav and the Prince arrived to visit Eleonora, and found her crying over a court summons for unpaid rent from years earlier. Straight away Lvov handed the writ to his lawyers who dealt with the creditors and settled the debt. When Eleonora tried to offer to repay him, he said that Nijinsky could pay him back when he was making more money and he regularly sent her and Bronia lavish gifts: French wine, hampers of foie gras, caviar and cheese, boxes of chocolates and huge baskets of fresh fruit.

With Vaslav too Lvov was magnificently generous. Assuring him that he could repay him later, when he was a star and could demand whatever he wanted for performing – a powerful vote of confidence in itself – he persuaded Vaslav to stop giving society children dance classes. For the past few years Vaslav had been teaching so that he, Bronia and Eleonora could afford an apartment in which he had his own room, a mark of maturity he longed for. Lvov furnished two rooms for him in the Nijinskys' large new apartment on Bolshaya Konyushennaya Ulitsa:

a study papered in dark raspberry with bottle green velvet curtains; a mahogany desk with secret drawers that glided open at the touch of a finger, upon which stood a bronze Narcissus; leather armchairs, a full bookcase and an enamelled stove. A brass bed and a marble washstand stood in his bedroom, along with a wardrobe full of new clothes and rows of pairs of custom-made shoes.

In St Petersburg they went most Saturday evenings to concerts together, attended various sporting events – Bronia thought perhaps Lvov and Vaslav had met through Mikhail Fokine, whose brother was a champion cyclist – and went to the theatre. The Prince took Vaslav and Bronia to see the first aeroplane to come to St Petersburg. In the summer of 1908, instead of taking an engagement at a summer theatre Vaslav spent a few months at Lvov's dacha on the islands outside St Petersburg where Lvov taught Vaslav to play tennis. Here he was described by one visitor as being bad-tempered and sulky, with a penchant for making scenes – still a teenager, even though he was now living in an adult world.

Saying that it was a privilege to help his young friend realise his potential, Lvov also insisted on paying for private lessons with the great Enrico Cecchetti, Anna Pavlova's mentor. Cecchetti was a legendary dancer who, in his late fifties, had become an equally legendary master of ballet. An intelligent, charming and whimsical man, he was adored by his pupils over whom he ruled with absolute authority. He was quite capable of reducing any of them to tears in class but, as Lydia Lopokova said, 'it was a bad sign not to be abused, for that would show that one had no gifts, no possibilities' and this was the start of an immensely productive working relationship. Cecchetti saw his role as helping his students reach 'perfection in the mechanics of dance technique, yet the ultimate artistic perfection – the feel for the movement and the interpretation of the dance – that, the artist must achieve and create for himself'.

Bronia's memoirs record that she saw nothing more in Lvov than the kindest of friends, a man whose devotion to Vaslav and the arts inspired him to great acts of generosity, and whose thoughtfulness to Eleonora and Bronia only demonstrated his disinterested affection for

Vaslav. When a schoolfriend whispered to her the rumours circulating about Lvov and her brother, she was so innocent that at first she did not understand what the friend was trying to tell her.

Eleonora could scarcely have pleaded such naiveté but everything in Vaslav and Bronia's lifelong devotion to their art suggests that they believed (as she had taught them) that people who loved art and admired artists would happily bestow gifts on them and would assist them financially to help them achieve their creative ambitions, expecting nothing in return except the pleasure of knowing they had been involved. Indeed, this was the principle by which Sergey Diaghilev would later run the Ballets Russes. Not many people had been kind to Eleonora or her children and she was evidently deeply touched by Lvov's generosity. Besides, she knew her son was a genius; surely it had only been a matter of time before someone appeared who would count himself proud, as Lvov put it, 'for the rest of my life to know that I had contributed to the development of this great talent'.

Yet it is hard to avoid the conclusion that Eleonora did understand what Lvov wanted from Vaslav in return for his patronage. Of course he liked the glamour and cachet of being associated with the arts; quite probably (although there is no evidence to corroborate this) he was also in thrall to the emotions that art and beauty stimulate in us all. But alongside these impulses often come more carnal compulsions and Lvov was clearly subject to these too. The benefits to Vaslav, to his career and to his material security – as well as to his mother and sister – evidently outweighed any unspoken worries Eleonora might have had about sanctioning her young son's intense new friendship.

She would not have been alone in tolerating a homosexual relationship like that of Lvov and Vaslav. Homosexuality in imperial Russia was illegal after 1835, but before that serfs had been used to call sex with their masters 'gentleman's mischief' and it was commonly accepted that lower-class men like coachmen, waiters, cadets and apprentices would, for a small sum and out of a certain deference, have sex with men of higher social standing and that young men of all classes might experiment before marriage without it meaning much to anyone.

Bath-houses were St Petersburg's most common pick-up spots, though a covered gallery off Nevsky Prospekt and the Tauride and Zoological Gardens were also well-known cruising areas. There was even a special name for the well-heeled, usually older gentlemen out looking for a young friend: *tyotki*, or aunties. In 1902 the penalty for sodomy between consenting adults (cases of which, for obvious reasons, very rarely came to court) was reduced to only three months in prison and, in the early 1900s, several grand dukes including one of the Tsar's uncles and Prince Volkonsky, Director of the Imperial Theatres between 1899 and 1902, barely bothered to disguise their homosexual preferences.

Although, according to his later diary and to Bronia's account of his adolescent crushes, Vaslav's real sexual urges were towards women, he adapted easily to his new life. 'Before, he had only known school. Now [he thought], this must be the way the rest of the world chose to behave.' Only one anecdote suggests that he may have felt uneasy about his initiation into Lvov's decadent world, perhaps suspecting too late that, unwittingly, he was being used for something he didn't quite understand. During Carnival in the spring of 1908, the Mariinsky held a masked ball and, telling him it was a prank, Lvov and his friends persuaded Vaslav to wear the costume of an eighteenth-century lady, powdered, laced and jewelled. 'With great ability he mimed a lady of the Rococo. He looked as if he had walked out of a Watteau, assuming the very air of the eighteenth century. Nobody could have told that this charming masquerader was not really a girl. For Vaslav this was all only a part to play, but not to the others, and only later was he shocked into regretting his ... innocence.'

One of Vaslav's early stage successes during this period was as Armida's favourite slave in the baroque fantasy *Le Pavillon d'Armide*; this is said to have been the performance that so dazzled Lvov, prompting him to pursue Vaslav in late November 1907. Mikhail Fokine – who had written the part of the slave especially for Nijinsky – brought the painter and set designer, Alexandre Benois, along to a rehearsal. Watching what he thought of as his ballet come to life, Benois experienced 'that very rare feeling – not unmixed, somehow, with pain – that occurs only when something long wished for has at last been accomplished'. But when Fokine introduced him to his young protégé, Benois was surprised at Nijinsky's ordinariness: 'He was more like a shop assistant than a fairy-tale hero.'

Another visitor to the rehearsals for *Le Pavillon d'Armide* was Sergey Diaghilev, who had told his friend Benois that he was 'dying of curiosity' to see how his first ballet as set designer was coming together. Members of the public did not usually attend rehearsals, though, and, perhaps because six years earlier he had been ignominiously dismissed from the Tsar's service, on the day Diaghilev appeared the police also turned up and asked him to leave. Despite this inauspicious introduction, it seems likely that this was the first time that Nijinsky met Diaghilev in person. It is possible that Diaghilev may have wanted to come to the rehearsal to catch a glimpse of the young dancer all St Petersburg was waiting to see; it is impossible to imagine that Nijinsky would not have known exactly who Diaghilev was when he walked into the rehearsal room, only to be ushered out unceremoniously by a police officer.

At thirty-five, Sergey Pavlovich Diaghilev cut an imposing and idio-syncratic figure. Though the streak of white in his black hair led the young artists of the Imperial Theatres to call him (behind his back) 'Chinchilla', he resembled 'a magnificent bear'. In fact he invited com-parisons with animals: Jean Cocteau would describe his smile as that of a very young crocodile, 'one tooth on the edge'; Karsavina said he reminded her of a sea lion; and Bronia thought he looked like a bulldog with black eyes that smiled but were always sad. Those eyes, said one lover, 'looked one through and through … saw everything, and yet, at times, gave the impression that they were not even looking at you'. When I try to imagine Diaghilev I am assailed by smells: the almond-blossom brilliantine he wore in his hair, a faint powdery whiff of the vio-let bonbons he habitually chewed, the smoke of his gold-tipped 'Black Russian' Sobranie cigarettes, a waft of Mitsouko.

Diaghilev was born in 1872 in the province of Novgorod, in a vil-lage near where his father, then a soldier, was stationed. His mother died soon after his birth and so her nanny took sole charge of the little boy until Pavel Diaghilev married again two years later, giving Sergey a stepmother he adored and two younger brothers. For some years Pavel and his family lived in St Petersburg, funded by the Diaghilevs' vodka-distilling business, but when bankruptcy loomed they returned to Pavel's father's house in Perm, several days' travel east by rail and then by river from St Petersburg.

Despite the loss of his mother and the family's hopelessness with money, Sergey remembered his childhood, surrounded by music and loving relations, as a happy one, an idyll of genteel rural Russianness, of wooden *dachas* encircled by wide verandas, of driving through snowy forests on sledges in winter, of sudden, longed-for spring thaws and golden autumns spent collecting mushrooms. This almost mythical Russia, so dear to his heart throughout his life, was the place he described in an article about the landscape artist Isaac Levitan: 'his bluelit nights, his avenues of sleeping, century-old birches, which slowly lead one to that old house in the country, which all of us know so well, where Tatyana [the heroine of Pushkin's *Eugene Onegin*] waits and dreams ...'

Even as a boy Sergey was supremely self-confident, with what Karsavina called a 'peculiar lazy grace'. At school his classmates 'looked up to him as a distinctly superior person' and, although when he returned to St Petersburg as a law student in 1890, his new friends considered him by turns provincial, a dandy, a dilettante and even a boor, he soon carved out a role for himself as leader of their group. At times they might rail against his tyrannical tendencies but they could not fail to respect his astonishing ability to accomplish exactly what he set out to do regardless of the obstacles in his path. 'It is the Seryozhas [an affectionate diminutive of Sergey] in life that make the world go round; all glory and honour be unto him,' wrote Alexandre Benois in 1897 after admitting defeat in an argument, though only months later he would again be wondering if Sergey was his friend or his enemy, and the same year he called him, 'the only one of us capable of furthering his aims by making really wicked decisions'.

From his childhood music, literature and painting were everything to Diaghilev. 'The dream and purpose of my life is to work in the field of art,' he wrote on his twenty-first birthday. A year earlier, in Bayreuth, he had seen Wagner performed for the first time. 'Everything is here: pettiness, intrigues, grief, anger, love, jealousy, tenderness, cries, groans – all of this goes on until eventually the whole of it mingles to present life as it flows on for each of us, and above it all triumphs the truth of beauty,' he wrote to his stepmother.

According to Benois, it was during one of these art-immersed trips to Europe in the mid-1890s that Diaghilev gave up his dream of becoming a composer and decided that his vocation in life was as a promoter of the arts – not an impresario, heaven forbid, that sounded like a thief – but as a Maecenas. He wanted to be 'part of history' and he possessed, as he famously put it, almost every quality required to succeed in this ambition. The one thing he lacked was money (or rather, enough to create his dreams) but he was certain that would come.

In 1898 Diaghilev secured the backing of two important patrons of Russian art, the fabulously rich railway tycoon Savva Mamontov and Princess Maria Tenisheva, for a new journal, *Mir iskusstva*, or *The World of Art*. He laid out his individualistic, art-for-art's-sake manifesto in an article in the first issue: 'We are a generation that thirsts for beauty. And we find it everywhere, both in good and evil ... We must be free as gods in order to become worthy of tasting this fruit of the tree of life. We must seek in beauty a great justification for our humanity, and in personality the highest manifestation of beauty.'

While Diaghilev was the founder and presiding genius of *Mir iskusstva*, it was always a collaborative achievement, the work of a group of passionately idealistic friends known to posterity as the *miriskusniki*. They included the artist Léon Bakst, with his ginger moustache, 'sly dandified primness [and] imperturbable good nature', constantly sketching something on the back of a menu or a paper napkin; clever, opinionated Walter Nouvel, who could have been a professional musician, and whose wit made 'one think of champagne'; the refined and rather superior Benois, ever-watchful for a slight; and Dmitry or Dima Filosofov, Diaghilev's high-minded cousin and closest companion.

They met in Diaghilev's large apartment, which was furnished in the lush, aesthetic fashion Prince Lvov had echoed in the rooms he decorated for Vaslav, with grey and beige striped wallpaper, a piano, velvet-covered armchairs, bronze statues and a huge black sixteenth-century Italian table covered with papers, pens and pots of glue which Diaghilev used as a desk. Diaghilev's ancient nanny in her black lace cap presided over a steaming samovar while Diaghilev, resplendent in a flowered dressing gown, drifted in and out dispensing opinions and infusing everyone with his energy and vision.

He possessed, said Benois, 'an individual gift of creating a roman-tic working climate and with him all work had the charm of a risky escapade'. One element of this was Diaghilev's inability to distinguish between his professional and private lives. For him 'there could be no bourgeois distinction between work and leisure, between the busi-ness of breadwinning and the life of the mind and soul'. He lived a life devoted to art and he expected everyone around him to do so too.

By the mid-1900s, *Mir iskusstva* had run its course and Diaghilev had embarked on another stage in his career as a Maecenas, as curator and exhibition organiser, personally amassing over 4,000 eighteenth- and nineteenth-century portraits from more than 550 lenders all over Rus-sia for an exhibition to be held in St Petersburg's Tauride Palace. His vigour, knowledge and organisational skills were extraordinary. As an artist who assisted him in setting up the show commented, the remark-able thing about him was that 'for all his "commander's" ways, Diaghi-lev had an eye for detail; nothing was trivial for him, everything was important, and he wanted to do everything himself'.

Diaghilev's exhibition opened in January 1905, the month of Bloody Sunday. Although he did not make a speech at the opening, he did speak at a dinner afterwards, summing up the *fin de siècle* feel of his times and his own attitude to it. 'I think many of you will agree that the idea of a reckoning, of things coming to an end, is one that increasingly comes to mind,' he began. As he journeyed across Russia in search of these lost and unappreciated masterpieces, he had found that, 'The end was here in front of me. Remote, boarded-up family estates, palaces frightening in their dead grandeur, weirdly inhabited by dear, mediocre people no longer able to bear the weight of past splendours.'

His conclusion was as surprising as it was characteristic, no lament for the lost world he still cherished but a call to arms for the new: 'Without fear or doubt, I raise my glass to the ruined walls of those beautiful palaces, and in equal measure to the new commandments of the new aesthetic. And the only wish that I as an irredeemable sensualist can make is that the coming struggle will not insult the aesthetics of life, and that death may be as beautiful and as radiant as the Resurrection!' The idea of himself as an 'irredeemable sensualist' was at the core of the mature Diaghilev's understanding of himself. As a young man he had struggled with his homosexuality, just like his tormented heroes Nikolay Gogol and Tchaikovsky, who had bemoaned his 'damned buggeromania' in letters to his brother and lamented the predilections which were 'my greatest, my most insurmountable obstacle to happiness'. Through his stepmother, Diaghilev had had some childhood contact with the great composer, whom he proudly called Uncle Petya, and would have understood the causes of his lifelong depression and possible suicide.

Diaghilev was lucky to live in slightly more tolerant times. In 1902 he visited the German clinic of the psychiatrist Richard von Krafft-Ebing and arrived at some kind of acceptance of what Dr Krafft-Ebing would have called his 'deviant' sexual nature. Perhaps he came to believe, as his friend the writer Vasily Rozanov would argue, that homosexuality was not unnatural, just another facet of human nature. Whatever decision he came to, from this point forward he would make no effort to disguise his true self. Though he was never camp or effeminate, he made a point of appearing to be exactly what he was – a grand, rather old-fashioned bachelor, as Léonide Massine would later put it, 'elegant but unremarkable'.

Though this dichotomy between his imposing and almost respectable exterior and his debauched private life was what made him so fascinatingly 'wicked' in the eyes of many of his contemporaries, his friends learned to accept him as he was. After several years' acquaintance with

Diaghilev, Tamara Karsavina remembered walking through the gardens at Versailles, discussing him with Sergey Botkin, a mutual friend and Bakst's brother-in-law. Hitherto, she confessed to him, she had shied away from certain aspects of Sergey Pavlovich's character, but Dr Botkin 'made me see that it was the quality of love that makes it beautiful, no matter who the object'.

The great love of Diaghilev's early life was his cousin Dima Filosofov. As young men they had travelled extensively together and as literary editor to Sergey's editor-in-chief Dima had worked by his side on *Mir iskusstva*. By 1905, after a decade together, their relationship had broken down, with Filosofov leaving Diaghilev to live in an even more unconventional arrangement, a *ménage à trois* with Zinaida Gippius, a woman who wore men's clothes and described herself as a male intellect in a female body, and her asexual husband Dmitry Merezhkovsky, a philosopher and mystic.

Their separation was devastating to Diaghilev but he consoled himself by cruising the parks and bath-houses of St Petersburg with friends of similar tastes, Walter Nouvel and Mikhail Kuzmin. Kuzmin's explicit diaries and 1905 autobiographical novel, *Wings*, give a detailed picture of the confident and promiscuous homosexual subculture Diaghilev and his friends inhabited, comparing notes on boys they picked up and sharing and swapping lovers. Over the next year Diaghilev's secretary, Aleksey Mavrin, would become his regular lover and travelling companion.

After the triumphant exhibition of Russian portraiture, Diaghilev had turned his attention to Europe, organising a series of five concerts of Russian music in Paris in the summer of 1907. Following its success, he returned to St Petersburg where he was planning a 1908 Parisian season of Russian opera, possibly using Russian dancers in some of the acts. This was the moment when he met Nijinsky.

The *miriskusniki* had long been interested in ballet. As early as 1897 Walter Nouvel had speculated that ballet would one day realise 'the clamorous demands of the modern spirit', but only when it moved away from the ideals of thirty years earlier and came into line with the 'decadent aesthetic and sensual demands'of the day. Soon afterwards, in *The World of Art*, Benois deplored the ruination of ballet: fairies (he did not mean homosexuals).

Diaghilev had made his own attempt to bring ballet into line with his artistic vision when in 1899 he was appointed special assistant to the then-Director of the Imperial Theatres, Prince Sergey Volkonsky. It was a disaster. Volkonsky and Diaghilev came up against Mathilde Kshesinskaya and lost; the one ballet Diaghilev tried to commission – *Sylvia* – was never made; and both he and Volkonsky resigned in 1901 feeling deeply aggrieved by the entire experience. This period at the Imperial Theatres, Volkonsky wrote, was difficult and unpleasant, marked by envy, plots, ill-will and no support from above, and Diaghilev's hopes for a career in the state theatres were dashed by a specific injunction against him ever again holding a position in the civil service.

It is more than likely that their sexuality was an unspoken element in the 'unpleasantness' of this period. Neither Volkonsky nor his protégé, Diaghilev, made a secret of their preferences; indeed, gossip about Diaghilev had reached such a pitch in the 1890s that someone had anonymously sent him a powder puff. Kshesinskaya would not have been above using her certain knowledge of their private lives to influence the Tsar when she was seeking to exert her backstage control of the Theatres. This may have been an element in Diaghilev's decision in the mid-1900s to turn away from Russia, where he could not hope to be restored to favour, towards Europe, and Paris in particular – partly because it was known to be a city receptive to new creative endeavours but also because homosexuality was not illegal there.

While rumours about his sexuality may have been affecting Diaghilev's career, Nijinsky was plagued by different troubles. His successes – his brilliant interpretation of the Blue Bird in the coda from *La Belle au bois dormant*, a role more senior dancers considered their own; his increasingly regular pairings with Pavlova and Kshesinskaya; and his selection by Fokine for the only male part in *Chopiniana* (what would become *Les Sylphides*) – were provoking jealousy among the artists of the Imperial Theatres. Gossip about his relationship with Lvov was also circulating. Sensing disapproval and hostility, never that easy in company, Nijinsky withdrew from the camaraderie of his peers, mostly former schoolmates, and earned himself a reputation among them as a snob.

Instead he spent his time with Lvov and his friends, though they seem to have warmed to him little more than his contemporaries. He and Lvov dined with Diaghilev and Walter Nouvel several times over the winter of 1907 and Nouvel visited them at Lvov's *dacha* in 1908. Nouvel thought Vaslav a dull-witted oaf; his view is corroborated by Benois who found him 'uninteresting ... [he] seldom spoke, blushed furiously and got muddled when he did, and usually understood that it would be better for him to return to silence'.

But on stage this awkward creature became something else entirely. Even though Nouvel and Benois were scathing about Nijinsky's hesitant efforts to contribute to their sparkling discussions, they had to admit that he was an extraordinary artist. One of his most important roles in his first year as an Artist of the Imperial Theatres was as the Blue Bird. Cecchetti had created the part in 1890 and Nijinsky's former teachers Oboukhov and Nikolay Legat had also danced it to great acclaim but instead of learning from them Vaslav chose to work alone on his interpretation of the role. Though he didn't change Petipa's steps, there was enough space in the original choreography for him to mark out his own creative path, including persuading the usually rigid Mariinsky to change the costume so it was actually bird-like and to allow him to do his own make-up. It was a triumph: as the Blue Bird Vaslav's whole body seemed 'to lose its human contours and design a bird's flight in the air'.

For his part, Nijinsky was 'greatly impressed' by Diaghilev, telling Bronia what an exceptional person he was and how much he learned whenever he was with him and his friends. When Sergey went to Paris in the spring of 1908, as a token of their friendship he gave Vaslav a full set of *Mir iskusstva* and the catalogues from his exhibitions, and when he returned that autumn Vaslav began spending most evenings with him and his circle, ardently listening 'to their conversations, discussions and arguments about the theatre, about art and music'. Diaghilev's commitment to art was in line with Nijinsky's own; meeting him made him feel he had discovered the place he belonged. Nouvel confirms this. From their meeting in late 1907 and throughout 1908, he wrote, Nijinsky did all he could 'to please Diaghilev and attract his attention'. At first Diaghilev was unsure about him – evidently sharing his friends' assessment of the young dancer – but as early as December 1907 he was interested enough to ask Kuzmin for advice about the situation.

From the start Lvov was determined to push Nijinsky into Diaghilev's path, urging his young friend to be unfaithful to him with Diaghilev. Swapping or handing lovers from one man to another was quite usual among this group of grand homosexuals – Diaghilev, Nouvel and Kuzmin did it all the time – and given the social inequalities between the parties there was very little the junior partner could do about it except acquiesce. Lvov had already introduced Vaslav to one friend, Count Tishkevich. Although Bronia, who also met this Polish patron of the arts, insisted that he spent his time with her and Vaslav lecturing them as if they were children, Vaslav's diaries record preferring Prince Pavel to the 'Count' – which suggests that the count was a lover, or made an attempt to be. In Diaghilev's case, Lvov recognised how much he could 'help cultivate [Nijinsky's] culture and talent', impressing on Nijinsky how useful Diaghilev could be to his career, and he told Nouvel that it was 'his most fervent wish' to bring them together.

Throughout the autumn and into the winter of 1908, Nijinsky and Diaghilev's lives became more closely entwined as Diaghilev's plans for a second season of Russian opera in Paris became plans for a season of ballet and opera. The ballet Diaghilev most wanted to mount there was *Le Pavillon d'Armide*, in which Nijinsky shone and which was almost certainly the first role Diaghilev saw him dance (he was sitting beside Benois at its premiere on 27 November 1907). Taking it to Paris would guarantee that Nijinsky would accompany him there.

Isadora Duncan had returned to St Petersburg in the spring of 1908, and Vaslav and Bronia watched her at the Mariinsky from Prince Lvov's box with Tamara Karsavina and her husband. On this second viewing, the Russians were more critical of Duncan's lack of technique. With her usual thoughtfulness Karsavina admired her ideas and thought they would enrich ballet, while still considering her 'a child who knows the alphabet but cannot yet read the book'. Vaslav was more strident. To him, Duncan's 'barefoot childish hoppings and skippings should not be called an art'. He also noticed an overwhelming void at the heart of her performance: although she was occasionally accompanied by female dancers and had founded a dance school for girls, male dancers did not feature in her work.

Since the early nineteenth century, ballet had been an art that predominantly showcased women. Male dancers were on stage to enhance their partners' loveliness, rather than to be acclaimed as artists in their own right: according to the nineteenth-century critic Jules Janin, they were merely 'the green box trees surrounding the garden flowers'. It was this that made Foma Nijinsky's use of the word *porteur* to his son so derisive, although ironically it was Vaslav who had already begun to change the audience's perception of male dancers. For the first time, audiences were calling Nijinsky's name as loudly as they cried out any ballerina's – if not more loudly. Fokine was as responsive to this trend as he was to the powerful influences of Duncanism. He choreographed for men, and for Nijinsky in particular, as well as he choreographed for women.

The combination of Fokine's innovative choreography, Nijinsky and Pavlova's dancing, and Benois's exquisite set designs gave Diaghilev something fresh and magical to export while the constrained atmosphere of the Imperial Theatres under Telyakovsky and their frustrated desires for greater creative control of their careers gave the dancers a reason to leave, at least for part of the year. Adolph Bolm described feeling helpless to criticise or even make suggestions to the Theatres' reactionary administration. Even before Diaghilev planned his ballet season, some artists had been looking to the West in the months of their holidays from the Mariinsky: Pavlova and Bolm had toured Germany and Scandinavia in 1907–8 and Kshesinskaya had danced in Paris in 1908 (Vaslav had been unable to accompany her because of an illness).

Vaslav signed his contract to dance in Diaghilev's Saison Russe in Paris in the summer of 1909 on 10 October 1908, not once but an emphatic five times. He was to be paid 2,500 francs for the two-month season and given his second-class train ticket; any other expenses would be met by Diaghilev. As a comparison, although Nijinsky was among the highest paid dancers, the celebrated bass Fyodor Chaliapin, who was to be the star of Diaghilev's opera programme, received 55,000 francs for the season.

It is more than likely that Nijinsky and Diaghilev had become lovers by the time this contract was signed. In his diary Nijinsky remembered Lvov 'introducing' him to Diaghilev by telephone. Although he makes it sound as though he had not met Diaghilev before this telephone call, his writing in the diary is impressionistic and I think it occurred after they already knew each other a little (and by the time Vaslav knew Lvov well), perhaps as late as the early autumn of 1908. Vaslav did not meet Lvov until the autumn of 1907 and by the winter of that year they had dined with Diaghilev several times.

Over the telephone Diaghilev summoned Vaslav to come and see him at the Hotel de l'Europe where he was staying. Nijinsky describes their meeting in an often-quoted passage from his diary: 'I hated him for his voice, which was too self-assured, but I went in search of luck. I found luck there because I immediately made love to him. I trembled like an aspen leaf. I hated him, but I put up a pretence, for I knew that my mother and I would starve to death. I understood Diaghilev from the first moment and pretended therefore that I agreed with all his views. I realised one had to live, and therefore it did not matter to me what sacrifice I made … but Diaghilev liked boys and therefore found it difficult to understand me.'

These words were written more than ten years after the event, at a time when Nijinsky was deeply troubled by sexual and moral issues, but they do carry a weight of authenticity. He was being over-dramatic about starving, since it must have been clear even to someone as inexperienced and impractical as him that a rich lover like Lvov would keep him better than a hopeful Maecenas, but the sense that this was a sacrifice is clear: a sacrifice he was willing to make for many reasons but a sacrifice nonetheless. Elsewhere in the diary he remembers at this time, aged nineteen, having to limit his masturbating again (to what he considered an acceptable level, once every ten days), because he was seeing 'many beautiful women who flirted' and made him nervous – women, not men. There is no record of him fantasising about men and because of this he and Diaghilev would never be entirely compatible.

Still, having lived happily with Lvov and admiring Diaghilev as he did, Nijinsky knew that he could give Diaghilev what he wanted and what he would receive in return, and he was used to acting a part. In the same way, when the young Anton Dolin was engaged as a dancer by Diaghilev in the 1920s, his bags were moved out of his single, second-class compartment and into Diaghilev's first-class double for the train journey down to Monaco. 'I knew perfectly well what was expected of me,' wrote Dolin.

For Nijinsky and Diaghilev it was not a case of instantly moving in together, though. Diaghilev's relationship with his secretary Mavrin continued throughout this period and, though Nijinsky's affair with Lvov had become less intense over the second half of 1908, they were still seeing each other irregularly until, in late April 1909, Nijinsky left for Paris with Diaghilev, Aleksey Mavrin and Walter Nouvel: a cosy little quartet for the two-day journey.

The incident Vaslav would remember about this first trip abroad demonstrated his anxiety in the presence of his sophisticated and often unwelcoming new friends, the social gulf that yawned between them. Eleonora, afraid her darling boy would be hungry on the journey, had cooked Vaslav a chicken and wrapped it in waxed paper along with bread rolls, butter and oranges: a feast she would not have been able to afford until very recently. Neither she nor Vaslav knew that there was a dining car for the wagon-lit passengers. Vaslav wanted to ask the others to share his meal but he was too shy; and Eleonora had only packed him one plate, one fork and one knife.

When Diaghilev stood up and said that he was going to the restaurant car, Vaslav – embarrassed by his ignorance of the ways of the world and fearing the others would make fun of him – waited until he was alone to throw the lovingly wrapped packet out of the window, raging inwardly against his innocent mother. Later, he would laugh about it; at the time he burned with humiliation.

Just after their departure, Prince Pavel came to see Eleonora and stayed with her for some time, telling her that Diaghilev had asked him to give Vaslav up. Diaghilev had said that if he sincerely wished Vaslav success he would not accompany him to Paris. With great sadness, Lvov had agreed and had given Diaghilev money for his season there. Bronia found Lvov standing alone in Vaslav's study, the room he had decorated for him.

'I came to say goodbye to you. I am leaving.'

'But when will we see you again?'

'I do not know. Probably we will not see each other for a very long time.' His eyes were filled with tears as he kissed her hand and left.

CHAPTER 3

Dieu de la Danse
1909–1910

THE FIRST EXPERIENCE OF PARIS was overwhelming. The following year, 1910, Lydia Lopokova had barely arrived there before fainting
at 'the lovely sight of the Gare du Nord' and having to be revived by
Léon Bakst with whom she was travelling. It was a beautiful, bustling,
modern city: the Métro had been running nearly a decade and, on the
crowded boulevards, motor-cars sped between 'the tangled mass of cabs
whose drivers wore shiny top hats of waxed cloth, and the horse-drawn
double decker buses'. The smell of gasoline mingled in the air with the
traditional scent of horse manure. It had felt like winter in St Petersburg
when they left, still cold and damp, but in Paris the sun was warm, the
trees were all coming into leaf and Karsavina said that she couldn't
remember a cloud in the sky the whole time they were there.

Diaghilev made his headquarters in the Hotel de Hollande near the
Opéra. Nijinsky stayed in the cosier Hotel Daunou around the corner
and, when they arrived in early May, the other dancers – including Bronia and Eleonora, as her chaperone – lived in smaller hotels around the
Boulevard St Michel. Amid all the excitement of being in Paris, Bronia
had barely enough time to buy a hat at Galeries Lafayette before rehearsals began.

The company had spent March and April rehearsing in St Petersburg.

Once again Diaghilev had managed to offend his old adversary Mathilde Kshesinskaya, this time by offering Pavlova better roles in Paris than her. In a huff she withdrew from his programme altogether and demanded that the Tsar refuse to allow Diaghilev's company to rehearse in the Hermitage Theatre, or to take the Mariinsky's sets and costumes to Paris, or to receive generous state funding for the season. Diaghilev's patron, Nicholas's uncle Grand Duke Vladimir, had just died and Diaghilev had no other friends at court to argue his case. Hastily he arranged for his small company to rehearse in a hall on Yekaterinsky Canal and raced to Paris to find donors to ensure that the Saison Russe could go ahead as planned.

In Russia, Diaghilev had raised money by introducing rich merchants who wanted titles to grand dukes, like Vladimir, with access to patents of nobility; his friends sniggered about his enterprises being sponsored by rubber barons (*galoshisty*, or rubber-makers, with the word 'rubber' having the same connotation in Russian as in English). In Paris, initially through Grand Duke Vladimir and his wife, he had become friends with a small group of rich lovers of music, particularly of opera, who would become the Ballets Russes' sponsors. These included Misia Edwards, the Comtesses de Chevigné and Greffulhe, models for Proust's Duchesse de Guermantes (he began writing *À la recherche du temps perdu* in 1909), and Winnaretta Singer, the American sewing-machine heiress and devoted Wagnerian, who was married to the Prince de Polignac.

These women were fabulously rich but they were also unconventional. The formidable Princesse de Polignac may have been married to one of the pillars of French society but it was a *mariage blanc*; she was known to her friends as Tante Winnie – *tante* in the same way as the St Petersburg *tyotki* were aunties. Madame Greffulhe, descended from the Thermidorian beauty Thérésia Tallien, was a trained classical musician and the President of the Société des grandes auditions musicales de France. When her husband took to frequenting the company of what she called 'little ladies who enjoy jumping on mattresses' she simply raised a graceful eyebrow, and she told a friend she considered it of no importance whatever whether someone slept with 'a man, a woman or a canary-bird'. She took Diaghilev at first for an adventurer, but he won her over with his knowledge of art and his wonderful piano-playing.

Voluptuous, flame-haired Misia Edwards (later and best known as Misia Sert) was the most important of the women Diaghilev befriended in the mid-1900s, the most steadfast champion of the Ballets Russes and for the rest of his life his closest woman friend – in many ways the replacement for his beloved stepmother. As the muse for a roll-call of artists including Vuillard, Bonnard, Renoir and Toulouse-Lautrec, friend of the poets Verlaine and Mallarmé, student of Liszt and patron of Fauré and Ravel, her artistic credentials were impeccable and must have impressed even Diaghilev.

Her disregard for convention was a match for Diaghilev's – married twice (the second time to the immensely rich newspaper magnate, Alfred Edwards) and divorced once by 1909, she was living adulterously with the man who would become her third husband, the Spanish painter José-Maria Sert – and, also like Diaghilev, her friends loved and despaired of her in equal measure. She was 'a fairy godmother one moment and a witch the next, frightfully malicious, adorably generous', inspiring nicknames like Tante Brutus and Tante Tue-Tout, as well as Proust's dreadful Madame Verdurin – though her best qualities were also revealed in Princess Yourbeletieff, Proust's exquisite patron of the Russian ballet. She and Diaghilev plotted together on the telephone every morning – the drawing room of her rue de Rivoli apartment, with its vast Bonnard mural, would become Diaghilev's unofficial headquarters whenever he was in Paris.

Two men were also essential to the business side of Diaghilev's enterprise in 1909: Baron Dmitry de Günzburg, introduced by Walter Nouvel, who stepped in with generous funds after the Tsar withdrew his backing from the Saison Russe; and Gabriel Astruc, the French impresario who brought Artur Rubinstein and Mata Hari to Paris and who had secured 100,000 francs from each what he called a 'tournée des mécènes' for Diaghilev's 1908 opera season. Astruc knew everyone, 'mes chers snobs', without whom no venture could prosper in Paris, and had done the deal for Diaghilev's 1909 Saison Russe with the shabby and rather unfashionable Théâtre du Châtelet, known principally as a home for operetta.

In St Petersburg, Diaghilev's committee had been drinking weak tea since the previous autumn while they planned their season. Diaghilev, his exercise book in front of him, was omnipresent. Other regulars were the *miriskutnik* artists Alexandre Benois, Nicholas Roerich and Léon Bakst; Walter Nouvel, a gifted amateur musician; and Mikhail Fokine, who was choreographing every new piece they would present. Fokine had suggested his friend Sergey Grigoriev as company *regisseur* or manager. A 'benevolent giant', Grigoriev saw everything that went on in the company, noting it down (along with the relevant fine) in the little notebook he always carried.

'A conference was like a council of war,' wrote one observer of these meetings. 'Each would pour out his ideas into a common pool, but Diaghilev – have no doubt of it – was the supreme commander, he imposed a unity of form and aesthetic conception, he turned a mass of brilliant projects into an ordered and coherent work of art,' inspiring each of his collaborators to produce for him their best work. 'It was impossible to know where the work of one began and another ended.'

When Karsavina signed her contract with Diaghilev the following year, he took her into his bedroom so they could discuss it in private, and she was fascinated to find the room 'bare of adornment ... I could not realise then that the glamour of his personality spent itself in creations of fancy'. Diaghilev was uninterested in ownership. His friend, the critic Michel Calvocoressi, asked him why he hadn't bought some *objets d'art* that he had admired and he replied that he 'did not want to own them. I have no possessions and wish for none. To own things is cumbersome and tedious. A couple of trunkfuls of personal effects is all I have in the world.' Even then he knew that what he created would be more important than anything he might own: his vocation was the ephemeral.

Benois remembered the company's rehearsals in St Petersburg's

Catherine Hall in the spring of 1909 being infused by a picnic spirit, an atmosphere of adventure and excitement, of joy and hope at watching something mature 'that would amaze the world'. Fokine, composing the Polovtsian Dances for the opera *Prince Igor* in a matter of hours, was at the top of his form, inspiring everyone around him. He 'shouted himself hoarse, tore his hair, and produced marvels'. Benois, who, despite seeing Diaghilev almost daily for the past year, had never seen him with Nijinsky before, noticed at these rehearsals an intimacy between the two which surprised him.

In Paris the almost celebratory mood continued during two weeks of frenetic rehearsals at the Châtelet before their first night. It was so hot in the theatre that Karsavina said you could have bred salamanders and they danced through the dust and drying paint while the builders made trap doors, extended the orchestra pit, removed seats, added boxes, resurfaced the stage with fresh pine boards and laid thick new carpet in the lobbies. Rather than breaking for meals, Diaghilev would order roast chickens, paté and salad from Larue's and the company would eat on packing boxes amidst the scenery, as if they were picnicking in the porcelain colours – apple green, rose pink and duck-egg blue – of Armida's enchanted garden.

Diaghilev was tireless. He could spot a single bulb that had burned out among the stage lights or hear when the orchestra's second trumpet was playing flat. Shadowed by the spectral Grigoriev, he supervised costumes, hair, make-up, musicians, backdrops, press briefings and photography sessions, complimentary tickets to potential sponsors – and everything else that had to be done. Karsavina said that she 'had seen a Japanese performer once, exhibiting feats of quadruple concentration. I failed to be impressed by him: I had seen Diaghilev at work.'

A few days before the dress rehearsal, Anna Pavlova, who featured in a graceful arabesque on Saison Russe posters all over Paris, informed Diaghilev that she would arrive in Paris two weeks later than planned, missing the opening night, perhaps because she wanted to see how the company would be received before joining it. If so, it was a tactical misjudgement, allowing Karsavina to step into her roles and providing

Diaghilev with the perfect excuse to present Vaslav Nijinsky to the already fascinated newspapermen as his company's star.

Every seat at the Châtelet was taken on the night of 19 May 1909. Astruc had even arranged for the prettiest actresses in Paris to be seated around the front row of the balcony, alternating blonde and brunette. (The next day the press called them Astruc's *corbeille*, or flower basket, and since then the dress circles of French theatres have been known as *corbeilles*.) Bronia watched her brother waiting on stage for his role in *Le Pavillon d'Armide* – the first performance of the first night – to begin. 'His whole body is alive with an inner movement, his whole being radiant with inner joy.' At the end of his *pas de trois*, Nijinsky, in what looked to Karsavina like an explosion of delight, leapt instead of walking off stage, landing out of sight and giving the impression that he had flown off the stage. The audience gasped audibly: 'a storm of applause broke; the orchestra had to stop'.

For the second piece, the Polovtsian Dances, Nicholas Roerich's depiction of a nomadic camp on the steppes of southern Russia, with long, low, dark tents from which a few thin columns of smoke rose into a vast, sulphurous sky, transported the audience from the refined rococo loveliness of Armida's palace to a place of barbaric wilderness. The warlike dances of the Tatar warriors and their maidens, led by Adolph Bolm, provoked such an enthusiastic response from the audience that in the interval that followed admirers flooded backstage. The stage became so crowded that Nijinsky and Karsavina could not practise their lifts from the *pas de deux* they were about to perform as part of *Le Festin*, adapted from the Blue Bird variation which Nijinsky had danced with Pavlova in St Petersburg the previous season.

When the curtain fell for the last time, pandemonium broke out. 'The familiar barriers between the stage and the audience were broken.' Karsavina had been so swept away by the moment that she had not noticed cutting herself on Nijinsky's jewelled costume while they danced and backstage afterwards she remembered someone 'exquisitely dressed' using his 'cobwebby handkerchief' to staunch the blood trickling down her arm. 'Somebody was asking Nijinsky if it was difficult to stay in the air as he did while he was jumping; he did not understand at first [if only he had paid better attention to his French lessons at school], and then, very obligingly: "No! No! Not difficult. You have just to go up and then pause a little up there."' From that night on, Karsavina said, a proud Diaghilev called her and Nijinsky his children.

The second programme premiered on 4 June. Pavlova and Nijinsky floated ethereally through the melancholy beauty of *Les Sylphides*, Fokine's masterful *ballet blanc*, an homage to the age of romanticism. Here Nijinsky dazzled as the only male dancer on a moonlit stage inhabited by ghostly maidens in long tutus and delicate gauze wings. This was a demonstration of faultless poise, in which 'every movement was so graceful that he seemed ideal, almost god-like'. Writing many years after seeing Nijinsky as the poet, one critic could still recall 'the billowing of his white silk sleeve as he curved and extended his arm'.

Until the Russians' arrival in Paris, ballet had been seen as an all but dead art form. The dancers Edgar Degas painted at the old Paris Opéra were popularly known as Petits Rats (and in fact were taught by a woman called Madame Rat). Far from being objects of beauty to their contemporaries, they were seen rather as drab, miserable little creatures waiting to be selected to become the mistresses of wealthy philistines on a stage that was hardly more than a brothel. Even the physical layout of the Paris Opéra encouraged this association of ballet with selling sex: interested gentlemen could examine the goods on offer in the *foyer de la danse* as the ballerinas warmed up before a performance.*

The reserved, thoughtful elegance of La Karsavina (as she quickly became known) was very far from this popular idea of a ballerina and, because there were no classically trained male dancers outside Russia,

---

* The Jockey Club was founded in 1833 by a group of these gentlemen in a site next to the Opéra. It was 'purportedly devoted to Anglophile equestrian affairs, although the activities of its members tended more towards gossip and the "protection" of ballerinas' (J. Homans, *Apollo's Angels: A History of Ballet*, 2010, p. 145).

Nijinsky, Fokine, Bolm and the other male dancers of Diaghilev's troupe were a revelation. Until their arrival in Paris, dancing had been seen as so unmasculine that even male roles were usually danced by women *en travesti*. Not since Auguste Vestris in the early nineteenth century had male dancers of their calibre been seen on a European stage. The critic Henri Gauthier-Villars (Colette's husband) called Nijinsky a 'wonder of wonders' and *Le Figaro* hailed him the God of the Dance – a title the French had last given Vestris.*

Russia was already an established French ally and the object of some fascination in Paris. The great Russian novelists of the nineteenth century had been translated into French and were read avidly. Exhibitions in 1900 and 1907 of Russian arts and crafts had been huge successes and Diaghilev's concerts and opera season had stimulated this interest still further. Russian folk dances had even been shown on film in France in the late 1890s (Degas had painted them). Kshesinskaya had danced at the Opéra in 1908. Still, what Diaghilev's company gave Paris in 1909 was something entirely new. No one had 'seen anything like it before,' said the pianist Artur Rubinstein. 'The music, the daring colours of the décor, the explosive sensuality of the dances – it was overpowering, and quickly became the talk of Paris.' This was particularly true of Bakst's *Cléopâtre*, possibly the greatest success of the season, which had its premiere the same night as *Les Sylphides*.

Although Pavlova had the central dancing role, as the slave Ta-Hor who watches her beloved, Amoun (Fokine), share a night of love with Cleopatra, knowing that he will be killed in the morning, the star of the piece was Ida Rubinstein as the licentious queen. Rubinstein was a rich, eccentric beauty who was determined to be a famous actress. To that end, aged twenty, she had enlisted an adoring Bakst as her personal set designer and he had introduced her to Mikhail Fokine, who taught

---

* Years later, in his memoirs, Fokine would insist that the three most acclaimed pieces of the 1909 season were Bolm in the Polovtsian Dances, the Jesters from *Armide* and the Bacchanal (danced by his wife) from *Cléopâtra* – none of which were danced by Nijinsky. The accounts of Karsavina, Grigoriev and Benois, as well as the press reports, contradict his claims.

her the dance of the seven veils for her own production of *Salomé* in St Petersburg in 1908.

Rubinstein had little to do as Cleopatra except exude a fatal sex appeal, a skill which came naturally to her. Six slaves carried a gold and ebony chest onto the stage, then lifted a mummy out of it which they placed upright and carefully began to unwind. Veil after veil of shimmering colours – red embroidered with silver crocodiles, shot orange and deep blue – were removed until a semi-naked Rubinstein was revealed wearing a heavily fringed blue wig and blue-green body paint, one jewel-encrusted hand resting on the dark head of her favourite slave – Nijinsky (in danger of being typecast) – crouching like an adoring panther beside her. The audience were spellbound by her 'vacant eyes, pallid cheeks, and open mouth' and powerful sense of drama.

Like Pavlova, Rubinstein wasn't pretty according to the conventions of the day – Jean Cocteau described her legs as being 'so thin you thought you were looking at an ibis in the Nile' – but she gave off an irresistible essence of enchantment. Paris became obsessed: she was seen swathed in furs, her eyes rimmed with kohl, walking her pet leopard on a chain; it was said that she drank only champagne and ate only biscuits; she declared that when she left Paris she would go lion-hunting in Africa; she gave the bohemian Italian poet D'Annunzio a live tortoise with a gilded shell; her romantic conquests reputedly included not just husbands but their wives as well.

Diaghilev and Bakst's association of the Orient with unrestrained sensuality was nothing new. Since Napoleon's Egyptian campaign over a century earlier the French had been in thrall to the colour-saturated exotic. By 1909 the designer Paul Poiret was dressing his clients in oriental-style tunics; Henri Matisse had been painting in Tangier for years; and recently a new French edition of the *Arabian Nights* had been released. Even in St Petersburg fashionable Prince Lvov had an oriental room, complete with tiled walls, tropical plants, goldfish swimming in a fountain and stars twinkling down from a blue-painted ceiling.

But while to the French the Orient was foreign, for Russians it was part of their heritage. Their empire, after all, included Bukhara, the Caucasus and Siberia. When Bakst and Diaghilev were looking for costumes for *Prince Igor* in 1908, they found everything they wanted – brocade shawls, embroidered collars, kilim coats, fantastic headdresses – in the Tatar markets in St Petersburg. Fokine had amassed a collection of Islamic miniatures when he visited the Caucasus in 1900. And to French eyes, even Russian folk culture as reimagined through the Talashkino workshops of Princess Tenisheva looked unimaginably exotic.

Understanding and absorbing these trends was one aspect of Diaghilev's particular genius. Lopokova described 'the cunning with which he knew how to combine the excellent with the fashionable, the beautiful with the chic, and revolutionary art with the atmosphere of the old regime' – all at the same time as being obsessed by the box office. Most important of all, 'he couldn't stand anything that wasn't absolutely first class'.

The real power of Diaghilev's artistic achievement, though, was its coherence. The exquisite scenery and costumes, the music, the skill of the dancers and the innovative choreography combined seamlessly to create the impression with each ballet of a single work of art that had reached a new height of perfection, in which the whole surpassed the sum of its individually marvellous parts: as Benois said, 'not this, that or the other all in isolation, but everything together'. 'We really did stagger the world,' he remembered, and Sergey Grigoriev, not naturally given to hyperbole, agreed. During those weeks in the late spring of 1909, 'we all lived in an unreal and enchanted world, which was shared not only by those in close touch with us but even by the public, over whom we seemed to have cast our spell'.

Parisian socialites fell over one another to rhapsodise about the Ballets Russes. 'Right away I understood that I was witnessing a miracle ... [they] took possession of our souls,' wrote Anna de Noailles. Elegant Madame Greffulhe, one of the season's sponsors, may have been appalled by how 'drably provincial and uncultivated' the dancers were when she gave a dinner at the Hotel Crillon for them (Bronia had been right to worry about her hat), but seeing the dress rehearsal won her over – she was captivated. Perhaps the society composer Reynaldo Hahn best summed up the mood: 'When one has seen Nijinsky dance, nothing else matters.'

Wherever he was, Vaslav's day began with class and in Paris it was no different. After a few cups of tea at his hotel he would go to the Châtelet and go through his daily routine while Maestro Cecchetti* watched over him with bright, critical eyes, his cane banging time on the floor, shouting out instructions in his fabulously idiosyncratic mixture of Italian, French and Russian. The other dancers said that he could walk upright between Nijinsky's legs when Nijinsky jumped.

Bronia, who knew her brother's practice intimately and recognised its intensity, described how he would work through the barre exercises at an accelerated tempo, double the speed of other dancers. Vaslav 'applied maximum tension to every muscle', practising each movement that he would make on stage with exaggerated force, 'building up a reserve of strength so that' when he performed it would appear entirely effortless. Even Bronia, with her trained eye, could never spot his preparation for spins and jumps.

His aim was perfection. As Susan Sontag would write in 1986, 'In no other art can one find a comparable gap between what the world thinks of a star and what the star thinks about himself or herself, between the adulation that pours in from outside and the relentless dissatisfaction that goads one from within … Part of being a dancer is this cruelly self-punishing objectivity about one's shortcomings, as viewed from the perspective of an ideal observer, one more exacting than any real spectator could ever be: the god Dance.'

Years afterwards he would try to teach his little daughter, Kyra, what he knew: 'how perfection lay in the strength of the toe, the perfect

---

*Cecchetti did not travel with Diaghilev and his dancers as their Ballet Master until the following year, but since he was Nijinsky's most regular teacher throughout his career from 1907 onwards I have included him in this description as a way of trying to recreate Nijinsky's daily routine during his career as a whole.

"pointe"; that the secret of being light as a feather lay in one's breathing'. Dancing, he believed, 'should be as simple as one breath taken after another, and, though every step is a separate action, it must seem to be the natural and harmonious consequence of all previous action'.

He did not need a mirror to correct his faults because his muscular control was so finely tuned. Someone once said to him that it was a pity 'he could never watch himself dance. "You are mistaken," he replied. "I always see myself dancing. I can visualise myself so thoroughly that I know exactly what I look like just as if I sat in the midst of the audience."' After class he would spend an hour or two rehearsing with Fokine and the other dancers.

Lunch was always late, about four in the afternoon, once Diaghilev had roused himself from the hotel room with its curtains drawn and electric lights blazing, where, 'like an old Marquise afraid of the daylight', he had been drinking coffee in bed, reading and dispatching telegrams, scanning the papers and conducting conversations on several telephones at the same time. When he appeared at rehearsals, often with a small group of friends, the dancers fell silent and any who were sitting stood up. He radiated an almost regal self-assurance. 'With Grigoriev following discreetly a yard or two behind, he passed through the crowd … stopping here and there to exchange a greeting. Any male dancer to whom he spoke would click his heels together and bow.' Nijinsky, of course, was the one exception to this custom, confirmation (if any were needed) of the chasm that existed between him and the other dancers.

After lunch Vaslav might drive through the Bois de Boulogne with Nouvel or Bakst or go to the Louvre with Diaghilev, who was 'incapable of loving someone without trying to educate him', before a massage and a rest. Every day she was with them he had tea with his mother.

On the nights he was performing, Vaslav would arrive at the Châtelet at about half past six or seven. He would change back into practice clothes – slim black trousers and a loose silk shirt – and go through class alone at the back of the stage, avoiding any conversation. Then he would return to his dressing room, to which only Diaghilev's valet Vasily Zuikov was admitted – even Diaghilev was barred. Benois described

Zuikov as independent-minded but totally devoted to his master, 'a capacity Diaghilev perceived at once, for he possessed a wonderful gift of detecting all kinds of talent'. He relayed all the company gossip back to Diaghilev and was charged with keeping a close eye on Diaghilev's 'pride and joy' – Nijinsky.

Vaslav kept his dressing room austerely tidy, with his sticks of Leichner greasepaint and new pairs of shoes laid out in neat rows. Zuikov was in charge of these glove-leather shoes, ordered specially from Milan (and later London), and of his costumes. Vaslav might go through two or three pairs of shoes a night. It was here, while Vaslav dressed and put on his make-up (something he always did himself, part of his creation of the character), that a metamorphosis took place and the awkward young man would enter into a 'new existence'. Which of these creatures, the tongue-tied boy in one of his two slightly ill-fitting suits or the graceful, composed artist who seemed to breathe different air from his audience, was the real Nijinsky?

His mother, dressed in a newly bought evening gown, paid for by her son, came backstage to bless him before the curtain rose but Nijinsky – unusually for dancers at this time – didn't cross himself before a performance. The dancers' real sacrament was coating their shoes in rosin so they wouldn't slip on stage, pressing their toes into the box with a distinctive grating sound. One of the dancers in her troupe gave a marvellous description of Pavlova quivering on pointe in the rosin box at the side of the stage, grinding her toes into the rosin as deeply as possible while crossing herself with fluttering, 'uncanny swiftness' as if 'doing a special little *divertissement* for the pleasure of Jesus'. She would do this once on a normal night or over and again if she was nervous.

Vaslav preferred to stand still and silent for a moment with his eyes closed before going onstage, calming what Deborah Bull has called the 'tight, nervous energy' that takes over as a dancer waits for his cue, 'like a thousand gyroscopes in one small space'. Bronia would watch him, 'standing in the wings, immersed in silence and concentrated in himself. He seemed unaware of anything around him, as if in a meditation, gathering within himself an inner soul-force that he could carry onto the stage and offer wide to the audience.'

Diaghilev usually watched the performance from Misia Sert's box, sitting behind her with a 'very small pair of mother-of-pearl opera glasses' to look out over 'that murmuring ocean of jewels, feathers and heads'. Everyone on stage danced differently – better – if Diaghilev was watching. 'We always knew as soon as we were on stage or in the theatre if he was in the front of the house. It went round like a grapevine. Diaghilev's here, everybody knew. Ping, up, you had to be, as he was in the house.'

While Vaslav was dancing, Zuikov waited in the wings, holding 'a glass of water, a towel, a mirror, a powder box, or some eau de cologne'. During the intervals, he watched over Vaslav 'like an anxious nurse, wiping perspiration off his face, handing him the soap, turning on the faucet, throwing his dressing gown over his shoulders'.

After the curtain fell, Vaslav took his bows humbly, gently, revealing deep appreciation for the reception he received and never giving the impression that he thought it was his due. 'His bearing was modest and dignified, his features were composed ... contrast the quietly bowing figure on stage with the frenzied applause and excited gestures of the enraptured audience.' It may have been another role or perhaps for this brief instant, on stage but not in character, Vaslav was closest to his truest self: neither the exalted being he became when he danced nor the awkward boy he appeared afterwards but simply himself, what he wanted to be, no more and no less.

If he felt his performance had not been perfect, Vaslav might stay on in the darkened theatre after everyone else had left, practising his steps again and again. Even when he was satisfied, he continued dancing for a while after taking his bows 'just as a horse is trotted up and down with decreasing momentum after a race gradually to calm its quivering muscles'.

Diaghilev presided over dinner after the show. He tended to favour the same restaurants – 'their' corner table at Larue's, because Larue had once been chef to the Tsar, where Astruc remembered them devouring chateaubriand; Prunier; Viel – and the same faces were usually there:

Léon Bakst, Alexandre Benois, Walter Nouvel. The dance critic Valerian Svetlov, so vain he refused to smile for fear of wrinkles, had accompanied the committee from St Petersburg. He wielded immense power in this world. Vaslav said that 'all the ballerinas went to bed with him because they were afraid of him', the most notable exceptions probably being Karsavina, who, having refused Fokine to please her family, had in 1907 married Vasily Mukhin, a civil servant, and Bronia.

Alone among the other dancers, Karsavina was sometimes invited to dinner – she was always amused by the fact that Eleonora left the theatre every night to take her naive daughter home, kissing Vaslav goodnight and leaving him with Diaghilev – but the most regular of Diaghilev's female guests was Misia Sert. After the champagne-drenched first-night dinner at Larue's, Vaslav told his sister what fun the evening had been: during supper Diaghilev had flirted with Misia, kissing her and playfully poking a banana in her cleavage. Misia spoke Polish, and Vaslav told Bronia they had become 'great friends'.

Another young man was often there too, the poet Jean Cocteau, known to his friends as *l'ange du mensonge*. Although they were the same age and Cocteau still looked like a mop-haired schoolboy, he suffered from none of the shyness that plagued Vaslav. From his rouged lips witticisms as dazzling as fireworks burst forth and to Vaslav's amusement he urged Vaslav to make up too; this was Paris, after all. At the party after the premiere, high on the colours with which he said Diaghilev had splashed Paris (and God knows what else), Cocteau danced on the back of Larue's velvet banquettes, earning himself the nickname 'Jeanchik' from his new hero.

When dinner ended, Vaslav went back to his hotel with Zuikov dispatched to see he got into bed safely and alone, while Diaghilev and the others would stay out later, sampling – as Romola would knowingly put it – 'the peculiar specialities of Paris'. There is only evidence of Nijinsky accompanying the others on this type of late-night tour once. Cocteau told a friend that he, Nijinsky, Diaghilev, Astruc and Bakst went to Le Chabanais, the most famous and opulent brothel in Paris. 'Bakst thought the women were superb. The women fought over Nijinsky, screaming, "I want the one that's never done it!"' (History does not relate whether one of them got him; if one had, I half suspect Diaghilev might have made her regret it.)

It was an intoxicating time. Diaghilev appeared one morning while Karsavina was working alone on the Châtelet's unlit stage, a graceful figure in her long white practice tutu and darned pink tights, and said to her, 'We are all living in the witchery of Armida's groves.' Gradually the bond between him and Vaslav was growing closer. Vaslav had stopped wearing the diamond ring Prince Lvov had given him and replaced it with a huge sapphire ring made by Cartier from Diaghilev that he took off only as he was going on stage.

Although nothing survives in writing to document how Vaslav felt in these heady months, the extensive evidence of how everyone around him said they all felt suggests that he, too, must have been drunk on success, springtime and possibly love. The one piece of evidence we have is that leap off-stage after his first variation in *Armide*, recalled by Karsavina and other witnesses, which she saw as an outburst of joy. For Vaslav, this must have felt like the beginning of life. Everything he had hoped for lay waiting for him: cheering audiences, critical acclaim, creative fulfilment (probably not in that order). Whatever sacrifice he thought he had made in becoming involved with Diaghilev must surely have seemed more than worthwhile; and, in this heightened state of excited anticipation, perhaps he began to love Diaghilev as well as admire him.

The neglected Aleksey Mavrin, Diaghilev's secretary and up to now his acknowledged lover, turned for consolation to a dancer called Olga Fyodorova. Deliberately or not he had selected one of the few women Diaghilev had publicly singled out as attractive, apparently telling Benois the previous year 'that she was the only woman with whom he could fall in love'. When Mavrin and Fyodorova eloped, Diaghilev sacked them both, but more for form's sake than anything else: it was his pride rather than his heart which was wounded.

After their season at the Châtelet closed on 18 June, Vaslav had two more performances – a gala at the Opéra and a performance at a private party given by Maurice Ephrussi (he was the son of Charles, Proust's

Swann, who bought the netsukes described by Edmund de Waal in *The Hare with Amber Eyes*). The Ephrussis were loyal supporters of Diaghilev's enterprises, though Karsavina was embarrassed by the attention – Gabriel Astruc made it quite clear to her that Madame Ephrussi, née Rothschild, was enamoured by her and when she arrived she found her admiring hostess had covered her dressing table with white roses.

These salon performances were important parts of the Ballets Russes programme, allowing Diaghilev to display his productions to even more potential sponsors and audience members from this sophisticated group at the apex of French society. Exposure to their rarefied world was also good for his dancers. Karsavina remembered watching Nijinsky marvelling at Emmanuel Bibesco's collection of Gauguin paintings: 'Look at that strength!' Finally, they provided the performers with welcome additional income. Diaghilev had negotiated a thousand francs for Nijinsky's appearance at the Ephrussis', almost half his salary for the entire season, and Madame Ephrussi saw to it that Karsavina got a thousand too, double what Diaghilev had agreed to on her behalf.

Vaslav managed to get through the Opéra gala but was too ill to perform in the Ephrussis' electrically lit garden in the avenue du Bois. Diaghilev was so distracted by worry that he barely noticed the beauty of *Les Sylphides* – his favourite piece – being performed in an illuminated garden on a summer evening and could not enjoy the party that followed. Leaving behind the crowds waiting to congratulate him on his triumphant season, he rushed off early to check on Vatsa.

Parisian water was not clean and Vaslav, used to being able to drink from the tap in St Petersburg, had not known to stick to bottled or boiled water. He developed typhoid and, although they caught it early, he still spent a month at the Daunou convalescing. His mother sat by his bedside every day and by the time Bronia was allowed in to see him, when his temperature had fallen, he was sitting up in bed wearing a white nightshirt, thin and with a shaven head, but very cheerful, looking like a little boy and eating cream of asparagus soup. He was enjoying everyone fussing over him and he told Bronia laughingly that Sergey Pavlovich, who was mortally afraid of illness, had not ventured into his room all the time he was ill but had spoken to him through a crack in the door. Even once he was allowed visitors Diaghilev maintained a cautious distance.

When he was almost better, Diaghilev finally came into his room and made him an offer – of business and pleasure combined, the two being interlinked as they always were with Diaghilev. He invited Vaslav to live with him and be supported by him. Although he would no longer pay Nijinsky a salary, he would take care of all his expenses and give Eleonora 500 francs a month. It sounds rather bald, all these years later, but I think that for Diaghilev at least, this was a romantic moment: the acknowledgement of a serious commitment, significantly of a personal as well as a professional nature – a kind of public bond that had hitherto not existed between two men. As Proust's Baron de Charlus would declare of Robert Morel, the protégé over whom he felt a possessive pride not unlike Diaghilev's for Nijinsky, 'The mere fact that I take an interest in him and extend my protection over him, gives him a preeminence.'

'I did not want to agree,' remembered Vaslav. 'Diaghilev sat on my bed and insisted … [he] realised my value and was therefore afraid that I might leave him, because I wanted to leave even then, when I was twenty years old. I was afraid of life.' But elsewhere in the Diary he wrote that he 'loved Diaghilev sincerely, and when he used to tell me that love for women was a terrible thing, I believed him. If I had not believed him, I would not have been able to do what I did.' In the end he accepted, perhaps more because there didn't seem to be any alternative than because he was really afraid of Diaghilev or because he loved him and actively wanted to be with him.

He knew that he couldn't cope with life in the real world – he had no idea how to book a train ticket or find a hotel room, let alone organise his working life; he had been effectively institutionalised by his time at the Imperial Theatre School – and he also understood that nowhere else, with no one else, could he live the sort of life that he could with Diaghilev. As he said to Bronia, 'this world of art was where he belonged'.

And while he may not have found Diaghilev physically attractive, he admired him profoundly, telling someone years later that Diaghilev meant more to him than anyone else he had known. Léonide Massine, Diaghilev's next lover, described being unsure of himself when Diaghilev was courting him, if courting is the right word, 'but exhilarated at the prospect of working with such a man'. Vaslav must have felt this too. (Massine also told a mistress that sex with Diaghilev was 'like going to bed with a nice fat old lady': boring but not exactly a trial.)

Finally, under Diaghilev's aegis he was becoming a star, far more quickly than he would ever have been allowed to rise at the rigid Mariinsky, and only as a star would he be granted control over his creative life, which meant choreography as well as performing. This, I believe, was the bargain Vaslav struck with himself when he accepted Sergey Pavlovich's proposal in the summer of 1909.

Though he no longer queued up with the other dancers every two weeks to collect their salaries from Grigoriev, sitting backstage behind a table piled high with gold and silver coins, his new position in Diaghilev's life gave Vaslav a new insight into the runnings of Diaghilev's marvellously haphazard operation. It was probably at this meeting or soon afterwards that Diaghilev told him that, despite every seat at the Châtelet being taken throughout their season, they had made significant losses. None of the other dancers knew because he had managed to pay them all in full before putting them on the train back home.

Diaghilev's insistence on the 'first class' had cost over 600,000 francs, leaving a gap of 86,000 francs between income and expenditure. In an effort to recoup his losses, Gabriel Astruc, Diaghilev's sponsor in Paris, pawned the ballet's entire stock of sets and costumes to Raoul Gunsbourg, Director of the Monte Carlo Opera, for 20,000 francs. If he wanted to present another season in Paris, Diaghilev would have to buy everything back from Gunsbourg as well as repay Astruc. But instead of negotiating with Astruc, Diaghilev incensed him still further by making plans to present the 1910 Saison Russe at the Opéra rather than the Châtelet. Furious, Astruc wrote to Mathilde Kshesinskaya, whom he knew despised Diaghilev, hoping to undermine his reputation in Russia. Eventually that winter Baron Dmitry de Günzburg (not to be confused with Raoul) came to Diaghilev's rescue as he had the previous year, repaying Astruc and restoring relations between the two men.

Diaghilev rose above the impending financial Armageddon, blithely pressing ahead with preparations for his new season. In July he asked Maurice Ravel and Claude Debussy to write pieces for his ballet. Diaghilev urged Debussy to finish the scenario as quickly as possible so that he could take it to Venice to show it to a choreographer there. Fokine was not in Venice: the choreographer to whom Diaghilev was referring could only have been Nijinsky. Bronia Nijinska disagreed with this interpretation of events but, since Nijinsky's first ballet, *L'Après-midi d'un faune*, was accompanied by Debussy's music, it is not inconceivable that this was the first mention of it – perhaps even a promise given by Diaghilev to Nijinsky in their talks about their future in his room at the Hotel Daunou, only weeks before.

Accompanied by Bakst, Diaghilev and Nijinsky stayed first in the spa at Carlsbad and then at the Grand Hotel des Bains in Venice during what amounted to an unconventional honeymoon. They made a strange pair: an impressive, middle-aged, rather *ancien régime* gentleman (in his summer uniform, a black jacket with a gardenia in the buttonhole, his tie held in place by a black pearl and 'an eyeglass dangling against his waistcoat', a silver-topped malacca cane, narrow white trousers, white shoes and a straw hat, which he kept lifting to sponge his forehead), accompanied by a twenty-year-old boy whom he obviously adored, described variously as looking like a stable lad, a plumber's apprentice, or a clerk. As Cecil Beaton would observe of Serge Lifar, it didn't matter how immaculately Diaghilev dressed him (as he also dressed Vaslav), he always looked 'like a street urchin'.

Michel Calvocoressi took Nijinsky shopping for a bathing suit, translating for him at the tailor. Vaslav was as exacting about the fit 'as if it had been a stage costume', while Monsieur Calvo took the opportunity, when they were in the changing room together, to marvel at 'how powerful and harmonious Nijinsky was in build. Although his muscles were on the big side, his body suggested that of a Greek athlete, reposeful as well as strong, and in sharp contrast with the mobile, monkeyish face. It had none of the almost feminine grace which he so often showed when appearing in stage costume.' Calvocoressi, like most of Diaghilev's friends, found Nijinsky quiet and almost childlike – hardly surprising, given that they were all fifteen to twenty years his senior* – but 'pleasant'.

Venice in August was *en fête* and full of Diaghilev's friends and acquaintances. At a party given by the flamboyant Marchesa Casati – 'to society what Ida Rubinstein was to the stage' – Isadora Duncan told a surprised and rather disapproving Nijinsky what beautiful children they would have together (but she was prone to say this to anyone she admired). After they danced together, she enthused to a friend that 'it was more wonderful than making love with a Negro boxer on Mr. Singer's billiard-table'. Mr Singer was Paris Singer, Winnie de Polignac's brother, Isadora's lover at the time and the father of one of her children.†

When they arrived at St Petersburg that autumn, Alexandre Benois was disappointed to find (probably retrospectively, as his memoirs were not published until over thirty years later) that 'Diaghilev's attitude towards his own enterprise had ceased to be that of Olympic

---

*The only person of Vaslav's age in Diaghilev's circle was Jean Cocteau, who, though he never saw Nijinsky after 1914, returned to him as a subject again and again throughout his life. His biographer Francis Steegmuller speculates (in *Cocteau: A Biography*, 1970, pp. 72–3) that Cocteau's initial efforts to get closer to Nijinsky when they first met (he had a habit of visiting Nijinsky at the time he knew he was being massaged) were firmly squashed by Diaghilev.

†Duncan was another enthusiastic hostess. On a rainy summer's night in 1910 she threw a party in the gardens of the Palace Hotel, Versailles. Guests drank champagne and ate caviar in tents in the illuminated gardens while gypsy music and an orchestra from Vienna played. Duncan presided over everything in flaming Fortuny silk and gold sandals. In the *New Yorker*, Janet Flanner recalled her once giving 'a house party that started in Paris, gathered force in Venice, and culminated weeks later on a houseboat in the Nile. She was a nomad *de luxe*'. (Flanner, *Paris was Yesterday*, 2003, p. 36.)

objectiveness; thanks to his friendship with Nijinsky, he had become *personally* interested in the success of the ballet.' I would argue that Diaghilev had always been personally interested in his ballet – and that this may have been his reason for pursuing Nijinsky, rather than the other way around – but Benois was jealous of his influence over Diaghilev and perhaps already sensed it slipping away.

There was a new face at the conference table in Diaghilev's apartment that winter of 1909: the owlish young composer Igor Stravinsky. He was almost unknown, but Diaghilev with his customary confidence in his own taste had entrusted him (along with Fokine) to write a self-consciously Russian ballet tailored to the French market: *L'Oiseau de feu*.* Pavlova, he hoped, would take the title role. Despite her late arrival for the 1909 season, she was still the biggest draw in ballet and if she could be tempted to star in his 1910 season Diaghilev had to put her first, even though Nijinsky begged to be allowed to dance the Firebird himself, offering to dance *en pointe*, something no male dancer had done before. (In the end Pavlova refused Diaghilev's offer, preferring to set up her own company, and Karsavina became the first Firebird.)

Stravinsky was welcomed by Diaghilev's collaborators. Benois, predictably, remembered liking him because 'in those days he was a charming and willing "pupil"'. Stravinsky and Diaghilev developed a deep friendship, though he did not appreciate Diaghilev's insistence that loving women was morbid and that he would be a better artist if he were homosexual; it was, Stravinsky said later, 'impossible to describe the perversity of Diaghilev's entourage – a kind of homosexual Swiss guard'.

But he liked Nijinsky, who was only seven years younger than him, immediately. Vaslav's 'extraordinary physical presence' was the first thing Stravinsky noticed, but his 'shy manner and soft Polish speech' were endearing and 'he was immediately very open and affectionate

---

* Prince Lieven said of the folklore pastiche that was *L'Oiseau de feu* that it was 'as if Alice of *Alice in Wonderland* was partnered with Falstaff in a Scotch jig'. (Quoted in L. Garafola and N. V. N. Baer (eds), *The Ballets Russes and its World*, 1999, p. 120.)

with me', though Stravinsky thought he detected 'curious absences in his personality', perhaps immaturity, perhaps something deeper.

This may have been down to Nijinsky's lack of confidence in Diaghilev's circle. Diaghilev and his friends and colleagues were all highly distinguished in their own right, 'the elite of the St Petersburg intelligentsia'. Much as he enjoyed being part of this group and eagerly soaked up their ideas, Vaslav froze in their company and could not 'overcome his timidity. He did not behave like a famous artist. He did not realise that he had achieved fame on his own merit and that he was great in his own art.' He remembered never being able to speak in their meetings, though he always attended them, 'because I was considered a silly kid'; and it almost certainly suited Diaghilev to keep him feeling like this.

It worried Bronia. The carefree boy she had known, 'at ease and unconstrained' and a special favourite with her girlfriends, had disappeared. She put it down to Vaslav's pride and sensitivity: he would be so devastated at having 'made the slightest social blunder' that he retreated altogether so as not to risk embarrassment.

But on his own ground, Nijinsky suffered from none of these anxieties. When Fokine gave Bronia the role of Papillon in his new ballet, *Carnaval*, but had no time to do more than show her the basic steps, Vaslav helped her create the butterfly's fluttering lightness to match Robert Schumann's *prestissimo* tempo, working out the placement of the body and the flickering hand movements himself and then helping her to learn them. It was his first piece of choreography for another dancer. As Richard Buckle, Nijinsky's first biographer, would put it, Nijinsky's first 'essay in choreography was embedded in a work of Fokine's, just as Leonardo's angel is said to smile from the corner of Verrocchio's Madonna in the National Gallery'.

Throughout the autumn of 1909 Nijinsky and Pavlova rehearsed *Giselle*. Being chosen to dance the prestigious role of Albrecht while still so young and untried a dancer was a great honour for Nijinsky. Bronia, who watched their rehearsals, described the creative union between her brother and Pavlova as the most 'supremely right' of all the performances she ever saw in her life. 'The unreal quality and beauty of the dance, so ethereal and weightless, charmed the eye and moved one to heartache.' Other dancers at their rehearsals were reduced to tears.

But so powerful was Vaslav's interpretation of Albrecht that in the end Pavlova refused to dance opposite him, insisting that they perform *Giselle* on different nights. She was straightforward when Bronia asked her why: 'I do not wish to share with Nijinsky my success before the public. I do not wish to see ovations being given Nijinsky for a performance in which I too dance. Let the public that comes to see Pavlova see only Pavlova! Vassia has enough of his own public to fill the theatre to overflowing ...'

That winter, even more than in previous years, the Mariinsky was a hotbed of intrigue and jealousy. Diaghilev's innovative young dancers were known as the 'Diaghilevtsy-Fokinisty', set against the old guard 'Imperialisty' led by Kshesinskaya and Nikolay Legat, with their antiquated ideas and close connections to the court. Nijinsky, hailed by the St Petersburg press on his return from Paris that autumn and known to be the particular intimate of Diaghilev, was a special focus of Imperialisty hostility despite the boyish modesty with which he responded to his stardom.

Leaving St Petersburg and the stifling atmosphere of the Mariinsky in May 1910 came as a relief. The company travelled first to Berlin for two weeks of dates there, and from there on to Paris. Despite his sublime performances Vaslav was evidently troubled. Bronia was concerned that his mood was increasingly serious and preoccupied. 'He was almost always alone now, and seemed to be avoiding people ... More and more I felt him to be Nijinsky, "le dieu de la danse," rather than Vaslav, my own brother and dear friend.'

As Diaghilev's chosen one he was set apart from the camaraderie of the *corps*, several of whom he had danced with since schooldays, but he never felt he truly belonged at Larue's either. Vaslav seldom contributed to Diaghilev's debates with his friends, having learned 'that it is better to be silent than to talk nonsense'. Later he said Diaghilev had realised he was 'stupid and told me not to speak'.

The atmosphere in Paris was different in 1910, too. Diaghilev's 'magic lantern for grown-ups' may have been relit, but rivalries and resentments were also glowing patiently, waiting for the spark that would blow them into life. Fokine went first, even before the season had officially begun. Jealous of his pre-eminence, throughout the preparations for the summer he had been demanding to play the lead parts in his ballets – which meant that Nijinsky could not dance some of the roles Diaghilev wanted for him. It was agreed after extensive negotiations that for certain performances Fokine could have the Chief Warrior in the Polovtsian Dances and Harlequin in *Carnaval* as well as Ivan Tsarevich in *L'Oiseau de feu*. Next an article on the Ballets Russes in *Comoedia Illustré* listed him merely as a performer, not as *premier danseur* or choreographer. Furious about this slight, Fokine insisted that for all future publicity material his name be written in larger letters than anyone else's and above the composers, designers and artists. Astruc, who was in charge of promoting the season, refused these demands.

Benois was next. At the opening night, having left his family in Italy and travelled to Paris especially for the occasion, he was horrified when he opened his programme to find that *Schéhérazade* was listed as being by Bakst, who had designed the sets but not written the libretto. When he asked Diaghilev about it the next day, Diaghilev replied, '*Que veux-tu?* Bakst had to be given something. You have *Le Pavillon d'Armide* and he will have *Schéhérazade*.' Diaghilev considered that since everyone in his committee contributed to all the ballets, everyone should take their turn to be recognised and rewarded for them. Bakst had worked just as hard as Benois on the 1909 season and received none of the plaudits or royalties. Anyway, he was late paying Bakst again – this would go some way to making up for the delay.

Besides, it was Bakst's designs rather than Benois's story or even Fokine's choreography which made *Schéhérazade* such a phenomenal success. His set was an Arabian Nights harem in glowing blues, emerald greens, fuschias and crimsons that looked as if they should clash but created instead a fantastical riot of colour. The exquisite watercolour sketches he made for the costumes show Schéhérazade's attendants in

Creatures of perfect grace: Nijinsky as Harlequin and Karsavina
as Columbine in *Carnaval*, by Ernest Oppler, *c.*1910.

sheer filmy fabrics that reveal delicate traces of rosy nipples, the curve of a buttock and shadowy pubic hair. Their heads are thrown back in abandon, arms ecstatically raised to reveal their armpits, their nails and lips darkened. But Benois was unconvinced by Diaghilev's view that everyone should share in the Ballets' rewards and hated to admit a rival's talent. He wrote from Italy to tell Diaghilev that their friendship was over; not for the first time, and nor would it be the last.

In *Schéhérazade* Nijinsky was again playing a favourite slave, but this time his role was all about sex. In gold harem trousers, his skin painted a dark grey-blue, 'not unlike the bloom on black grapes', he stalked the stage like a creature half animal, half snake, crazed with desire, ravishing Ida Rubinstein as Zobéïde and then dying at her feet. He was 'inexpressibly wild, a cat caressing, a tiger devouring … His lightness and swiftness were unbelievable, but it was sensuality all the way.'

Here one senses Diaghilev understanding even better than they did what his audiences wanted to see and giving it straight to them. 'Nobody will believe me of course, but Diaghilev did not know anything about dancing,' George Balanchine told Robert Craft in 1958. 'His real interest in ballet was sexual. He could not bear the sight of [Alexandra] Danilova and would say to me, "Her tits make me want to vomit." Once when I was standing next to him at a rehearsal for *Apollo* [1928], he said, "How beautiful." I agreed, thinking that he referred to the music, but he quickly corrected me: "No, no. I mean Lifar's ass; it is like a rose."' But Stravinsky did not believe Nijinsky was ever 'conscious of his performances from Diaghilev's point of view': for him ballet was art and art alone, never commerce or sex.

It was a measure of Nijinsky's versatility that his other two roles in the 1910 Paris season were so different. In his hands Albrecht, traditionally just an auxiliary part, became a major acting role, 'the grief of the repentant seducer [made] profoundly pathetic' while he watched his abandoned beloved go mad. As Harlequin in *Carnaval*, 'his dancing was music made visible'. He came on stage with his arm around Columbine's tiny waist, mischievously taking one big step for every two of hers. That incredible *entrechat-dix*, which he was the first dancer to achieve on stage, was executed with elegant, negligent wit. Cocteau was delighted: Nijinsky's Harlequin was 'an acrobatic cat stuffed full of candid lechery and crafty indifference, a schoolboy wheedling, thieving, swift-footed, utterly freed from the chains of gravity, a creature of perfect mathematical grace'.

CHAPTER 4

Petrushka
1910–1911

DURING THE SUMMER OF 1910 Vaslav and Diaghilev returned to Venice where Vaslav swam every day at the Lido.* Bakst painted him on the beach in red briefs, with a handkerchief covering his head and one arm upraised, suntanned muscles rippling: Calvocoressi's Greek athlete. A bad case of sunstroke – or rather a disinclination to jump when the Mariinsky told him to, after a second triumphant season abroad – meant that Vaslav missed the opening of the Mariinsky's season in September, passing up the opportunity to dance Albrecht opposite Pavlova's Giselle. He did not get back to Russia until the end of November after stopping in Paris with Diaghilev for several weeks en route. When they finally did return, he was regularly – insolently – late for class and, as in the previous year, fined for every tiny infringement of the rules. The critics were quick to spot that in the non-Diaghilev repertoire he did not display 'his usual brilliance'.

The atmosphere at the Mariinsky had worsened since the previous spring. Supported by the dress-circle audience, Kshesinskaya was still at war with Diaghilev and his dancers, and the younger members of the

---

*Diaghilev never did. Lifar reported that Diaghilev would not have appeared naked for anything in the world, quite apart from hating water with a superstitious passion.

audience who sat up in the gods, students and admirers of Nijinsky, Pavlova and Karsavina, now refused to applaud her. When word got out that Kshesinskaya had said, 'I spit on the gods,' they sent her a collective letter saying, from 'up here, it is much easier to spit down on you than for you to spit up at us'.

On his return to St Petersburg, Bronia found Vaslav still silent and withdrawn, holding himself aloof. 'But there was also a new air of happiness about him, a certain inner glow.' Gradually, he began to confide in her about what he and Diaghilev had been discussing over the months they had been away. The Ballets Russes' successes had made Diaghilev determined to create a permanent company that would work for ten months of the year, rather than just a touring troupe available to him in their summer vacations. His putative company would consist of well-paid dancers on three-year contracts but, except when the artist was a big enough name to demand time away from the Imperial Theatres, this would require them to relinquish their positions as Artists at the Mariinsky, losing all the security and status that rank carried with it.

Implicit in these talks was the fact that Nijinsky would, of course, be the star of Diaghilev's new company – although he would not be free to leave the Tsar's service altogether until 1912, having performed for him for the obligatory five years. That was a problem Diaghilev would deal with when he had to.

Next were the ballets Diaghilev intended his new company to put on. The first would be *Petrushka*, to music composed by Stravinsky and with the libretto and design by Benois (Diaghilev was using the promise of the project to lure him back into the fold) and Vaslav was to play the eponymous hero (or anti-hero).

Most thrilling of all, from Vaslav's point of view, was that secretly, so as not to antagonise the temperamental Fokine, Diaghilev had entrusted him with his first choreographic work. It was to be *L'Après-midi d'un faune*, from a poem of Stéphane Mallarmé, set to the music of Debussy, and he was already bubbling over with ideas for it. 'I want to move away from the classical Greece that Fokine likes to use. Instead I want to use the archaic Greece that is less known and, so far, little used in the theatre,' he told Bronia. 'Any sweetly sentimental line in the form or in the movement will be excluded. More may even be borrowed from Assyria than Greece. I have already started to work on it in my own mind ... I want to show it to you ...'

Bakst was encouraging him in other creative endeavours, too. Vaslav attended his painting classes where his easel was next to that of the young Marc Chagall. He smiled at Chagall, 'as if to encourage me in my boldness, of which I was not yet aware', but his own drawings, wrote Chagall, were childlike in their simplicity.

Nijinsky danced *Giselle* for the first time at the Mariinsky in January 1911 to thundering applause and rave reviews. He performed opposite Karsavina, his partner in the Ballets Russes's Paris version of the ballet, and he wore the costume Benois had designed for him earlier that year. The next morning, according to Bronia's account, he was awakened by a telephone call summoning him to the offices of the Imperial Theatres. Bronia and Eleonora waited for him at home, hoping that he would return promoted to the coveted rank of *premier danseur*; Karsavina had told them she had just been made *prima ballerina* with a corresponding rise in salary to 6,000 roubles.

Instead he reappeared pale but with an excited determination in his eyes and told them that he had been dismissed for wearing 'an indecent and improper costume' in the presence of her Imperial Majesty Maria Fyodorovna, the Tsar's mother. When Vaslav did not respond, he was told that if he issued an apology to the Minister of the Imperial Court and requested a reinstatement he would be taken on again. As Vaslav turned to leave, still without saying anything, the official panicked and offered him a contract for 9,000 roubles for twenty performances a year, leaving him ample time to perform abroad. Still Vaslav said nothing. The offer was raised to 12,000 roubles. Finally he bowed and said haughtily that he did not wish to remain at 'the Imperial Ballet from which I was thrown out as if I was useless'. If they wanted him to return, he said, *he* would expect an apology and a petition requesting his return. 'I am no longer an Artist of the Imperial Theatres. I am now only an artist of the

Diaghilev Ballet,' he told Eleonora and Bronia when he got home. 'I will telephone Seryozha and tell him … I can imagine how happy he will be.'

The Mariinsky's official costume for Albrecht was a long tunic worn over a pair of tights, with short trunks worn over the tights so that nothing untoward could be glimpsed beneath the tunic. Benois's costume, intended to be a more accurate approximation of medieval clothing (*Giselle* is set in Germany in the Middle Ages), had a shorter, belted tunic and no trunks. In Paris, Diaghilev had ordered Benois to shorten the tunic a further two inches from his original design to show off Nijinsky's bottom. But, as Telyakovsky, the Director of the Imperial Theatres, would observe in his diary, 'Paris is tolerant of things that would be out of the question in St Petersburg, especially on the Imperial stage.'

Nijinsky, though, would have seen the Mariinsky's costume as out of date. He and the other dancers of the Diaghilevtsy-Fokinisty set were passionately attached to the idea of ballet being authentic, rather than pandering to the audience's tastes or prejudices: he simply would not have worn a costume he considered wrong. When Grand Duke Sergey, one of Mathilde Kshesinskaya's lovers, had come backstage between the first and second acts to demand that Nijinsky change the offending outfit, Nijinsky, furious at this interference in his artistic domain, had rudely refused. Benois had a different perspective. Even though he had designed the disputed costume, he called Nijinsky that 'conceited artist' for taking offence over the issue and resigning.

There has been much speculation since about whether Diaghilev persuaded Nijinsky to appear in an improper costume in order to provoke a crisis between the dancer he considered his property and the theatre which still effectively owned him. Diaghilev may well have encouraged Vaslav to wear the costume they both considered appropriate for Albrecht; it is hard to imagine they hadn't discussed it, given the importance of this Russian debut of what was effectively their production of *Giselle*. Probably, too, without the knowledge that Diaghilev was waiting to offer him a position in his new company, Nijinsky would not have dared to reject the Imperial Theatres' offer to take him back. In reality, though, all this incident did was clarify the fact that Nijinsky's fate was inextricably tied to Diaghilev's: from the moment in the Hotel Daunou two summers earlier this confrontation had been inevitable, in one form or another. 'Vaslav,' said Benois, 'was now entirely at his [Diaghilev's] disposal and under his control.'

Whether or not he had a hand in Nijinsky's dismissal from the Imperial Theatres, Diaghilev was quick to capitalise on it. He telegraphed Gabriel Astruc in Paris days later, detailing the intrigue: 'Appalling scandal. Use publicity.' When Telyakovsky called repeatedly to try and persuade Vaslav to change his mind, Diaghilev reminded him how he had been insulted and urged him to leave behind the petty jealousies and tedious administrative demands of the Imperial Theatres, to live instead with him in a world of art 'where ballets would be created by great musicians and great painters under [his] personal guidance and direction', and where Vaslav would be a central figure in all their works.

In a matter of weeks Bronia had tendered her resignation on the grounds that she no longer had confidence in the artistic direction of the Imperial Theatres. Adolph Bolm followed and others, including Karsavina, promised to dance for Diaghilev when they were not required to be at the Mariinsky.* Enrico Cecchetti was engaged as *maître de ballet* – though his tastes were more traditional than Diaghilev's he would become the company's 'dance-conscience' – and the volatile Benois and Fokine were given grandiloquent titles, *directeur artistique* and *directeur choreographique* respectively. Diaghilev had headed writing paper printed with the words 'Les Ballets Russes de Serge de Diaghilew'. 'A completely new path was opening in front of us ... the future uncertain but so exciting.'

There was one unhappy footnote to this episode, a kiss from Carabosse. Vaslav was due to be called up for military service, but no one close to him foresaw that outside the influence of the Imperial

---

* When Karsavina tried to protest that she might need some time off, Diaghilev raged at her, telling her she had all eternity to rest in. 'Why could you not have married Fokine? [Then] You would both have belonged to me.' (T. Karsavina, *Theatre Street*, 1948, p. 284.) Fokine and Karsavina had in fact hoped to marry in the early 1900s, until, at her parents' behest, she turned him down.

Theatres, and bearing in mind Diaghilev's unpopularity at court and the manner of Vaslav's dismissal from the Theatres, it would be almost impossible for him to procure an exemption. Once he left Russia he would not be permitted to return without performing this service. From 1910 onwards he was effectively stateless, belonging nowhere but the stage.

Nijinsky and Diaghilev left St Petersburg in March for Paris and then Monte Carlo, where the new company would be based for the spring. Having left behind the tensions surrounding their departure from Russia – Vaslav's proud refusal to compromise and his mother's anguish over his decision – this was, like their first season in Paris, a time of excited hopefulness.

It was decided while they were in Monte Carlo that *Petrushka* would be put on hold while they prepared for the premiere of the new season, *Le Spectre de la rose*, which was first performed in late April at the Monte Carlo Opera, a last flourish of art nouveau style. Its premise, based on two lines from a poem of Théophile Gautier's, was wonderfully simple: a young girl, returning home from her first ball, falls asleep on a chair in her bedroom, dreaming of the boy who has given her the rose she still holds.* The spirit of the Rose comes through her window and dances with her as she sleeps; the music is Carl Maria von Weber's swirlingly romantic 1819 'Invitation to the Waltz'. The Rose flies out of the window when the girl wakes, wondering whether it had all been a dream.

Léon Bakst designed the set, a pretty blue and white bedroom in the style of the 1830s, and Tamara Karsavina as the girl wore a ruffled ivory satin gown trimmed with lace. On the first night Bakst was rushing around trying to find a spot for a canary in a cage that he

---

*This is the same premise as the opening scene of one of the classic nineteenth-century ballets, but with the masculine and feminine roles inverted: at the start of *La Sylphide*, the hero, James, is asleep in an armchair, dreaming of the otherwordly sylph. (A. Macaulay, *Matthew Bourne and his Adventures in Dance*, 2000, p. 192.)

was determined would provide the final touch to the scenery, but he couldn't hang it in the window through which Nijinsky would jump and there was nowhere else for it to go. It recalled the exquisite yellow drawing room in the house belonging to his glamorous but irascible French grandfather, which had canaries in four gilded cages – one of those Proustian details at which the designers of the Ballets Russes so excelled. Impatiently Diaghilev told him to do without it: 'You don't understand, Seryozha; we must create the atmosphere.' The cage was lost in transit before they reached Paris.

Benois described Diaghilev in top hat and tails, 'looking very pompous and solemn as he always did on first nights, [standing] by, giving directions with growing anxiety' as silk rose petals were sewn onto a squirming Nijinsky's pink and mauve tricot body stocking beneath Bakst's watchful eye. Bronia thought this process of transformation into the Rose was like watching the creation of a work of art. Vaslav had made up his face to look like 'a celestial insect, his eyebrows suggesting some beautiful beetle ... his mouth was like rose petals' and he wore a close-fitting cap of silk petals. It was probably just Diaghilev creating a story, but Nijinsky was even said to have sprinkled himself with attar of roses before he went on stage.

As the Rose, Nijinsky 'suggested a cluster of leaves wafted by a slight breeze', his hands and arms unfolding around his head like petals or tendrils. 'When he danced *Spectre* he was the very perfume of the rose, because in everything he extracted the essence,' recalled Marie Rambert. It was, said the critic Cyril Beaumont, 'the most perfect choreographic conception I have ever seen ... It seemed too beautiful, too flawless, too intangible to be real; and when it was over you had a feeling as though the warm theatre had caused you to doze and you had suddenly awakened from an entrancing dream.'

The most demanding of teachers, Enrico Cecchetti loved this piece. For him Karsavina embodied 'grace, freshness and trembling thoughts', while Nijinsky exuded 'all the luscious beauty and sensuous perfume of the Rose'. But Fokine – whose attitude to Nijinsky would become so begrudging that he mentioned him in his memoirs only when exclusion would have been unthinkable – laced his praise with plenty of vinegar. 'The fact that Nijinsky was not masculine gave a special charm to this role, making him all the more suitable for it,' he wrote, before conceding that Nijinsky 'never displayed any effeminacy on the stage, no matter how effeminate he may have been in his personal life'.

In truth, despite the sensuality of the piece, Nijinsky seems to have been an ethereally genderless presence as the Rose – a creature removed from humanity, as otherworldly as his Blue Bird or the Firebird he had hoped to be able to dance. But for an audience of 1911 it was challenging to see a girl dancing with a man pretending to be a flower: yet another reason for Nijinsky, however well he danced, to be suspect.*

The *pièce de résistance* was Nijinsky's final leap offstage, recalling that triumphant jump as Armida's slave during their first night in Paris in 1909. Considering that he had just danced what was effectively a nine-minute solo – Karsavina's part was minimal; *Spectre* was really the first solo ballet created for a man – this *grand jeté* was an extraordinary feat of strength and control. What watchers were astonished by was 'the artistry by which he contrived to give the impression that having once taken off with an infinite continuity of grace, he was never going to come down'.

There was more than mere artistry at work, though. The conductor, Pierre Monteux, 'played the chord before last with a slight *point d'orgue*, thereby creating an illusion of a prolonged elevation of the dancer. When I played the final chord, you may be sure, the Spectre was already reclining on the mattress placed there to receive him. Ha, ha!' In the wings, Nijinsky was caught almost upright by Zuikov and then lay panting on his mattress as Zuikov mopped his brow and let him have small sips

---

*Three years later, in London, Nijinsky's dancing provoked an indignant letter to *The Times*, which concluded: 'Against Nijinsky personally, of course, nothing can be said. He is a conscientious artiste devoted to his work. But is not the influence of his dance a degenerate one? It is luscious and enervating. The type of young man who likes it and the type it will breed is precisely that which loves the languor of a rose-lit apartment with the curtains drawn all day, with the smoke of opium curling, and the heavy breath of strange perfumes in the air. And that means rottenness!' From John Julius Norwich's 2011 *Christmas Cracker* (my thanks to Peter Carson for passing on this quotation).

Nijinsky as the Rose, backstage, by Jean Cocteau, *c.* 1911. Zuikov
is tending to his panting charge while a monocled Diaghilev,
Stravinsky and Misia Sert, her aigrette waving above her head,
are clearly recognisable in the group surrounding him.

of warm water while Diaghilev watched on, 'all solicitude as if Nijinsky was in serious danger'.

Jean Cocteau said seeing *Spectre* from backstage was like watching a boxer between bouts. 'What grace coupled with what brutality! I can still hear the thunder of that applause, still see that young man smeared with greasepaint, sweating, panting, one hand pressed to his heart and the other clutching a stage brace. He collapsed on a chair, and in a few seconds, slapped, drenched, pummelled, he walked back out onstage, bowing, smiling.'

If *Schéhérazade* had made Nijinsky into a sex symbol, *Spectre* sealed his status as an unlikely romantic hero. Audiences adored it. Unmasculine he may have seemed, and his life with Diaghilev was hardly secret, but that did not stop women as well as men fantasising about him leaping through their bedroom windows. Zuikov was said to have built himself a house on the proceeds of the rose petals shed nightly by Nijinsky and he was no longer able to keep admirers out of his charge's dressing room: they were a part of the tyranny of success to which Nijinsky knew he had to submit. Vaslav's recourse was silence. With Zuikov anticipating his habits, he learned to dress and make up in a room crowded with well-wishers before, during and after a performance without saying a word to anyone.

The other success of the 1911 season, possibly Nijinsky's greatest role, was *Petrushka*, the unhappy clown: a Russian version of a folk hero common to all European cultures – Punch, Pierrot, Pulcinella – part fairy tale, part *commedia dell'arte*, well-harvested sources of ballet inspiration. Benois and Stravinsky drew on their shared memories of the frosty Shrovetide fairs of St Petersburg and added a sinister dash of the absinthe-soaked world of Paul Verlaine, whose first Pierrot poem was published in 1868 ('no longer the lunar dreamer of the old song … his spectre haunts us today, thin and luminous') and his second – in which Pierrot is explicitly associated with his lover Arthur Rimbaud – in 1886 ('A pale face lit by cunning grins … Accustomed, one might say, to contemplating every outcome').

The germ of the ballet was Stravinsky's creation in the summer of 1910 of what would become 'Petrushka's cry'. He, Diaghilev, Benois – and Nijinsky, silent but watchful – worked on the scenario through the autumn and winter, in person and by letter, while Stravinsky continued to compose the music (it was not finished until mere weeks before the premiere). Fokine joined them in Rome in May to begin blocking out the ballet in earnest.

Again, a mood of excited optimism infused them all during the creative process. Stravinsky wrote to one friend during this period, vigorously denying that ballet was 'the "lowest sort" of scenic art', but instead the only form of theatre 'that sets itself, as its cornerstone, the tasks of beauty, and nothing else', and asked another to send him the tunes of two popular songs that he would insert into the fairground scenes.

Bronia remembered visiting Vaslav in his hotel room and finding him surrounded by spring flowers – radiant; and Benois also used the same word to describe this period. Vaslav and Karsavina practised daily with Cecchetti, unless Arturo Toscanini needed the theatre for rehearsals. Occasionally, to Cecchetti's irritation, they were swept off by Diaghilev to see an arch, a view or a monument.

As yet, Fokine's dissatisfaction with his place at the Ballets Russes had not been directed towards Nijinsky, and in his memoirs he recalled working together 'in perfect harmony' on *Petrushka*. Unaware that Diaghilev had promised Nijinsky *Faune* (on which Nijinsky had been working for months) and that Diaghilev was already telling people he considered Fokine a spent force, he put their happy working relationship down to the fact that 'Diaghilev had not yet persuaded Nijinsky that he was a choreographer, and therefore he strove only for perfection of execution'.

But the fact that Fokine came to the proceedings late pleased Stravinsky, who later said Fokine was the most disagreeable person he ever worked with (though this was probably partly because, for his part, Fokine found Stravinsky's music – especially *Petrushka*, the last piece on which they worked together – undanceable). It also allowed him and the others to form a good idea of the ballet before Fokine began the final choreographic process.

As ever with one of Diaghilev's premieres, the first night, in Paris in June 1911, was plagued by hitches. On their arrival in Paris it was discovered that the set for the second scene of the ballet, which takes place in Petrushka's cell, had been damaged in transit. A key part of Benois's decoration was the malevolent portrait of the Magician that watched over everything poor Petrushka did. This had been destroyed. Because Benois had an abscessed elbow, Bakst offered to repaint it. On dress rehearsal night, when Benois saw the new portrait for the first time, he was furious because Bakst had painted the Magician in profile, ruining his effect. Though the artist Valentin Serov repainted it again according to Benois's instructions in time for the opening night, and Diaghilev and Bakst apologised, the hysterical Benois launched into an unforgivable anti-Semitic attack on Bakst. Benois and Diaghilev eventually patched up their friendship but never again would Benois be at the heart of Diaghilev's group of trusted advisers.

On the night itself, a befeathered and bejewelled Misia Sert was sitting in her box, waiting for the ritual three knocks of the call boy that signalled the curtain was about to rise, when Diaghilev burst through the door, drenched in sweat and with his coat-tails flying out behind him. 'The costumier refuses to leave the clothes without being paid. It's ghastly. He says he won't be duped again and he'll take all the stuff away if he isn't paid at once!' Sert raced downstairs, ordered her driver to go home and collect the requisite 4,000 francs, and 'the show went on, impeccable and glamorous'.

This first performance of *Petrushka* was conducted by Pierre Monteux, who had met Stravinsky in the months leading up to the premiere and become fascinated by the dynamic, dragonfly-like figure of the young composer, as well as by ballet which he had previously considered a lower art form. After a few rehearsals, Stravinsky declared, 'Only Monteux will direct my work.' For his part, Monteux came to regard *Petrushka* with a proprietary air, saying that he never liked seeing anyone else conduct it.

Nijinsky, who claimed not to get stage-fright, was so nervous before the premiere that he asked Fokine to stay in the wings to prompt him if he went wrong, something he had never done before. He needn't have worried. Benois – the most critical of audiences – was 'enchanted' by his performance. He was particularly impressed by the way Nijinsky, who had hitherto played only *jeune premier* parts, had bravely embraced the grotesque half-human, half-puppet, resisting any temptation to make himself attractive to the audience. Even Fokine said he never saw a better Petrushka.

The set was a vivid picture of an entirely Russian world: a jostling crowd of coachmen dancing in the snow to keep warm, of trained bears, troupes of gypsies, wet-nurses in their distinctive headdresses, staggering drunken soldiers, fur-capped *muzhiks* and organ-grinders; where stalls sold caramels, sunflower seeds and doughnuts, tea from steaming samovars, and vodka; and where the sound of silver bells tied to sleigh reins hung in the cold air. Children rode on the painted horses of a wooden carousel. Over a hundred people were on stage in the crowd scenes, almost all of them in costumes designed for their specific role and each acting an individual part rather than dancing in sync like a traditional *corps de ballet*, their apparent spontaneity echoing Stravinsky's complex multiplicity of musical themes. There was even space for in-jokes: Bronia, as one of the street dancers, parodied Kshesinskaya's acrobatic demonstrations of virtuosity in *Le Talisman*, a ballet by Marius Petipa loathed by the Diaghilevtsy-Fokinisty.

Petrushka is one of three puppets who belong to the fair's showman, the Magician. He loves the empty-headed ballerina (Karsavina), who flirts with him but then abandons him for the vain and brutish Moor. The Moor challenges him to a fight and kills him; the last scene showed Nijinsky as Petrushka's ghost, blowing a final, futile kiss to the world that had destroyed him.

Each of them had steps that corresponded to their characters: pretty *pizzicato* steps for the ballerina; florid gestures and clumsy movements for the Moor, whose body language is *en dehors*, turned out; and stiff, restricted motion for the tormented Petrushka, who is all turned in, *en dedans*. When Petrushka danced, his heavy wooden head hung awkwardly from his shoulders, his feet in their blue boots dangled loosely at the end of shabby stuffed legs, his hands in black mittens were as stiff as wooden paddles. 'Only the swinging, mechanical, soul-less motions jerk the sawdust-filled arms or legs upwards in extravagant motions to indicate transports of joy or despair.' Given what we know of Nijinsky's later choreographic style (and Fokine's own tendency to lyricism), the dislocated, fragmentary quality of Petrushka's movement is likely to have been Nijinsky's contribution.

For all the acclaim Stravinsky's score and Benois's set received, Nijinsky was *Petrushka*'s undisputed star. Somehow he had managed to create the illusion that he was a puppet aping a human being, while even Karsavina and Alexandre Orlov, as the Moor, could do no more than appear as humans pretending to be puppets.

His clown-like clothes were worn and shabby and his face was ashen, the paint that gave him an expression chipped away. 'Of the once bright-red cheeks only a faded trace remains ... the eyebrows look as though they were hurriedly pencilled in, one eyebrow flies up across the forehead; there are no eyelashes on his blank face.' 'A friend pointed out that the only role in which one recognises Nijinsky's civilian face is that of Petrushka, where he is most heavily made up,' observed the American dance critic Edwin Denby. 'He is never showing you himself ... He disappears completely, and instead there is an imaginary being in his place. Like a classic artist, he remains detached, unseen, unmoved, disinterested. Looking at him, one is in an imaginary world, entire and very clear.'

While *L'Oiseau de feu* was composed as a self-conscious attempt to bring a Russian subject to French audiences, *Petrushka* was a more sincere artistic creation. Stravinsky had meditated 'an entire poem in the form of choreographic scenes ... of the mysterious double life of Petrushka, his birth, his death, his double existence – which is the key to the enigma, a key not possessed by the one who believes that he has given him life, the Magician.'

Though there were political connotations too – Nijinsky was said to have 'amplified the crazy doll into the spirit of the Russian people, oppressed by autocracy, but resurgent and unconquerable after all its abuse and frustration' – this was the key to the extraordinary resonance of the piece. It is impossible to know whether Stravinsky, the primary author of the ballet, recognised the way his story mirrored the relationship between Diaghilev and Nijinsky, but observers spotted it at once. Cyril Beaumont was amazed at how Vaslav 'seemed to have probed the very soul of the character with astonishing intuition. Did he, in one of his dark moods of introspection, feel conscious of a strange parallel between Petrushka and himself, and the Showman and Diaghilev?'

And even though Nijinsky, in the months before Fokine arrived to stage the ballet, had plenty of time to develop his own ideas about how to play Petrushka, one of the remarkable things about Fokine's choreography is how insightful it was. Again and again he took a stock character and made it into something vitally evocative, distilling something of a dancer's essence in the roles he created for them. He did it for Pavlova with the Dying Swan, and he did it for Nijinsky with Petrushka, turning a wooden puppet into an existential hero, oppressed by his fate, scrabbling for a vestige of dignity, meditating on the precariousness of freedom and the tragedy of its loss.

Lydia Lopokova agreed. Petrushka had become, she wrote, the symbol of Nijinsky's 'personality, the imprisoned genius in the docile body of the puppet struggling to become human and falling back again'. He was, Richard Buckle quipped, 'a Hamlet among puppets'.

If, as Valery Bryusov had proposed in an essay in 1902 in the *World of Art* magazine, the sole task of the theatre was 'to help the actor reveal his soul to the audience', then it had triumphantly succeeded with *Petrushka*. Nijinsky was acclaimed not just as a great dancer, but as a great actor. On seeing his Petrushka, Sarah Bernhardt declared she had 'seen the finest actor in the world'. Stravinsky said that as Petrushka Nijinsky was perfection, 'the most exciting human being I have ever seen on a stage': 'his beautiful, but certainly not handsome, face, could become the most powerful actor's mask I have ever seen'. He was haunted by Nijinsky's final, futile gesture, asking the critic Nigel Gosling years later which was the real Petrushka, the puppet or his ghost.

Nijinsky was under no illusions about who Petrushka represented and how closely they were linked. He gave a friend photographs of himself in everyday clothes and in costume as Petrushka, to have side by side, describing Petrushka as 'the mythical outcast in whom is concentrated the pathos and suffering of life, one who beats his hands against the walls, but is always cheated and despised and left outside alone'. Years later he would repeatedly refer to himself in his diary as a 'clown of god'.

In June 1911, Diaghilev took his company to London for the first time, performing at the Opera House in Covent Garden under the aegis of Sir Thomas Beecham. Accustomed to the grandeur of Paris and St Petersburg, they were amazed to find the theatre 'in the midst of a vegetable market ... hemmed in by greengrocers' warehouses and vast mountains of cabbages, potatoes [and] carrots'.

Like the French, the English had long given up on ballet. Just five years earlier, in *A History of Dancing*, Sir Reginald St-Johnston had proclaimed that 'ballet is now a thing of the past, and ... never likely to be resuscitated'. But London society was as overwhelmed by their first glimpse of the Russian ballet as Paris had been. 'People thought and talked of nothing but ballet'; wide-eyed duchesses left the theatre 'with their diamond tiaras all awry'; society girls dreamed of dancing in the *corps de ballet*. A critic timed the applause at their last performance: the cheering, clapping and handerchief-waving went on for twenty minutes. After seeing *L'Oiseau de feu*, Osbert Sitwell knew he had found the thing that would give his life meaning. 'Now I knew where I stood. I would be, for so long as I lived, on the side of the arts.'

Here, too, Diaghilev was surrounded by friends and sponsors. After Sir Thomas's mistress, society hostess Lady Cunard, known as Emerald (who had her house in Cavendish Square redecorated in the Bakst style with huge Chinese incense-burners hanging on the wall, a lapis lazuli dining table and arsenic green lace curtains at the windows), the most important of these was Lady Ripon, patron of Nellie Melba and friend of Oscar Wilde. She had arranged for the Ballets Russes to appear as part of a Coronation programme to mark George V's ascent to the throne. Tall, elegant – she smoked cigarettes through a long amber holder – excitable and extremely kind-hearted, she was bored by politics and shooting but devoted to the arts, and to Diaghilev and the Ballets Russes in particular, perhaps because of her Russian grandfather.

Another friend was Muriel Draper, a young American with an English husband whose bohemian household in Edith Grove was always full of artists, writers, actors and musicians including Henry James, John Singer Sargent (who made drawings of Nijinsky and Karsavina), Artur Rubinstein and Gertrude Stein. The modern, Bakst-inspired styles Draper wore, with turbans or a jewel dangling on her forehead, suited her slender pallor. Once she asked Diaghilev how he achieved his magic on stage. '*Je ne sais pas, je ne sais pas, ma chère Muriel. Je ne sais pas. Un toooout petit peu de la connaissance peut-être, et beaucoup de l'amour … Je ne sais pas.*'

Nijinsky accompanied Diaghilev to the Drapers' where 'he ate and drank with incurious stolidity, moved unnoticeably from room to room, smiled without meaning, and spoke rarely. So he maintained and nourished the living automaton that belonged to him, in order to use it for living during the segment of eternity vouchsafed him on the stage. There he remains alive forever.'

Barely two years into their relationship, and despite their shared professional triumphs and plans for the future, as well as Vaslav's total dependency on Diaghilev for all the practicalities of his life, their incompatibility in private was becoming unignorable. Diaghilev was not content merely with running Nijinsky's career: he wanted to control his entire world. Lifar described him being at once the most rewarding, but also the most exacting, of friends. 'Always he demanded the whole of a person, and in return would shower back everything it was in his power to give, *everything*. But on one condition, and one condition only, that all should come from him, be given by him or through him.' Later he would think nothing of sacking dancers who flirted with Lifar and Léonide Massine and everyone in the company knew that his valet Zuikov, who acted as Vaslav's dresser, was also Diaghilev's spy, posted to watch over every movement Vaslav made.

So devoted was he to his art that Vaslav seems barely to have noticed that Diaghilev kept him in 'the most rigorous seclusion', but the relentless pampering and surveillance made him both spoilt and rebellious. Count Harry Kessler, who met Diaghilev and Nijinsky in the summer of 1911 to discuss Nijinsky posing for a sculptural monument to Nietzsche, was fascinated to see how slowly Vaslav made his way along the hotel's breakfast buffet, pausing before each item to ask Diaghilev in detail if he thought he, Vaslav, would like it or not.

Jean Cocteau witnessed a scene in the wings in which Vaslav, dressed in the gold harem pants of Zobéïde's Favourite Slave, was refusing to go on stage unless Diaghilev promised 'to go to the hockshop tomorrow and get my Kodak'. 'Certainly not,' Diaghilev replied, but Cocteau said he knew Nijinsky meant it and knew Diaghilev would give in. Stravinsky, too, began to find Vaslav 'childishly spoiled and impulsive' and Bronia thought Diaghilev was deliberately encouraging her brother's vanity 'on the pretext that it will make him work harder and develop his talent'.

Sexually they were already living separate lives, sleeping in separate rooms – rooms to which, when they were in London, Diaghilev invited at least one young male visitor whom Kessler observed him addressing as '*mon petit*'. When he visited St Petersburg briefly in the autumn of 1911, Diaghilev accompanied Kuzmin on the usual boy-chasing tour around the bath-houses, but his mood struck his friend as restless.

Vaslav meanwhile had spent his time offstage in Paris trying to elude the faithful Zuikov. Diaghilev 'thought I went out for walks, but I was chasing tarts [*cocottes*]', sometimes several times a day. After his bout of gonorrhoea in St Petersburg in early 1908 he was wary of disease, but because the police monitored the prostitutes in Paris he thought he was safe. Still, 'I knew that what I was doing was horrible'. Once, near the Galleries Lafayette with a girl, he noticed a man in a cab with his two children staring at him, and was certain he had been recognised. 'I received a moral blow, for I turned away and blushed deeply. But I continued to chase tarts.'

He did not despise these women. On the contrary, he admired them for their beauty and simplicity and spoke of women in general – even his use in the diary of the word *cocotte* is as un-derogatory as slang for prostitutes gets – with the greatest respect. He simply had no other way of getting close to them, guarded as he was by Zuikov, shy, immature and impractical. Probably in a way these encounters were as intimate as he had ever been with other people; he even described making love to one woman during her period. But the power of his sexual urges terrified him: 'A man in the grip of lust is like a beast.'

As early as 1910 Diaghilev had known things weren't right. One evening he appeared in Karsavina's dressing room to apologise – most unusually – for allowing another dancer to play her role in *Les Sylphides*, a mournful monochrome spectre in her mirror.

'You have slapped one cheek. Here is the other.' Then he added sadly, 'Tata, I am desperately in love.'

'Who with?'

'She [sic] doesn't care for me any more than for the Emperor of China.'

CHAPTER 5

Faune and *Jeux*
1911–1913

NIJINSKY HAD STARTED on *L'Après-midi d'un faune* with Bronia in St Petersburg in early 1911. They worked at home, after hours and without a pianist because no one – least of all the already disgruntled Fokine – could be allowed to know of Vaslav's plans.

As soon as Nijinsky resigned from the Mariinsky, Alexandre Benois had foreseen the future, worrying about the possibility that Fokine, jealous of his pre-eminence, might leave the Ballets Russes. When he voiced his concerns, Diaghilev replied, 'That's not so great a calamity. What is a ballet-master [choreographer]? I could make a ballet-master out of this ink-stand if I wanted to!' This, said Benois, was conviction, not bravado, on Diaghilev's part, but he thought it showed wilfulness and conceit. His own influence, he wrote (wrongly), 'was still the decisive one' but because he had never believed Diaghilev really '*understood* the ballet' (Benois didn't tire of remembering that Diaghilev had taken longer than him to discover ballet), he did not trust him not to grasp how valuable Fokine was to what he still considered their project.

But Diaghilev had decided that Fokine was finished, and that anyway he had been the true source of whatever Fokine had been getting right. Although he later praised him to Serge Lifar for the extraordinary originality of his early works, the freshness, vividness and fire of compositions like the Polovtsian Dances, *Le Pavillon d'Armide*, *Les Sylphides* and *Schéhérazade*, he also said that Fokine and Nijinsky, as choreographer and dancer, did no more than 'carry out my artistic ideas' (an odd boast, given than Fokine had created *Armide* and the early version of *Sylphides* at least, before he ever met Diaghilev). Both Benois and Bakst always thought they contributed more than Fokine to the ballets they created together. 'Oh, he was like the rest of them, you know, he had no imagination,' said Bakst. 'I had to show him what was wanted scene by scene. He just arranged the steps.' Besides, so the Diaghilev argument ran, though Fokine may have had genius he lacked taste. All that emotion, that poetry, that lyricism: it was, as Vaslav said dismissively to Bronia, too 'sweetly sentimental'.

Lifar (who did not meet Diaghilev until the early 1920s) described a bolt of inspiration striking Diaghilev as he and Nijinsky sat in the Piazza San Marco one afternoon in the autumn of 1910. 'Leaping to his feet there and then, between two pillars, he began to depict the dense angular plastic* movements of this ballet, and so enthused Nijinsky that for a time all else was ousted from his mind.' Leaving aside the visual incongruities of this scene, it seems clear that while they toured Europe between them, Diaghilev and Bakst, with Nijinsky present and eagerly absorbing their ideas, formulated the idea for a new ballet that would be not romantically classical (like the dances of Isadora Duncan – her dances were emphatically not ballets – in her filmy tunic and sandals, as well as those of Fokine) but avant-garde and austere, inspired by Bakst's visits to the remnants of the muscular ancient cultures of Crete, Knossos and Mycenae.

Indebted to the radical theories of the director Vsevolod Meyerhold, it was to be a 'moving bas-relief, all in profile, a ballet with no dancing but only movement and plastic attitude' – an approach that echoed both the 'sonorous, monotonous and empty line' of which Mallarmé's Faun

---

* *Plastique* was the standard Russian term for the acting, as opposed to the dancing, elements of ballet: free dance, or free movement, rather than choreographed ballet steps; the form and line the body makes in space.

was dreaming and the archaic Greek vases and sculpture Bakst had studied. Since this was Nijinsky's first attempt at choreography, Diaghilev and Bakst were hoping to keep as much creative control as possible in their experienced hands; they chose the music and Nijinsky apparently never even read the poem that was its source.

Even so, Vaslav had absorbed their ideas by the time he spoke to Bronia about his ballet for the first time, although he was determined, as he told her, that Greece would be only 'the source of my inspiration. I want to render it in my own way.' Night after night, in front of Bronia's dressing-table mirror, set on the floor in their mother's living room, he moulded her body and his own into the shapes of the Faun and his Nymphs, taking the first bold steps towards abstraction in dance.

His method of almost sculptural choreography – worked out on the artist's own body and then communicated to the other dancers – is commonplace today, but no one had worked in this way before Nijinsky. The painter Mikhail Larionov described watching him work in subsequent rehearsals, what he described as 'laboratory experiments in movement, attempts at creation. Sometimes after an hour's work only a single movement would be fixed. Like a sculptor or a painter with a lay figure, he took hold of the dancer, moving his limbs in different directions, stepping back to judge the effect. "No use, no use. Wait; hold it; not bad like that. That's right now." Sometimes nothing at all would please him, then suddenly came a pose that would seem interesting; he would retain it and begin to build around it, always experimenting and groping for something that was not quite articulate.'

Marie Rambert participated in the process Larionov described. 'Explaining [what he wanted from a dancer] is the wrong word when applied to Nijinsky. He spoke very little, and words did not come easily to him, which is why the rehearsing of his ballets took so long. But he demonstrated the details of the movement so clearly and perfectly that it left no doubt as to the way it had to be done.'

Despite the intuitive understanding between Bronia and Vaslav, it was not an easy process. Bronia was amazed by how her brother, 'without any preparation, is in complete mastery of the new technique of his ballet. In his own execution, each movement, each position of the body, and the expression of each choreographic moment is perfect.' But what he was demanding of her was difficult – the usually reverent Bronia actually used the word unreasonable – and Vaslav, impatient to see his vision realised, was 'unable to take into account human limitations'. While she understood the delicate precision of his work, knowing that 'any undue tension in the rhythm of the movements, any small mistake, could destroy the whole composition, leaving only a caricature of the choreographic idea', still she often found it impossible to 'master the refinements of each detail of the movement'.

Before they left St Petersburg in February they showed their work to Diaghilev and Bakst. Bakst was immediately supportive, understanding as Bronia did the monumental newness of what Vaslav was creating, but Diaghilev had doubts: the 'inkstand' had gone rather beyond his remit. He was uneasy about the 'unexpected and unusual severity of the composition and the lack of dance movements' and worried about presenting to the public someone so young – Vaslav was only twenty-two – as a choreographer. Finally, having signed Fokine up for the 1911 season as *directeur choreographique* (though this year Vaslav, as the company's official *premier danseur*, would be dancing all the leads), Diaghilev was reluctant to antagonise him. He postponed *Faune* for a year.

In the spring of 1911, on their way to Paris, Nijinsky and Diaghilev visited Émile Jaques-Dalcroze's school for eurythmics outside Dresden, interested to hear more about his new theories on the relationship of music to movement – particularly pertinent at this moment as they embarked on the experiment of *Faune*, although its main choreography was already in place. Dalcroze did not teach dance but he believed music could only be fully understood through movement and had developed a system of education incorporating singing, games and improvisation, based on new psychological and physiological insights, that was intended to develop an integral and creative musicality.

Richard Buckle suggested that Diaghilev was taken aback by the 'remoteness of music from movement' in Nijinsky's early sketches for *Faune*, while Diaghilev's most recent biographer, Sjeng Scheijen, speculates that Diaghilev may have hoped Jaques-Dalcroze's rhythmical exercises would 'compensate for Nijinsky's lack of musical knowledge'. But I think attacking Nijinsky for lacking musicality (as Diaghilev later did, to Lifar and others, and as Stravinsky did) was just an easy way of undermining him. All the evidence suggests that Nijinsky was perfectly musically literate at the very high standard required by a dancer. He played the piano by ear, remembering music that he had heard only a few times, according to his sister, with exceptional facility; he was quite capable of playing four-handed pieces with Maurice Ravel, as shown in a photograph from about 1912. The dance notation system on which he worked throughout his career, according to its modern student, Ann Hutchinson Guest, reveals a deep understanding of the intricacies of music notation. Further, the critical response to Nijinsky's performances praised his musicality: Cyril Beaumont called his dancing 'music made visible'. Even Fokine, who did not like *Faune*, congratulated Nijinsky with his customary backhandedness for having in it 'the courage to stand still when the music seemed to demand agitated movement'.

More importantly, the radical nature of what Nijinsky was trying to do with *Faune*, and indeed in his choreography as a whole, demanded a new and radical approach to music and its relationship to dance. The composers to whom Vaslav was drawn – Arnold Schoenberg, Richard Strauss and Stravinsky, in particular – created music to which it seemed almost impossible to dance. Pavlova had refused to dance *L'Oiseau de feu* because the music was 'horribly decadent', meaning too modern; Karsavina did it, but she recognised that contemporary music and choreography did not always do justice to her lyrical, elegant style. Fokine, Grigoriev and others thought Stravinsky's music undanceable. But Nijinsky, trying to fashion something totally new, required this level of difficulty from the music for which he wanted to create movement.

This debate did not begin until Nijinsky started choreographing. Though his contemporaries agreed he was an extraordinary dancer, actor and performer, there was no consensus on the works he created for others. Very often, critical views were coloured by personal allegiances. Fokine praised his dancing but believed Nijinsky had ousted him from the Ballets Russes and therefore never credited him as a choreographer, and in any case his style was a reaction against (or an overt rejection of) Fokine's. Grigoriev had little faith in Nijinsky's talents but he was Fokine's friend, whom Fokine had brought into the company. Walter Nouvel, like Alexandre Benois, never saw Nijinsky as anything more than Diaghilev's creature – but Nouvel and Benois were both Diaghilev's friends before anything else. They had condescended to Nijinsky for years, and could not fathom the petulant adolescent they had first met blossoming into a creative artist. To them he was almost an idiot savant – the only genius they were willing to credit him with was subconscious. These prejudices would crystallise as Nijinsky's revolutionary (or ridiculous, for those who took the other view) ideas took shape.

The 1911 season had been dominated by two new ballets: *Le Spectre de la Rose* and *Petrushka*. That winter, for the first time, Nijinsky did not return to Russia and the company played in London and toured central Europe. Pavlova returned to Diaghilev for a few performances, finally agreeing to dance her celebrated Giselle opposite Nijinsky's Albrecht.

And after years of rivalry, Mathilde Kshesinskaya had permitted Diaghilev to win her over so that she too could taste the delights of the Ballets Russes's foreign triumphs, consenting – entirely on her own terms – to perform with his company for a limited season. Her performances were notable less for her dancing than for the staggering quantity of jewels with which she was encrusted (she brought her million-rouble collection with her, storing it at Fabergé's London shop, and the Savoy arranged for two plain-clothes detectives to guard the jewels whenever she wore them), but, swathed off-stage in ermine, even at forty her star quality was undeniable. As *The Times*'s ballet critic observed, unlike Karsavina or Pavlova, 'she never makes one forget that she is a *prima ballerina*'.

She and Diaghilev were well-matched sparring partners. One evening at dinner he said to her, 'Oh, Mathildoshka; yes. You are superb. You deserve all your success, even to the two Grand Dukes at your feet.'

'But Sergey Pavlovich,' she replied, not missing a beat. 'I have two feet.'

Their last stop, in March, was Budapest which, in its own way, would prove to be the site of an event as momentous in Nijinsky's life as Diaghilev's gift of *Faune*. Sitting in the audience at the Municipal Opera House with her then-fiancé's mother was a very determined and resourceful young lady of nineteen (later she would say she had been sixteen), Romola de Pulszky. Overwhelmed by the colours, the beauty, and the passion on stage in front of her, she decided to discover all she could about the Ballets Russes and its dazzling star – Nijinsky.

It was a piece of good fortune for Romola that her mother, Emilia Márkus, was Hungary's most celebrated actress. Using her theatrical connections, Romola made friends with Adolph Bolm, who told her about Nijinsky 'almost as a priest might speak of a divinity'. There was no opportunity to meet her idol – she could not have known that Diaghilev had constructed around his precious, troubling Vatsa an invisible but impenetrable wall – and anyway, she wasn't sure if she wanted to: though his 'genius' had swept her off her feet, he gave her 'an uncanny feeling of apprehension'.

In March 1912 the Ballets Russes reconvened in Monte Carlo to prepare for the upcoming year. This was the Riviera's high season and the ice cream-coloured hotels and restaurants overflowed with a glamorous, raffish set: portly American tycoons with money to burn on the baize-covered tables of the casino, French and English aristocrats, extravagantly moustachioed Maharajas and bearded Grand Dukes. One particular admirer of Diaghilev and his troupe was the Aga Khan, whom – in hopes of his backing – Diaghilev permitted to attend the meetings of what he called his 'heads of department': Nijinsky, Stravinsky, Bakst, Karsavina and Cecchetti.

One evening the Aga Khan took Karsavina out to dinner. 'When she unfolded her napkin, there was a huge emerald concealed in it. She gently but firmly pushed it away': Karsavina was no Kshesinskaya. Diaghilev urged her to accept it, on the grounds that a jewel from the Aga Khan was a bouquet from another man, but she would not. The disappointed prince consoled himself with another dancer, Josefina Kovaleska, nearly as pretty as Karsavina but importantly more interested than her in presents hidden in napkins.

Rehearsals for *Faune* now began in earnest. If Nijinsky had found it hard to explain to his sister what he wanted from her, the other artists were impossible. Grigoriev said the 'dancers dreaded the monotony and fatigue' of working on *Faune* and Bronia's memoirs corroborate this. 'Up to then the ballet artist had been free to project his own individuality [on a role] … he was even expected to embellish it according to his own taste, possibly neglecting the exactness of the choreographic execution.' What mattered was the mood of the piece and preserving the basic steps and the groupings on stage. But with *Faune* Nijinsky demanded that the artists perform exactly as *he* understood their roles: they were his instruments, not his collaborators, and he would permit them no freedom of interpretation. 'Each position of the dance, each position of the body down to the gesture of each finger, was mounted according to a strict choreographic plan.' For a nine-minute ballet this precision required ninety rehearsals – well above the usual number.

Marie Rambert remembered watching Nijinsky teach a new dancer one of the nymph's roles. When he asked her why she looked so frightened, she replied that she thought she was meant to be scared. Nijinsky retorted that he was not interested in how she felt: 'the movement he gave her was all that was required of her'. For him, the face was 'merely an extension of the body', as one admiring critic would write of his work. 'It is above all the body that speaks.'

Before they left for Paris Diaghilev wobbled again, asking Vaslav to change fundamentally his completed composition on the grounds that it would not appeal to the public and throwing his already defensive friend into a frenzy of self-justification. Angrily Vaslav insisted to Bronia that despite the complaints of the dancers who did not understand him, despite the shocking modernity of his work, he would stand by his art as he had conceived it or leave the company altogether. In a panic Diaghilev cabled Astruc in Paris to say that he had 'never seen him [Nijinsky] so firm and intransigent'.

It was not until Bakst saw a rehearsal and rushed up to Vaslav,

Nijinsky as Harlequin by Antoine Bourdelle,
*c.*1910. 'His dancing was music made visible'.

kissing him and saying loudly, 'You will see ... how wild Paris will be for this,' that Diaghilev's nerves were calmed. Later, excitedly, he told Bronia he had never seen Bakst so enthusiastic. 'Levushka said that *L'Après-midi d'un faune* is a "super-genius" creation and we are all fools not to have understood it.'

Initially *Faune* was scheduled for four performances in Paris but Diaghilev extended its run to eight performances, overshadowing the new ballet Fokine was to present, *Daphnis et Chloé*, unfortunately also on a classical theme. Fokine felt that Diaghilev's promotion of Nijinsky – '"creating" a choreographer out of' him, as he put it – was an effort to undermine his authority among the dancers and a bid to unite the Ballets Russes under Diaghilev's leadership, not Fokine's. Though it is surprising to think Fokine could ever have imagined that he rather than Diaghilev was the real leader of the Ballets Russes, it is true that by presenting Nijinsky as his modern choreographer there was nothing else for Fokine to be, by comparison, but old-fashioned and outdated. As Grigoriev put it, by prioritising *Faune* over *Daphnis*, Diaghilev was knowingly letting Fokine go.

'This was a very unhappy time for the ballet,' recalled the conductor Pierre Monteux, the reason Misia Sert was able later to call the Ballets Russes just a 'shabby, jealous little group ... [surrounding everything] with pettiness'. Fokine was furious about the lengths to which Diaghilev was going to make *Faune* a success and seething with conspiracy theories. Rehearsals for *Faune* and *Daphnis* were occasionally at the same time, so dancers who were in both had to choose which to attend; the argument between Fokine and Grigoriev over these rehearsals was so deeply felt that it ended their friendship. Spitefully, Fokine included in *Daphnis* parodies of what he was able to glean of *Faune*'s choreography, worsening the atmosphere for the confused dancers and forcing them to take sides between him and his young rival. The budget for new costumes and sets was so small *Daphnis* was required to share with the previous year's production of *Narcisse*. At *Faune*'s dress rehearsal, Diaghilev lavished his influential audience with champagne and caviar – an expense he had not considered worthwhile for Fokine's premieres. By this point, Fokine was no longer speaking to Diaghilev or Grigoriev.

Nijinsky, for his part, was unimpressed by Diaghilev's efforts on his behalf: he took them as his due, or more correctly, the due owed to art. All he minded about was the integrity of the performance. Cocteau watched Diaghilev and Bakst fret over him at dinner at Larue's one night shortly before *Faune* opened because he had a stiff neck. It turned out he had been practising 'with the weight of real horns ... This perpetual study for his parts ... made him irritable and sulky'. He and Diaghilev were bickering endlessly.

Materially as well as artistically, a great deal was riding on *Faune*'s success. It had been expensive to make – the dancers had to be paid for all those miserable rehearsals – and as ever, Diaghilev was sailing close to the wind, taking out high-interest, short-term loans to keep his company afloat and ensure, by expanding their repertoire, that it continued to attract large audiences. Each season had been costlier than the previous one and he was probably in debt for close to 300,000 francs in 1912 (he had even been forced to borrow money, just once, from Vaslav) and would be paying the money back for years to come even with sell-out seasons. But the first two premieres of the Paris season, *Le Dieu bleu* and *Thamar*, vehicles for Nijinsky and Karsavina respectively, were not the successes for which Diaghilev had hoped.

L'Après-midi d'un faune opened on 29 May 1912. After months of disagreement, resentment and distrust, the mood backstage was bleak. Bronia was nervous: 'doubts in the wings before a premiere reach out into the auditorium, to the public, and can lead to catastrophe'. Bakst painted the Faun's dappled hide directly onto the thin bodystocking Nijinsky was wearing, making him look '*plus nu que nu*'. On his head was a woven cap of golden hair and two small horns, his ears were pointed and elongated with wax, and heavy make-up made his face look uncannily, languorously bestial. 'In the costume, as in Nijinsky's expression, one could not define where the human ended and the animal began ... He did not imitate; he merely brought out the impression of a clever animal who might be human.'

Like *Petrushka*, this was Vaslav's story – a meditation, as the ballet historian Jennifer Homans writes, upon 'introversion, self-absorption and cold physical instinct'. It tells of the hesitant sexual awakening of a young faun who is fascinated by a group of bathing nymphs. At his approach they flee, one returning briefly to retrieve their discarded veils and to taunt him before being frightened away. The faun bears off a forgotten veil in triumph. For now, it is enough. Apparently without having read Mallarmé's poem, Nijinsky had summed up its premise: '*Ces nymphs, je les veux perpétuer.*'

As the Faun, Nijinsky was 'thrilling. Although his movements were absolutely restrained, they were virile and powerful, and the manner in which he caressed and carried the nymph's veil was so animal that one expected to see him run up the side of the hill with it in his mouth. There was an unforgettable moment just before his final amorous descent upon the scarf when he knelt with one knee on top of the hill, with his other leg stretched out behind him. Suddenly he threw his head back silently and laughed.'

This 'final amorous descent', in which in the last gesture of the piece an impassive Nijinsky, alone on stage, lowered himself face down onto the precious stolen scarf and shuddered with what clearly represented a masturbatory orgasm, caused a sensation.* The audience, already unsure whether to cheer or catcall, was stunned into momentary silence. 'Nobody was certain what had happened, who had won; was it a success or not?' For the only time in the Ballets Russes's history (as far as I have been able to ascertain), Diaghilev came onstage as the dancers waited to take their bows and told them to return to their places to repeat the piece. When the curtain fell for a second time the crowd applauded wildly, though loud whistles and hisses could also be heard among the cheers.

---

* Peter Ostwald, whose biography of Nijinsky focuses on his mental health, speculated that on the first night this 'final gesture' may have been unsimulated. 'Fear can and does lead to sexual arousal.' (Ostwald, *Vaslav Nijinsky: A Leap into Madness*, 1991, p. 61.)

The next day *Le Figaro* did not review the ballet but ran a front-page article denouncing Nijinsky's 'filthy' final gesture. The septuagenarian sculptor Auguste Rodin signed a letter published as a response the day after that in *Le Matin*, in which he praised Nijinsky's art, his beauty and expressiveness, and concluded, 'I wish that every artist who truly loves his art might see this perfect personification of the ideals of the beauty of the ancient Greeks.' Gaston Calmette from *Le Figaro* replied with an attack against Rodin himself, who was living at the exquisite Hotel Biron – funded by the French state – and creating works (according to Calmette) as indecent and shameful as Nijinsky's Faun. It was said that Calmette was seeking to obtain an injunction to prevent *Faune* being performed again, although he did publish a letter from Odilon Redon to Diaghilev regretting that his friend Mallarmé had not been at the Théâtre du Châtelet to see 'this wonderful evocation of his thought'.

With his eye on the box office, Diaghilev was thrilled with the debate; Misia Sert said he was so pleased with Rodin's (ghostwritten) article that he carried the cutting in his wallet for years afterwards. News of the scandal even reached the United States, with the *Pittsburgh Gazette*'s headline of 5 June howling delightedly, 'WICKED PARIS SHOCKED AT LAST'.

Later critics have seen in the Faun's fetishization of the scarf a fundamental ambivalence towards real intimacy, a preference for imagined rather than real consummation. Instead of engaging with the nymphs he so desired – indeed, they barely touch – Nijinsky as the adolescent Faun opted for the 'safe haven of self-gratification', a reflection of his own ambivalent experience of sex. When the Faun and the Chief Nymph dance – briefly – together, 'the seesaw of angled bodies suggests a host of competing desires: lust, fear, acquiescence, timidity, evasion, a will to dominate'. Despite the eroticism of their situation, the geometry of their coupling, the severe stylisation of their movements 'also unsexes them, as if form, like some higher morality, were a shield against instinct'.

Stravinsky saw it differently. 'Of course Nijinsky made love only to the nymph's scarf. What more would Diaghilev have allowed?' He 'adored the ballet': 'Nijinsky's performance was such marvellously concentrated art that only a fool could have been shocked by it.' 'I did not think about obscenity when I was composing that ballet,' Vaslav would write. 'I was composing it with love.'

In many ways, the most shocking element of *Faune* was not Nijinsky's notorious gesture but the powerfully abstract quality of the choreography and the disconcerting distance between music and motion. Nijinsky used stillness consciously, just as artists like Cézanne and Picasso used blank canvas and empty space consciously; for him not-moving was as important an element of the composition as moving. Despite the difficulties they had faced learning their parts, the nymphs had achieved what Nijinsky wanted from them, a way of dancing between the bars, as he put it, with the music trickling through their consciousness. 'Once you mastered it, and you ... could feel yourself dancing in sound, it was the most delightful thing to dance in that you could possibly imagine,' remembered one, years later. 'The sensation approached the divine.'

Faune was, as its three authors had intended, an anti-ballet, but although it might seem 'a refutation of technique', it was in fact 'the extreme understatement of a technique that was without parallel'. It required mastery of the classical canon which Nijinsky then rigorously, analytically, consciously broke down 'to his own purpose': a physical expression of what the Cubists were trying to achieve on canvas. As with the Cubists (the best visual parallel I can think of is Picasso's 1907 *Les Desmoiselles d'Avignon*, shimmering with similarly disturbing, almost menacing undercurrents and a distinctive combination of primitivism and ultra-modernism), *Faune* was a pointed repudiation of everything audiences loved about ballet in general and Nijinsky as a dancer in particular: virtuosity, exoticism, romance and sensuality. There were no jumps, no spins, no razzmatazz. But Nijinsky loathed that aspect of his celebrity. Angrily, he used to say when people raved about *Spectre*, '*Je ne suis pas un sauteur; je suis un artiste*'. With *Faune* he ruthlessly re-examined the traditions that had nurtured his talent, seeking to cleanse them of all their cloying decorativeness and sentiment.

Some – but by no means all – of his fellow artists understood his vision. Benois, predictably, found his work still-born: 'in spite of

Diaghilev's and Bakst's efforts to "feed" his creativity ... novelty and strangeness are not in themselves valuable'. But Léonide Massine, who learned the role of the Faun from Nijinsky in 1916, believed Nijinsky had 'evolved a sculptural line which gave an effect of organic beauty such as I had never before seen'.

Diaghilev's pride was mingled with jealousy. He told a condescending story about how he had sent his protégé to look at the Greek sculptures in the Louvre for inspiration, but Vaslav had got lost and spent the afternoon in the Egyptian rooms while Bakst waited for him as arranged on the floor above. This, Diaghilev liked to joke, was why the ballet was performed in profile. Later he would tell Lifar that during the making of *Faune* Vaslav had 'revealed not one ounce of creative talent'.

The strains of the last few months were obvious to their English friends when they arrived in London in late June 1912. Nijinsky was observed listening to Diaghilev's anecdotes with 'ill-concealed impatience' and others noticed how 'very nervous and highly-strung' he was, perpetually watched over by his 'guardian and jailer'. One afternoon, after an argument, Diaghilev appeared alone at Lady Ripon's and 'sat in the garden with tears dripping down his face, and would not be comforted'.

Usually Diaghilev kept Vaslav away from parties that might upset his delicate temperament (or where he might meet women – so unsettling for poor Vatsa), but he did permit him a few freedoms and in London Vaslav had something of a social life, despite his English being even more limited than his French* and his complete lack of polish. 'I do not know how to be polite,' he would write later, 'because I do not want to be.' He was 'naively – appallingly – honest', as Stravinsky put it, remembering playing a parlour game at Lady Ripon's in which everyone was compared to an animal. Diaghilev was a bulldog, Stravinsky a fox.

'Now, Monsieur Nijinsky, what do you think I look like?'

'*Vous, Madame – chameau.*' The answer was as unexpected as it was

---

*Diaghilev wasn't much good at English either. His only English words were said to be, 'More chocolate pudding!' (O. Sitwell, *Great Morning*, 1948, p. 247.)

Les Nymphes et le Faune by Ernest Oppler, *c*.1912.

precise, even though his hostess was a celebrated beauty; one has to assume that he did not know how rude it was in French to call a woman a camel. 'In spite of her repeating: "A camel? How amusing! I declare. Really. A camel?" – she was flustered all evening.'

Vaslav and Diaghilev would go down to stay for the weekend at Lady Ripon's house in the country and Vaslav actually became friends with Lady Ottoline Morrell, who courted him assiduously when her friends became his enthusiasts that summer. He came to tea with her – perhaps encouraged by his success with Lady Ripon, he was overheard by Diaghilev during one meeting comparing her to a giraffe – and thrilled her five-year-old daughter by dancing with her around the drawing room. 'He was so different from all the smart people at luncheon [at Lady Ripon's],' she wrote, 'for he was such a pure artist, a drop of the essence of art, and quite impersonal.' He had an air of being lost, as if he were looking on normal life 'from another world', but she could see that he noticed everything.

Lady Ottoline's friend Lytton Strachey sent Nijinsky a huge basket of flowers in the hope of attracting his attention and John Maynard Keynes – resolutely homosexual at this point, but eventually the devoted husband of Lydia Lopokova – was another obsessed fan. 'There were at this time fantastic fables about him; that he was very debauched, that he had girdles of diamonds and emeralds given to him by an Indian prince,' wrote Lady Ottoline, 'but on the contrary, I found that he disliked any possessions or anything that hampered him or diverted him from his art.'

It was in Lady Ottoline's garden in Bedford Square that the idea for Nijinsky's next ballet, *Jeux*, came to him. It was to be a contemporary ballet – actually a futuristic one, set in 1920, eight years away – depicting a game of tennis in a tree-filled garden at dusk, as moths danced in the arc-lights high above. There would be 'no *corps de ballet*, no ensembles, no variations, no *pas de deux*, only boys and girls in flannels, and rhythmic motions,' Vaslav told an anxious Diaghilev as they dined later at the Savoy Grill, while Bakst frowned at the sketches Vaslav was making on the tablecloth to illustrate his idea.

Stylistically, it would be as radical as *Faune*. At this early stage, Nijinsky planned for his three dancers, regardless of gender, to dance in the same way, as uniformly as possible. For a short time during rehearsals he worked in pointe shoes, but then discarded them because they were wrong for the athletic mood he wanted to create. As he would write in his diary, years later, 'A woman and a man are the same thing': human. Again, the facial expressions would be blank, giving nothing away. Everything he wanted to say would be in the movement.

The *Figaro* journalist Hector Cahusac was present at a lunch in the Bois de Boulogne in the spring of 1912 when Diaghilev, Cocteau, Bakst, Reynaldo Hahn and Nijinsky were discussing the difficulty of finding subjects for ballets and the virtues and shortcomings of historical as opposed to contemporary scenarios. When the talk moved on to movement, the normally silent Nijinsky came alive. 'The man that I see foremost on the stage is a contemporary man. I imagine the costume, the plastic poses, the movement that would be representative of our time,' he said. 'When today one sees a man stroll, read a newspaper or dance the tango, one perceives that his gestures have nothing in common with those, for instance, of an idler under Louis XV, of a gentleman dancing the minuet, or of a thirteenth-century monk studiously reading a manuscript.'

'Childish nonsense,' spat Bakst; but these were the ideas stimulating Nijinsky when he was creating *Jeux*. For the first time a ballet was to be about modern people going about their everyday life. In his 'waltz with changing partners', the three dancers would gossip, play tennis, show off, bicker, smoke, embrace – even briefly dance the turkey trot.

As with *Faune*, the mood was to be one of erotic anticipation, the theme desire – and Nijinsky's view of both, coloured by his life with Diaghilev, was ambivalent. 'The Faun is me, and *Jeux* is the kind of life Diaghilev dreamed of. Diaghilev wanted to have two boys. He often told me about this desire of his,' but Vaslav had always refused to go along with it. In *Jeux* he would play Diaghilev and the two boyish girls he flirted with would be the boys with whom Diaghilev dreamed of making love. He may also have been inspired by what he saw of the fluid love lives of Lady Ottoline and her friends – the androgynous Stephen sisters, Virginia and Vanessa, and their relationships with their husbands and lovers; and Lady Ottoline's own idiosyncratic approach to romance. As choreographer and dance historian Millicent Hodson writes, *Jeux* was a Bloomsbury ballet in theme as well as setting. On his copy of the piano score, where the music comes to a climax and the three figures embrace, for an instant bound together in ecstasy, Vaslav wrote, 'Sin'.

Despite his persistent concerns about Nijinsky's experimentalism, Diaghilev wrote to Debussy describing the ballet and asking him to provide a score. After the scandal of *Faune*, Debussy needed some persuading: Diaghilev had to promise to double his fee to get him to do it. Although the music Debussy would produce was sumptuously beautiful, fresh and youthful, he was scathing about '*le terroriste* Nijinsky' and his '*nyanya* [nanny] S. de D.' when they visited him later in the summer to hear how he was progressing.

Diaghilev had no option but to support Nijinsky because he had burned his bridges with Fokine, who had waited only for the premiere of *Daphnis et Chloé* at the tail end of the Paris season to resign, telling Diaghilev that his company (and his relationship with Vaslav) was making the fine art of ballet into a 'perverted degeneracy'. More worryingly for Diaghilev, his invaluable *regisseur* Grigoriev had also handed in his notice. Now there was only Nijinsky, whose style was hardly commercial and who had no idea of how to produce, as Fokine could, sure-fire successes at short notice with limited rehearsal time. Harry Kessler and Lady Ripon – both fans of Nijinsky's, but aware too of his limitations – had tried to convince Diaghilev that there was space for Nijinsky and Fokine in the company, but he was unrepentant and rudely refused to consider making concessions to popular taste. 'If we don't lay down the law for them [the public], who will?' He did, however, pull out all the stops to persuade Grigoriev to stay.

The summer of 1912 saw Diaghilev and Nijinsky touring Europe, half working, half holidaying: Deauville, Bayreuth, Lugano, Stresa, Milan and, as ever, Venice. They returned to Paris briefly so that Nijinsky could sit for Rodin, who had so publicly admired him as the Faun. For some reason the piece was never finished. Bronia said that Diaghilev, coming one day to collect Nijinsky from his sitting, discovered Nijinsky asleep on a sofa and Rodin asleep at his feet, and, jealous of this intimacy, refused to let Nijinsky return; in his diary Cocteau related a fruitier tale, in which Nijinsky heard strange noises as he posed with his back towards Rodin. Turning round he saw Rodin masturbating – a story Diaghilev found funny but Nijinsky hated hearing. '*Il ne supporte plus les désordes sexuels*': he could no longer stand such debauchery.

In Paris, presumably spending a bonus Diaghilev had given him for *Faune*, Nijinsky went on a shopping spree. Instead of buying dress clothes or *objets*, he ordered hundreds of pairs of dancing shoes, light braided kid sandals to practise in and practice shirts made to his own design from the softest crêpe de Chine in whites, creams, pale blues and greens, the same pastel colours in which the girls from the Ballet had their dancing dresses made. He also ordered himself a very thin watch from the watchmaker Benson, with which he was 'happy and proud as a child'. The gold watch awarded to him by the Tsar while he was at the Imperial Ballet School had long ago been pawned and this was its replacement, a present to himself upon reaching his artistic maturity.

Diaghilev and Nijinsky parted ways in the autumn of 1912, Diaghilev returning to Russia and Nijinsky going to Monte Carlo to begin work on *Jeux*. Bronia, who had married one of the dancers in the company, Alexander (Sasha) Kochetovsky, in London in July, was waiting there for him. She was delighted to find that for the first time since he had become involved with Diaghilev her brother was himself again, the Vatsa of their childhood: free from tension, expressing himself openly, his creativity flowing.

But the strains of Vaslav's life were increasingly intense. Diaghilev was always short of money – not because he was personally extravagant but because the needs of his company were so great – and so he was happy to commit to any engagement they were offered to bring in extra funds. Vaslav danced all the principal roles but also needed rest and stability in order to create new work. He found moving constantly, always among strangers and speaking unfamiliar languages, exhausting

– besides which Diaghilev disapproved of him making friends or learning new languages, even (according to Bronia) of spending time with his mother, as distractions from his work. Cocteau described them migrating 'from hotel to hotel, expelled by theatre closings' and Grigoriev remembered Vaslav fruitlessly demanding a more permanent home, if only for a few months. The Ballets Russes was a demanding mistress. 'I gave my whole heart to it,' Vaslav would write. 'I worked like an ox. I lived like a martyr. I knew that Diaghilev had a hard life.'

All too soon they were on the road again, performing in Cologne in late October 1912 at the start of another European tour. Just before the curtain went up for their first performance, Vaslav and Bronia received a telegram from Eleonora informing them that their father had died. Vaslav had not seen or spoken to him for five years. Bronia was grief-stricken, but Vaslav appeared almost unmoved; the only person he was worried about was his mother, who had remained behind in Russia to plead (to no avail) with the government to release Vaslav from his military service. Until he was freed from this obligation, he would not be able to return home.

The company performed in Budapest again and once more a breathless Romola de Pulszky sat in the audience. Since seeing the Ballets Russes for the first time the previous year, she had broken off her engagement, abandoned her acting training and begun studying dance. This time she concentrated her energies on winning over Enrico Cecchetti. 'I soon discovered I could win his heart through flattery. I had a genuine admiration for him and a very real affection, but I had to use him in order to achieve my purpose – to become permanently attached to the ballet.' Through Cecchetti she watched not only every performance and every rehearsal, but also every class he gave. She managed to manouevre an introduction to Nijinsky, though after a brief misunderstanding – he thought at first that she was the Hungarian Opera's *prima ballerina* – he showed no interest in her.

Adolph Bolm advised Romola's mother to send her with them to Vienna to meet the Wiesenthal sisters, concert dancers who might take Romola on as a student. There she was able to observe Nijinsky more closely, watching him listen to gypsy music one night 'with an aloof, distant air. His half-closed eyes gave an extraordinary, fascinating expression to his face.' To her indignation he refused to acknowledge Romola or show that he recognised her. 'Occasionally I caught his eyes resting on me, but as soon as I looked at him he quickly turned his glance elsewhere.' Bolm told her that even the other dancers did not dare approach him. He was always guarded by Zuikov and only spoke to them about work. Romola realised that if she were to remain with the company she would have to keep her passion for Nijinsky a secret, especially from Diaghilev. Only Cecchetti guessed, whispering to her, 'Beware, Nijinsky is like a sun that pours forth light but never warmth.'

Spring 1913 saw the company back in Monaco and Nijinsky working again on *Jeux*, this time with his two ballerinas, Karsavina and Ludmila Schollar, who was to replace Bronia. Debussy had finally finished the music, after wrestling through the autumn to convey 'a rather risqué situation! Even though in a ballet immorality passes through the ballerina's legs and ends in a pirouette.'

Although shouting, crying, gesticulating wildly and occasionally throwing furniture were accepted facts of Ballets Russes rehearsals (Michel Calvocoressi, finding that a group of Russian choristers was not responding to his direction, asked Walter Nouvel why; 'he replied that it was probably because I spoke to them politely'), Nijinsky was particularly bad at successfully communicating his ideas to the dancers. As ever with him, while the movements looked simple, they were difficult to execute and unlike the persuasive Fokine, Nijinsky never learned how to sweep dancers along with him in his conception of a ballet.

All her subtlety and intelligence could not help Karsavina understand what Nijinsky was trying to achieve if he could not explain it to her. She and Schollar were reluctant collaborators and Vaslav and Karsavina, 'the best of friends both onstage and off', argued frequently during rehearsals. 'Once I asked "What's next?" and Nijinsky said to me, "You should have known yourself a long time ago! I will not tell you!"'

Marie Rambert, a young teacher from the Dalcroze Institute with a dance background (she had studied with Isadora Duncan and, briefly, with the Paris Opéra's Madame Rat), was employed by Diaghilev in late 1912 to help Nijinsky work with the dancers, principally on *Le Sacre du printemps* but also on *Jeux*, her communication skills (she was Polish and Nijinsky's first language was Polish, and she spoke excellent Russian and French) as important as her Dalcrozian training. She described an argument in which, when Karsavina asked Nijinsky to explain something to her, he exploded at her for having a 'ballerina mentality'.

'How dare you insult that great artist?' Diaghilev said to him. 'You are nothing but a guttersnipe to her, go at once and beg her to forgive you.' Vaslav appeared with a huge bunch of flowers and peace was restored – but the subtext may have been more complicated than this. In a confused passage in his diary,* Nijinsky confessed that he had always admired Karsavina (and her beautiful body) but never dared approach her, because he 'felt that one could not court her' – for her honesty, as he put it, and because she was married. Her virtue was well known to be unassailable – another reason I suspect the idealistic Nijinsky would have been attracted to her.

When they quarrelled, Vaslav was unhappy because he sensed Diaghilev trying to influence Karsavina against him, having noticed that secretly he 'was courting her ... I wept bitterly because I loved Karsavina as a woman'. By this stage Nijinsky and Karsavina had worked closely together for five years. In a rare group photograph taken in Monte Carlo in April 1911 after a lunch party with Stravinsky, Diaghilev and some others at the Riviera Palace Hotel, they are standing so close together that his head is under her wide-brimmed hat. They look relaxed and

---

* Because Nijinsky was on the verge of insanity when he wrote his diary, and because he often contradicts himself in it, it is on the surface an unreliable document. For example, he writes of hating Diaghilev and loving him, of despising his artificiality and respecting his genius and knowing that Diaghilev was jealous of his talent. But he was always honest, and all of these impulses seem absolutely consistent with the multiplicity of fractured and refracted emotions Diaghilev stimulated in him. The same is true of the way he describes his feelings for Karsavina and, later, for Romola de Pulszky.

happy, at ease with one another, almost flirtatious. Although Karsavina did not dance in *Faune*, I see her as the Nymph the Faun desires but doesn't – can't – pursue. When he remembered working on *Jeux*, Vaslav described longing – perhaps for Karsavina – making him so weak he 'could not compose' it. 'In that ballet you can see three young people feeling lust.'

He was also feeling harried: racing to complete *Le Sacre du printemps* at the same time meant that he 'never finished' *Jeux*. *Sacre* was the great focus of 1913 and *Jeux* was just one of its victims. The ballet was still incomplete three days before its premiere and Nijinsky was exhausted and 'blank' in the rehearsal rooms until Grigoriev suggested a run-through, 'in the hope of stimulating his invention. This luckily produced the desired effect,' remembered Grigoriev. Typically, he thought Nijinsky was 'baffled by Debussy's score'.

For all the strains on their relationship and the distance between them, Diaghilev was still in thrall to Nijinsky's magic. Marie Rambert described sitting next to Diaghilev as they watched Nijinsky rehearse that spring. Diaghilev was mesmerised, almost unaware of her presence. Under his breath she heard him exclaim, 'What beauty!' and 'Isn't he at his most perfect in this?' as Vaslav went through each of his roles.

Jeux premiered in Paris in May at the grand opening of Gabriel Astruc's modern new theatre, the Théâtre des Champs-Elysées. The set was a large grey-green garden, an open space – not intimate enough, Bronia thought, for Nijinsky's subtle *pas de trois* in which so much is implied or implicit. Bakst's costume designs were rejected at the last minute – for some reason he had planned to have Vaslav in a red wig and unflattering long shorts – so instead he wore a white version of his practice clothes while Jeanne Paquin designed the girls' white tennis dresses. Again, the dancers barely touched; again the theme of male innocence and female knowledge was repeated. This 'second instalment of Nijinsky's erotic autobiography [revealed] no less urgently than *Faune*, the power of desire, the ambiguity of sexual identity, and his aversion to intercourse itself'.

Debussy walked out during thin applause (and some snide laughter), later raging against 'Monsieur Dalcroze ... one of music's worst enemies' and the 'young savage' Nijinsky. Although he was willing to admit the ballet 'had some good choreographic ideas in it', and that 'if he had had more time in which to work on it, Nijinsky might well have made something of it', Grigoriev found *Jeux* 'helpless and immature'. Pierre Monteux was even more brutal; he thought *Jeux* asinine.

The reviewers were underwhelmed too, criticising *Jeux*'s slightness, the contemporary dress and the strange quality of the movements. 'Everything in the choreography was new – free movements and positions of the body applied to classical ballet technique' – but it was not especially successful. Audiences were so accustomed to seeing Nijinsky as something otherworldly, unreal – an animal, a puppet, a bird, an Indian deity, a flower, even a slave; roles that may have dehumanised and emasculated him but somehow lifted him out of the sphere of ordinary life – that perhaps they could not get used to seeing him as something close to themselves, simply a young man of their own time; or perhaps without taking a leap into another world he could not achieve the transformation they had come to expect of him.

Nijinsky was conscious of its weaknesses and touchingly grateful for any support he received. One night, soon after *Jeux*'s opening, the artist Valentine Gross encountered Nijinsky backstage after performing *Spectre*. 'He was like a crumpled rose in pain, and there was no one near him. I was so touched that I left him alone and said nothing. Then he saw me and sprang up like a child taken by surprise and came smiling toward me. As he stood beside me in his leotard sewn with damp purplish petals, he seemed a kind of St Sebastian, flayed alive and bleeding from innumerable wounds. In a halting but quite accurate French he began to tell me how pleased he was with some pastels I had made of *Jeux* and to thank me for the article I had written to go with them.'

In fairness to Nijinsky, as Richard Buckle would put it, watching the first performances of *Jeux* must have been as strange a sensation as tasting 'Japanese food for the first time'. Though its choreography has been seen as Nijinsky's least effective work, *Jeux*'s importance lies in its place as the first contemporary ballet and the forerunner of neoclassicism, associating Nijinsky irredeemably with modernism. The choreographer John Neumeier saw *Jeux* as a visual version of Gertrude Stein's 'Rose is a rose is a rose is a rose' – with Nijinsky saying 'I am here, I am here, I am here'.

Jeux's modernist style was in line with other interests they were pursuing at the time. Vaslav and Diaghilev had met Marinetti and the Futurists in Italy two years earlier, when they were rehearsing *Petrushka*, and in the first plan for *Jeux*, sent to Debussy, a Futurist-inspired dirigible crashed in the background to bring the games of love to a close. They were also fascinated by the ultra-modern, atonal music of the iconoclastic composer Arnold Schoenberg, hoping in early 1913 that he would provide a score for them.

In December 1912, the poet and librettist Hugo von Hofmannsthal wrote to Richard Strauss about an idea they had discussed with Diaghilev and Nijinsky for a new ballet based on the story of Joseph and Potiphar's wife (yet another tale of an experienced femme fatale trying to entrap an innocent youth). 'I must make myself the spokesman of Nijinsky, who implores you to write the most unrestrained, least dance-like music in the world, to put down pure Strauss for this leaping toward God which is a struggle for God. To be taken by you beyond all bounds of convention is exactly what he longs for; he is, after all, a true genius and just where the track is uncharted, there he desires to show what he can do.'

Finally, looking back from a post-war vantage point, *Jeux* also contains within it a powerful sense of impending doom: some kind of premonition that flirtations in a moonlit pleasure garden were more precious than anyone in 1913 could imagine.

CHAPTER 6

Le Sacre du printemps
1910–1913

FAUNE AND JEUX were not the only ballets with which Diaghilev was preparing to entrust his young friend. In Vienna in 1912 they met Hugo von Hofmannsthal to discuss a ballet Richard Strauss might write for them (which became *La Légende de Joseph*) and Hofmannsthal was 'entranced' by their all-night conversations, writing to his friend Harry Kessler that 'since the evening of this Saturday I have actually only existed with no one else but Diaghilev and Nijinsky'. A few months later, in Paris (about the time of *Faune*'s premiere), they sat up together again, this time accompanied by Kessler, Reynaldo Hahn and Marcel Proust, debating which biblical story should accompany Strauss's composition and Bakst's Veronese-inspired setting. The backdrop of Larue's was almost exotic enough to inspire a ballet of its own, to read Kessler's description: 'Bowls of monstrous strawberries stood on the table, glasses of champagne and liquors glittered in all colours; the Aga Khan, the richest Muslim prince of India, sat, arriving from a masked ball, at the corner in an oriental costume completely covered with fabulous genuine pearls, and even larger rubies and emeralds ... A belated pair danced the tango.'

As early as 1910, Nicholas Roerich and Igor Stravinsky had been talking about a ballet that would show the ancient spring rites of pre-historic Russia, a great sacrifice as enacted by a Slavonic tribe. Both claimed to have been the originator of the initial concept for *Le Sacre du printemps*, and quite possibly they came up with similar ideas simultaneously; Stravinsky said a vision of *Sacre* came to him in a dream. What is clear is that during the spring of 1910, when both were in Paris, they had discussed their shared passions for Russia and for the primitive and embarked on the development of a ballet that at this early stage they called the 'Great Sacrifice'.

Diaghilev was irritated that they had come up with the idea without his involvement and though he insisted that he was interested in it, he pressed for *Petrushka* to be produced first, partly because he wanted to tempt Benois back to work with him again and partly because prioritising a ballet of his choice would bind Stravinsky closer to him. Roerich could wait. For the time being, the Great Sacrifice was put aside and it was not until the following September that Stravinsky settled down in a pensione in Clarens to begin composing it in earnest.

In the meantime he, Roerich and Diaghilev corresponded about their aims for the piece. Nicholas Roerich, whom Nijinsky called the Professor and whom Karsavina described as a prophet, was one of the most interesting of Diaghilev's collaborators. Diaghilev had known him since their college days in the early 1890s and he had been one of the *miriskusniki*. A distinguished painter and occasional set designer (he had staged the opera *Prince Igor* for Diaghilev), he was also a respected scholar, a writer, philosopher, mystic and anthropologist whose earliest passion had been excavating shamanic burial mounds. His paintings were almost exclusively concerned with ancient landscapes and their primitive inhabitants, hunting, fishing and participating in rituals.

In 1910 Roerich had written an essay setting out his thoughts on ancient Slavonic fertility festivities, when the people would go into the woods and array themselves in fresh greenery before dancing and singing to celebrate the coming of spring. He believed that enduring folk customs such as ritualistic dancing when the crops were sown, or in some places stripping a girl naked and leading her on horseback through the newly planted fields before burning her effigy, were literal remnants of Russia's original pagan culture. What he wanted, writes the historian Nicoletta Misler, was 'to present the power of images as the survival of memory'.

The following year he painted a study for a mosaic for the church at Princess Tenisheva's Talashkino estate called *The Forefathers*, which showed a man sitting on a sacred hill playing a wood or bone pipe to a group of bears hypnotised by his music – a reflection of the Slavonic tradition that men were descended from bears. Stravinsky came to work with Roerich at Talashkino where he met the singer and *gusli* player S. P. Golosov, who was also studying there. While Stravinsky composed, Roerich studied the Princess's large collection of folk art, embroidery and clothing for inspiration for the costumes for the tribal dancers who would enact their ancient mysteries. Although Stravinsky would later claim he had tapped into 'some unconscious folk memory' for the traditional melodies that he abstracted for use in *Sacre*, it is likely that Roerich and Golosov pointed Stravinsky in the direction of folk songs that were ethnologically appropriate for the piece, right for the season and the ceremony they planned to portray.

Though the overall impression the piece would create was more important to both composer and designer than strict academic 'correctness' – they did not want *Sacre* to be dry or museum-like – each relied heavily on what was then seen as authentic source material. Roerich studied a three-volume history of Russian dress and the folk way of life and the folklorist Alexander Afanasyev's monumental *The Poetic Views of the Slavs on Nature*, as well as a twelfth-century chronicle of pagan customs and Herodotus's description of the Scythians during the Persian Wars. Stravinsky used Rimsky-Korsakov's collection of *100 Russian Folk Songs* and an extensive anthology of Lithuanian folk tunes.

Both men were inspired by the poetry of Sergey Gorodetsky. A few years earlier Stravinsky had composed music to accompany some of his poems. The 1907 poem 'Yarila' described an ancient wise man attended by two young girls, one of whom he kills with a flint axe by a pale lime tree in the spring as a sacrifice to the sun god, Yarilo: 'a white bride' who springs out of her bloodstains to become 'a new god'. This imagery is repeated in a letter from Roerich to Diaghilev describing a tribe gathered at 'the foot of a sacred hill, in a lush plain ... to celebrate the spring rites ... there is an old witch ... a marriage by capture, round dances ... the wisest ancient [imprints] his sacred kiss on the new-flowering earth'. Then the young virgins dance before choosing one of their number to be 'the victim they intend to honour'.

The titles of the sections Stravinsky used as he began composing echoed these visions: 'Divination with Twigs' (he told Roerich that 'the picture of an old woman in a squirrel fur ... is constantly before my eyes as I compose'); 'Khorovod – Round Dance'; 'The Kiss of the Earth; 'Game of Abduction'; 'Round Dances'; 'Secret Night-games' (which would become 'Mystic Circles of the Young Girls'); and 'Holy Dance'. By January 1912 he had finished Part One, and on 17 March he wrote to tell his mother that when he had played the completed sections to Diaghilev and Nijinsky in Monte Carlo, 'they were wild about it'.

Two days later he told Roerich triumphantly that he thought he had 'penetrated the secret of the rhythm of spring'. The mood and sounds of the Russian spring were vitally important to the piece, as essential to its émigré creators as Roerich's shamanic studies or Stravinsky's complex modernism. Serge Lifar described spring in Kiev, where he grew up, being marked by the 'dull, rumbling explosions' of the dislodged floes of the thawing Dnieper crashing against one another in a torrent of melt-water. Later, an exiled Stravinsky would speak of 'the violent Russian spring that seemed to begin in an hour and was like the whole earth cracking. That was the most wonderful event of every year of my childhood.'

Diaghilev raved so enthusiastically to Pierre Monteux about Stravinsky's 'extraordinary new work' that he was desperate to hear it when Stravinsky played it to them in Monte Carlo in the spring of 1912, but he was totally unprepared for the sadistic novelty of what he heard. As Stravinsky, drenched in sweat, pounded away on a quivering, shaking upright piano, the sound dwarfed everything. Monteux listened 'in utter amazement', worried his friend might burst. 'I must admit I did not understand one note of *Le Sacre du printemps*. My one desire was to find a quiet corner in which to rest my aching head.* Then my director turned to me with a smile and said, "This is a masterpiece, Monteux, which will completely revolutionise music and make you famous, because you are going to conduct it."'

In June, Stravinsky and Debussy played Stravinsky's four-hand arrangement of *Sacre* at the Paris home of Louis Laloy, editor of *La Grande Revue*. 'When they finished, there was no question of embracing, nor even of compliments,' wrote Laloy. 'We were dumbfounded, overwhelmed by this hurricane which had come from the depths of the ages, and which had taken life at the roots.' Five months later, Debussy was still in thrall to what he had heard, writing to Stravinsky that he was haunted as if 'by a beautiful nightmare', trying 'in vain to recall the terrifying impression that it made. That's why I wait for the performance like a greedy child who's been promised some jam.'

When they first began discussing *Sacre*, Roerich and Stravinsky had assumed that they would use Fokine as choreographer. In 1910–11 he was still the Ballets Russes's *directeur choreographique* and although Nijinsky had begun work on *Faune*, no one apart from Diaghilev, Bakst and Bronia knew about it. But by early 1912, as he was finishing *Sacre*, Stravinsky was having doubts, writing to his mother from Monte Carlo in March to complain that Fokine was not up to the job. Each of his successive works was immeasurably weaker than the one before, Stravinsky said, and for *Sacre* 'new forms must be created and the evil, the greedy and the gifted Fokine has not even dreamed of them ... Genius is needed, not *habileté*.' It could only be Nijinsky.

Diaghilev agreed, though neither he nor Stravinsky was motivated solely by artistic concerns. At this time Diaghilev and Fokine were locked in conflict over *Faune* and *Daphnis et Chloé* and he had no intention of retaining Fokine for another ballet. Using Nijinsky as choreographer – he thought – would also reassert his authority over *Sacre*, about which

---

*Monteux was asked in the 1950s what he had thought of *Sacre* when he first heard it. 'I detested it.' And now? 'I still detest it.' (T. F. Kelly, *First Nights*, 2000, p. 274.)

he was still smarting because it had been conceived without him. He assumed Nijinsky, whom he still saw as his creature, would act as his cypher. For his part Stravinsky, who had resented being a junior partner in earlier collaborations with Diaghilev, thought he would have more creative control with the inexperienced Nijinsky staging *Sacre*.

Both men sought to assert their influence over Vaslav with (according to which source you choose to believe) varying success. Grigoriev thought that while composing *Sacre*, Nijinsky 'was as helpless as a child and relied entirely on suggestions from Diaghilev and Stravinsky'. Because Nijinsky's method relied upon working out movements on his own body and then demonstrating them to his dancers – 'something he brought with him and showed you and you could either do it or you couldn't do it' – rather than working spontaneously with them as Fokine had used to, many of the dancers assumed Diaghilev worked out the steps and showed them to Nijinsky, who was then expected to teach them to the company. However Diaghilev's faith in his taciturn friend's capacity for communication was so limited that he had brought in Marie Rambert to help him explain what he wanted from the dancers. That Diaghilev was the ultimate source of the ballet and only used Nijinsky as his interpreter is as unlikely as the image of the portly impresario stomping around a hotel suite demonstrating to Nijinsky the Chosen Maiden's solo, though this is what Serge Lifar would later claim on Diaghilev's behalf.

Throughout the choreographic process, Stravinsky worked closely with Nijinsky, attending rehearsals whenever he could – and once furiously pushing aside the fat German accompanist, whom Diaghilev had nicknamed Kolossal, to play the music the way he intended it: 'twice as fast as we had been doing it, and twice as fast as we could possibly dance,' remembered Marie Rambert. 'He stamped his feet on the floor and banged his fist on the piano and sang and shouted, all to give us an impression of the rhythms of the music and the colour of the orchestra.'

He annoyed Nijinsky, though, by his time-wasting assumption that he was the only one who knew anything about music. 'He explains the value of the black notes, the white notes, of quavers and semi-quavers, as though I had never studied music at all,' Vaslav complained to Bronia, who replied that since Stravinsky did that with everybody Vaslav shouldn't take it personally. While Stravinsky may not have believed that anyone other than himself understood music, he expected Nijinsky to listen to his ideas about dance. Luckily his ideas for *Sacre* were closely in line with Nijinsky's. Throughout the collaborative process Stravinsky declared repeatedly that he and Nijinsky were wholly in tune. His conviction that the movement should be all dancing with no mime was perhaps a response to *Petrushka*, in which emotions and drama had been conveyed as much through facial expression as by using the body, a style Nijinsky had already moved away from in *Faune* and *Jeux*.

Like Diaghilev and Nijinsky, Stravinsky was in contact with Jaques-Dalcroze, who wrote to him in January 1913 to argue that only when the musician understood the human body as fully as the dancer's body was impregnated by the music would the regeneration of ballet that Stravinsky had initiated be complete. All three of them were influenced by Dalcroze's idea that in dance each musical note should be expressed by a corresponding movement; this would become one of the defining, and controversial, ideas behind *Sacre*'s choreography. Using Dalcrozian theory as a starting point, Nijinsky would originate the important 'idea of the ballet as an organism broken up into interacting members, dancing in relation to itself and to each other, keeping the time of its unit in relation to the great pulse of the whole'.

Throughout the summer and autumn of 1912, when he had time, Vaslav was planning *Sacre*, writing out his ideas swathed in a hotel dressing gown, the hood pulled down over his face like a prize-fighter's. The solidity, strength and simplicity of modern art – especially that of Gauguin – fascinated him, reflecting as it did his own preoccupations with rejecting illusion and artifice. Like Stravinsky he wanted to challenge preconceptions, violate rules and redefine expectations to bring audiences to a new reality. Ottoline Morrell observed him 'incessantly thinking out new ballets, new steps ... absorbed by the ideas of the old Russian myths and religions'.

In November, as they toured Germany, Nijinsky began work on the second part of *Sacre* with Bronia as the Chosen Maiden. Immediately she understood what he wanted from her. 'As I danced I imagined above me the dark clouds in the stormy sky, remembered from the painting by Roerich. Around me I pictured the calm of nature before the onslaught of a hurricane. As I envisaged the primitiveness of the tribal rites, where the Chosen Maiden must die to save the earth, I felt that my body must draw into itself, must absorb the fury of the hurricane. Strong, brusque, spontaneous movements seemed to fight the elements as the Chosen Maiden protected the earth against the menacing heavens. The Chosen Maiden danced as if possessed, as she must until her frenzied dance in the primitive sacrificial ritual kills her.' In two sessions Vaslav had created the role for her; by the third, Bronia was dancing it alone while her brother watched, delighted.

When the Ballets Russes were in London in December 1912 Vaslav began working on *Sacre* with the whole company for the first time. An approving Stravinsky told a reporter that, 'Nijinsky works with passionate zeal, forgetting himself'. The dancers were less enthusiastic, however. The music was so difficult and unpredictable that even the orchestra had trouble with the rhythms – they needed seventeen orchestral rehearsals as opposed to nine for *L'Oiseau de feu* – and, on first seeing the score, some demanded to know if the music was correctly printed: they could not believe how complicated it was. Occasionally during rehearsals, when the music began an awkward crescendo, nervous giggles could be heard, infuriating Stravinsky who would rush to the piano, shouting, 'Gentlemen, you do not have to laugh, I know what I wrote!'

Because there was no melody, the dancers had to follow the rhythm, calling out the time as they danced – they loathed what they called these 'arithmetic classes' in which all they did was count.* To make it even more difficult, the polysyllabic Russian numbers they all used took so long to say that they couldn't keep pace with the music. The girls ran

---

* When things got too much for them, Grigoriev gave the *corps* old Fokine ballets to rehearse 'to maintain morale'. (S. Grigoriev, *The Diaghilev Ballet, 1909–1929*, p. 90.)

1. Nijinsky in the dress uniform of the Imperial Theatre School, *c.*1900. This was taken at the time that Nijinsky, aged eleven, entered the senior schoool as one of six male students in his year and won the coveted scholarship that would fund his education. The silver lyres, the school's insignia, are embroidered on his collar.

2. Nijinsky and Anna Pavlova in the first version of *La Pavillion d'Armide*, 1907. It was Armida's Favourite Slave, a role written especially for him the year he graduated, that eighteen year-old Nijinsky in his pearl choker bewitched Prince Lvov and Sergey Diagh

3. Nijinsky in Paris in 1909. Along with the rest of the Ballets Russes, the awkward boy found himself inhabiting 'an unreal and enchanted world'.

4. Nijinsky in playful mood, posing for publicity stills for the 'Danse Siamoise' for the photographer Druet in his garden in Paris, 1910.

5. The composer Igor Stravinsky and Nijinsky as Petrushka by Bert, 1911. Even posing off stage Nijinsky is in character, arms handing woodenly by his sides, his feet turned in, *en dedans*, and his expression as blankly quizzical as a puppet's.

6. Bronia Nijinska as the Street Dancer and Ludmilla Schollar as a Gypsy flank Kobelev, the Organ Grinder, in their costumes for *Petrushka*, 1911. Bronia's dance was a parody of Mathilde Kshesinskaya's style, an in-joke only devotees of the Ballets Russes would have understood.

7. Nijinsky as the Rose (1911) with his face made up to resemble 'a celestial insect, his eyebrows suggesting some beautiful beetle ... his mouth was like rose petals'.

8. *Plus nu que nu*: Nijinsky as the Faun by Bert, 1912, wearing a short tail, horns, pointed, elongated ears and the dappled body stocking which, before every performance, Léon Bakst painted directly onto him. He looked, as one observer said, even more than naked. 'One could not define where the human ended and the animal began'.

9. Playing *Daphnis et Chloë*, a ballet choreographed by Nijinsky's in-house rival, Mikhail Fokine, with its composer Maurice Ravel in Paris, 1912. Note Nijinsky's look of utter concentration.

10. Dancing the turkey trot with Tamara Karsavina while Ludmilla Schollar waits in *Jeux*, 1913, the first ballet set in the contemporary world. Karsavina and Schollar wear white tennis dresses designed by Paquin and Nijinsky is in a white version of his usual practise clothes.

11. A formal portrait taken in New York in 1916 when Nijinsky was twenty-seven and about to lead the Ballets Russes in Diaghilev's place on a catastrophic fifty-two city tour of the United States which would lose its sponsor, the Metropolitan Opera House, quarter of a million dollars.

12. Posing as himself in New York, 1916, in the pale crepe-de-chine shirt,
slim black trousers and woven sandals in which he practised every day.

13. Supervising every detail of his work: Nijinsky applying makeup to one of the dancers in *Till Eulenspiegel*, New York, 1916.

14. 'I am a father. I am a married man.' Vaslav with two-year-old Kyra and Romola in New York, 1916.

15. When Romola and Serge Lifar visited Nijinsky in 1939 (attended by press photographers) he astonished everyone by joining in when Lifar danced for him. While Lifar was warming up a watchful Nijinsky warned, 'You might fall into the air.'

16. With Romola in a hotel in Egham, Surrey, 5 December 1947, just after their arrival in England. His eyes are so expressive that he seems almost to be looking out from behind the mask of his face.

around 'with little bits of paper in their hands, in a panic, quarrelling with each other about whose count was right'. This was why Diaghilev had employed Marie Rambert, whom the company quickly nicknamed Rhythmichka. Her role was to explain to them what Nijinsky wanted, helping to link the movements directly to Stravinsky's complex score; but although she was popular with the dancers, hardly any of them, including Bronia, approved of her Dalcrozian ideas or understood her strange position within the Ballets Russes – neither really one of them nor part of Diaghilev's inner circle of tacticians.

The lack of melody was one problem for the *corps*; Nijinsky's steps were another. The flat-footed, straight-legged jumps, the pounding stamping that made up a percussion section of its own (so interconnected were the choreography and the composition that Stravinsky noted the rhythm of their steps on his piano score), the bent-over stance, turned-in feet and shuffling steps contradicted in every gesture the nobility and grace of classical ballet. Movement was disconnected, jagged, frenzied, apparently chaotic. The dancers found the steps physically painful and resented being asked to perform them.

Because they spent much of the time turned away from the audience, absorbed in their mystery, and there was only one short solo – most of the ballet was danced by the *corps* en masse – there was no chance for the dancers to shine individually. As Nijinsky would tell a journalist in February 1913, *Sacre* 'is the life of the stones and the trees. There are no human beings in it. It is only the incarnation of Nature ... and of human nature. It will be danced only by the *corps de ballet*, for it is a thing of concrete masses, not of individual effects.'

This depersonalisation, this denial of individual virtuosity and beauty for its own sake, was an implicit repudiation of the dancers' ideals and their years of training and discipline. Many saw Nijinsky's challenging choreographic style as an insult to the traditions their work celebrated. Karsavina was one of these. Though she did not dance in *Sacre*, she said that in it (and *Faune*) Nijinsky 'declared his feud against Romanticism and bid adieu to the "beautiful"' – which was about as disapproving as the diplomatic Karsavina could force herself to be.

But while his critics complained that his work was a rejection of beauty, Nijinsky knew they were wrong. He was, he wrote, 'the artist who loves all shapes and all kinds of beauty. Beauty is not a relative thing. Beauty is god. God is beauty with feeling ... Beauty cannot be discussed. Beauty cannot be criticised.' Instead he wanted to re-examine beauty: *'La grace, le charme, le joli sont rangés tout autour du point central qu'est le beau. C'est pour le beau que je travaille,'* he explained to a journalist. Grace, charm, prettiness – Karsavina's 'Romanticism' – could obscure what he considered the essence of the art to which he was devoted, and it was this to which he wanted to return, not unlike Cézanne painting and repainting the same view of Mont Sainte-Victoire in an effort to uncover its spirit, or Gertrude Stein re-examining the use and function of language by subverting what people expected to hear or read. As Stein would write of Picasso, 'Another vision than that of all the world is very rare ... to see the things in a new way that is really difficult, everything prevents one: habits, schools, daily life, reason, necessities of daily life, indolence, everything prevents one.'

As the rehearsals went on, Nijinsky became increasingly defensive, all too aware how inadequately the dancers grasped his concept for *Sacre*. Even with Rambert's help he was 'unable to reach them [the *corps de ballet*] personally and obtain their cooperation, so they might believe in him and be supportive of his work and ideas, so essential during the process of creation'. If they could not perfectly copy a movement he demonstrated, he would accuse them of deliberately working against him and Diaghilev would have to come and make peace. When he saw how unpopular *Sacre* was proving in rehearsal, Diaghilev remarked sanguinely, 'that it was an excellent sign. It proved the composition to be strikingly original.'

What he was seeking to convey, as Vaslav told Lady Ottoline, was the sense of 'pagan worship, the religious instinct in primitive nature, fear [and] ecstasy, developing into frenzy and utter self-oblation'. His inspirations were Stravinsky's extraordinary score and the spiritual and anthropological discussions he had with Roerich, whom he respected enormously. He was also indebted to the folk dances he had performed as a boy – the Ukrainian *hopak*, with side kicks, big jumps and powerful arm movements; the Caucasian *lezghinka*, in which men wearing soft leather boots dance almost on pointe, with fisted hands and turned-in legs; the *khorovod*, a circular dance used in ritual ceremonies, with flat palms and turned-in feet – and even to the costumes Roerich was designing. Roerich used folk motifs from the libretto like the firewheel and bundles of dry twigs used for setting fire to effigies, as well as rhythmical repetition, perhaps the main decorative element of Russian folk art. So important were his ideas that Nijinsky apparently waited to begin composing the ensemble sequences until he had seen Roerich's sketches so that he could incorporate their arcs and broken and concentric circles into his choreography.

Another element in the fractured, disconnected quality of Nijinsky's choreography for *Sacre* must have been his own increasingly fragile emotional state. Through the spring of 1913 the psychological pressures he was under, which had been building since he began composing *Faune* in 1910–11, were approaching a crisis point. It was 'as if he felt that a net was being woven around him and was about to envelop him'.

His schedule of performing, composing and rehearsing, never in the same place for longer than a few weeks, was ever more relentless. There had never before been a ballet-master as young as him. Although he was convinced of the importance of what he was doing, he was not always sure he was doing it right and he had no real support. Bronia was newly married; his mother could not begin to comprehend the complexities of his life with Diaghilev (he wrote in his diary that he avoided speaking to her and Bronia about Diaghilev because he knew how worried they were about him); and Diaghilev himself, it was becoming increasingly obvious – the man who was meant to be his patron and protector – had a private agenda that clashed with his own.

Lydia Sokolova, a young British dancer born Hilda Munnings (until Diaghilev transformed her into a Russian ballerina when she joined the Ballets Russes in early 1913), described Nijinsky as being like 'a wild creature who had been trapped by society and was always ill at ease'.

He barely spoke to anyone and, if addressed, looked 'as if he might suddenly butt you in the stomach'; he was always nervous, fiddling with his hands and nails, 'and seemed to exist on a different plane. Before dancing he was even more withdrawn, like a bewitched soul. I used to watch him practising his wonderful jumps in the first position, flickering his hands; I had never seen anyone like him before.'

What kept Vaslav going was the knowledge that he was creating something totally original. In late January 1913 he wrote to tell Stravinsky how pleased he was with *Sacre*'s progress. 'If the work continues like this, Igor, the result will be something great. I know what *Le Sacre du printemps* will be when everything is as we both want it: new, and for an ordinary viewer, a jolting impression and emotional experience. For some it will open new horizons flooded with different rays of sun. People will see new and different colours and different lines. All different, new and beautiful ... So, goodbye until we see each other. A bow to your wife. I kiss your hand. Vaslav.'

The first blow to Vaslav's hopes came a few weeks later, when Bronia told him that she could not dance the role of the Chosen Maiden. She had been feeling nauseous and faint for some weeks and the doctor had informed her she was expecting a baby. Nijinsky lost control, screaming violently at her, 'You are the only one who can perform this dance, only you, Bronia, and no one else! ... You are deliberately trying to destroy my work, just like all the others.' When Bronia's husband Sasha Kochetovsky came into the room, Vaslav turned on him as if he were about to hit him, calling him an 'uncouth *muzhik* [peasant]' despite all Eleonora's protests that it was perfectly normal for a married woman to have children. Later he told Rambert that '"a blackguard, a brigand ... has prevented Bronia from dancing *Jeux* and *Sacre*". "But who is he?" "Kochetovsky!"'

Marriage – the first time Bronia had deviated from the path of art to which she and Vaslav had jointly been devoted from childhood – had shaken the bond between brother and sister; this betrayal, as he saw it, hardened the rift, leaving him even more isolated. In her memoirs, Bronia also described arguing with him during this period about the Dalcroze system, which she thought had nothing to teach classical dancers. After his furious response to her pregnancy she avoided him altogether, even though she longed to tell him how much she admired *Sacre*'s choreography and realised 'how exhausting and fatiguing it was for him to be surrounded by uncooperative artists and try to create a ballet in such a hostile atmosphere ... what an effort it cost him to obtain from the artists such exactness in the execution of a choreography they did not understand'.

Diaghilev, Nijinsky and the ballet travelled to Paris for their final rehearsals before the season began, but the news that Isadora Duncan's two children had been drowned in the Seine on 19 April cast a dark shadow over their arrival. Their driver had left the car in gear when he got out to crank the engine and, when it started, it shot off the road, plunging into the river. It was impossible to reach the two children and their governess who were trapped inside. Vaslav, who had known the children, was very distressed by this tragedy.

Just as in 1909, the theatre they were using was under construction, so they were having to rehearse alongside all the dusty commotion of builders. But the atmosphere was very different from the holiday feel of four years earlier. With *Jeux* still unfinished and so much riding on *Sacre*, the overwrought Nijinsky was furious at any distraction from his work and the entire company was picking up its mood from him and Diaghilev.

The Théâtre des Champs-Elysées was Gabriel Astruc's baby, a vast new building intended to be a temple to modern dance and music. The sculptor Antoine Bourdelle had even used Nijinsky, alongside Isadora Duncan, as his inspiration for the bas-reliefs that adorned the monumental exterior, showing Vaslav tearing 'himself away with a wild leap from the marble still holding him fast'. He called Nijinsky 'more than human ... [with] something of the sacred animal' about him.

Astruc was so determined to have the Ballets Russes as his opening programme that he promised Diaghilev an astronomical fee for the season: 25,000 francs a night for twenty nights (when in earlier years he had received less than half that for a night's performance), as well as extra money for supplementary expenses – electricians, coiffeurs, costumiers, stage hands and so on. Diaghilev couldn't have accepted less. His existing debts and the number of rehearsals Nijinsky and Monteux needed for *Sacre* were crippling him. Even though the front row of seats had already been installed – and the tickets for them sold – when Stravinsky, 'in that sad delightful Slav voice of his', insisted that they be ripped out to make space for the extra musicians he needed for *Sacre* ('You know, old friend, it's done with the utmost ease nowadays by that powerful machine they have for cutting steel and reinforced concrete. And the upholsterers will patch up the damage very quickly'), Astruc had agreed.

It is to this period of their time together that Vaslav's most eviscerating memories in his diary about Diaghilev belong: his false smiles, the black hair-dye that stained his pillowcase, his two false front teeth which moved when he touched them nervously with his tongue, and which reminded Vaslav of a wicked old woman. 'I realised that Diaghilev was deceiving me. I trusted him in nothing and began to develop by myself, pretending that I was his pupil … I began to hate him quite openly, and once I pushed him on a street in Paris … because I wanted to show him that I was not afraid of him. Diaghilev hit me with his cane because I wanted to leave him.'

Misia Sert's letters to Stravinsky in the late spring of 1913 confirm the misery and unpleasantness between them. Diaghilev was 'going through a dreadful period' in which creditors were threatening to sue him and an insufferably rude Nijinsky was chafing against their relationship, recalling the deliberately provocative way the young Vaslav had behaved towards his father before he left Eleonora.

Bronia hoped a romance might blossom between Vaslav and Maria Piltz, whom they had known since schooldays and who was replacing her as the Chosen Maiden; she thought Piltz was 'a little in love with him'. Piltz told an interviewer in 1968 that Vaslav had asked her to come with him for a ride through Paris fifty-five years earlier, but as she got into the carriage someone pulled her from behind. It was Diaghilev: 'Get out. You're not going anywhere with him.' She remembered Vatsa fondly. 'He was so nice! But he was strange ... He used to joke around with me. Once I asked him, "What do you love best in the world?" He laughed and replied, "Insects and parrots."'

Vasily Zuikov was still shadowing Nijinsky on Diaghilev's instructions. When he and Rambert were working together, Zuikov would interrupt every few minutes to open or close the window, although Rambert recorded that 'Nijinsky didn't take the slightest interest in me as a woman. It never occurred to him, it never occurred to me. We were only discussing the work in hand.' Afterwards they would go to Pasquier's and drink hot chocolate and eat cakes. Rambert didn't realise then that she was falling in love with Vaslav, but Eleonora noticed. Ever watchful for women trying to ensnare her son, she warned Vaslav that Rambert admired him; he assured her there was 'no danger'. Something else would be needed to help him break free of Diaghilev's hold.

Whatever his feelings for her, Rambert was enthralled by Nijinsky, as a man as well as an artist. He possessed a great feeling for literature and she found him observant, with a gift for summing people up with a choice phrase, and was drily funny. One of the most fundamental things Nijinsky's life seems to me to have lacked was humour. Everyone around him took themselves so painfully seriously – unless the sources just conceal it (which is of course very possible) – perhaps easy laughter was yet another of the sacrifices they offered up on the altar of artistic immortality.

Many years later, Rambert remembered watching Vaslav's ecstatic performances when he taught the Chosen Maiden's solo to Piltz as 'the greatest tragic dance I have ever seen'. 'His movements were epic. They had an incredible power and force, and Piltz's repetition of them – which seemed to satisfy Nijinsky – seemed to me only a pale reflection of Nijinsky's intensity.' For Rambert, Piltz could be no more than a 'picture-postcard of a great painting'.

Others were less convinced. At one of the last rehearsals, Diaghilev asked Enrico Cecchetti, venerable *maître de ballet* and guardian of the old style of dance, what he thought of *Sacre*. 'I think the whole thing has been done by four idiots,' Cecchetti replied. 'First, Monsieur Stravinsky, who wrote the music. Second, Monsieur Roerich, who designed the scenery and costumes. Third, Monsieur Nijinsky, who composed the dances. Fourth, Monsieur Diaghilev, who wasted money on it.' Diaghilev just laughed.

The people who crowded into the Théâtre des Champs-Elysées on the unseasonably warm evening of 29 May 1913 (the anniversary of *Faune*'s premiere) were a mixture of types – as Cocteau would put it, 'the thousand varieties of snobbism, super-snobbism, anti-snobbism'. Many were bejewelled ladies from the highest ranks of society, accompanied by men in white tie, the grand music-lovers who had been Diaghilev's earliest supporters in Paris. Others were younger, intellectual and rebellious – refusing to wear stiff collars and tailcoats (which anyway they could not afford) as a mark of their rejection of the traditional and outdated. Although the seats had all been sold, at double the normal price, Diaghilev, seeking support for his radical programme, had given these artists, critics and poets free standing passes, so that inside the theatre they were mingling on foot amidst the boxes occupied by the *gratin*.

Stravinsky had given an interview (which he later disowned) which came out that morning, explaining the inspirations behind *Sacre* and what he, Nijinsky and Roerich hoped to achieve with it. He concluded, 'I am happy to have found in Monsieur Nijinsky the ideal collaborator, and in Monsieur Roerich, the creator of the decorative atmosphere for this work of faith.' This public show of confidence does not tally with descriptions of the final orchestral rehearsals (during which Nijinsky tried to throw a chair at a workman who interrupted them) and the dress rehearsal the previous day, which Rambert described as pandemonium, and during which the dancers heard the orchestra play the score for the first time.

'Whatever happens,' Diaghilev told Pierre Monteux and the dancers, 'the ballet must be performed to the end.' To calm everyone's nerves, the first piece was *Les Sylphides*: graceful, poised and beautiful. Then, after an interval, Monteux gave the signal for the orchestra to begin playing *Le Sacre du printemps*. Stravinsky said later that his conductor had been 'impervious and nerveless as a crocodile' but Monteux remembered keeping his eyes glued to the score in front of him, not daring even to glance at the stage. 'You may think this strange, *cherie*,' he told his wife, 'but I have never seen the ballet.'

Like Monteux, the dancers waiting on stage were nervous, sweating heavily in their thick costumes.* This is the Sotheby's description, from a 1968 sale, of a costume for one of the Maidens: 'Exceptionally long-sleeved robe [of cream-coloured flannel] stencilled all over in barbaric patterns of oxblood, scarlet, lemon-yellow, turquoise-blue, peacock-blue, ochre and bottle-green, the predominant effect being tawny; and an attached vermillion petticoat stencilled with an oxblood and white stripe and dashes of white and yellow.' The glowing, gem-like colours Roerich used recalled traditional Russian ikons. On their legs both men and women wore loose white leggings over which the ribbons of their soft shoes criss-crossed. The men wore false beards and strange, pointed, fur-trimmed caps, the women headbands and long false plaits. Behind them the set portrayed a lush green landscape dotted with the mystical symbols or 'memory signs' so important to Roerich: animal skulls, sacred rivers, hills and trees, magical stones and ominously gathering storm clouds.

The first strains of *Sacre*, a technically intimidating bassoon solo in an unusually high register, are hauntingly delicate, but the body of the score is wild, violent, powerful and provocative: complex rhythms layered over one another, pounding away in a remorseless, dissonant frenzy of primitive abandon. For an audience of 1913, even an audience as sophisticated as this one, hearing this kind of noise for the first time was overwhelmingly disconcerting, 'as irritating to the nervous system,' said one early listener, 'as the continuous thudding of a savage's

---

* *Le Sacre du printemps* was far from being the only one of Diaghilev's ballets which required the dancers to perform in unwieldy and uncomfortable costumes. In *Les Femmes de bonne humeur* (1917), Lopokova said she and the other artists 'felt like rugby football players dressed as Eskimos pretending to be the most elegant and dainty females of the eighteenth century'. (J. Mackrell, *Bloomsbury Ballerina: Lydia Lopokova, Imperial Dancer and Mrs Maynard Keynes*, 2008, p. 118.)

tom-tom'. Hisses, whistles, boos and disbelieving laughter broke out: was this some kind of joke? The composer Camille Saint-Saëns leapt out of his seat to leave, hissing to his neighbour, 'If that's a bassoon, I'm a baboon!' Debussy, who had so longed to hear an orchestra playing *Sacre*, was sitting in Misia Sert's box. After a few moments he turned to her 'with a sad, anxious face' and whispered, 'It's terrifying – I don't understand it'.

Onstage, as the audience reaction grew less inhibited, the frightened dancers struggled to hear the music over the noise of the crowd and forced themselves to keep moving. Trembling with fury, dripping with sweat beneath the stage lights, his face ashen, Nijinsky stood on a chair in the wings, frantically shouting out the time for them. Stravinsky, who had rushed backstage when the tumult began, was by his side. Astruc leant forward out of his box, his fist clenched, and screamed, 'First listen! *Then* hiss!' Desperately Diaghilev switched the house lights on and off several times, appealing for calm.

Nijinsky's willingness 'to exclude the audience', partly by denying them the lightness and sensuality they had come to expect from the Ballets Russes, partly by having his dancers apparently more absorbed in the ritual of their dance than the performance, caused fury. When the maidens held their cheeks as if in pain, hecklers shouted out, '*Un docteur! Un dentiste!*' One countess took their heavily rouged cheeks as a deliberate dig at her own make-up, and stood up, cheeks flaming, tiara askew, to shout indignantly, 'I am sixty years old, but this is the first time anyone has dared to make a fool of me!'

Defenders of the piece were equally vehement, believing like Harry Kessler that they were witnessing 'an utterly new vision, something never before seen ... art and anti-art at once'. They recognised that what they were seeing and hearing was as revolutionary as the writings of Nietszche, Proust and Freud, the scientific discoveries of Einstein or the art of Cezanne, Picasso and Brancusi. Fisticuffs broke out between opposing factions: one man hit another over the head with his cane; Monteux saw a man pull someone else's hat down over his face. Some witnessed *gendarmes* arriving to quell the riot. The music critic Florent

Schmitt cried, 'Down with the whores of the *Seizième!*' Finding herself in the midst of a battleground, Eleonora fainted.

At times, reading the accounts of the rowdy, roiling mob, it is hard to avoid the conclusion that they had all come spoiling for a fight. The *succès de scandale* was an established part of cultural life, particularly in Paris at the turn of the twentieth century – the first Impressionist painters made a virtue of being rejected by the establishment with the *Salons des refusés*, while both Oscar Wilde's 1894 *Salomé* and Richard Strauss's 1906 opera of Wilde's play caused their audiences to return again and again in delighted horror. Premieres of pieces by Wagner and Schoenberg had provoked riots. Diaghilev himself was hardly a stranger to courting commercial success by leading his audiences to the outer bounds of what they considered acceptable.

The audience at the Théâtre des Champs-Elysées was apparently restless from the start, whispering and giggling even before *Sacre* began. Roerich later observed that the real savages that night were not the dancers portraying on stage 'the refined primitivism of our ancestors, for whom rhythm, the sacred symbol, and subtlety of movement were great and sacred concepts', but the brawling mass watching them. 'What an idiot the public is,' Rambert heard Nijinsky muttering. '*Dura publika, dura publika.*'

The theatre did not quieten until Maria Piltz calmly faced the hooting, bellowing audience for her solo.* 'She seemed to dream, her knees turned inwards, the heels pointing out – inert. A sudden spasm shook her body out of its corpse-like rigour. At the fierce onward thrust of the rhythm, she trembled in ecstatic, irregular jerks.' Finally the Maiden collapsed, having danced herself to death, and six of the men lifted her

---

*There is no precedent in the myths of any ancient cultures (except Aztec, which Roerich did not mention in his notes) for female sacrifice. This was a modern construct, 'cousin to the invented myths of W. B. Yeats, T. S. Eliot, and Sigmund Freud' (see L. Garafola, *Diaghilev's Ballets Russes*, 1989, p. 72) – except for one arena in which young virgins had willingly and regularly sacrificed themselves for some higher ideal: classical ballet, both on stage and off. (T. Scholl, *From Petipa to Balanchine: Classical Revival and the Modernisation of Ballet*, 1993, p. 72.)

limp body to the skies and bore it off with 'no cathartic outpouring of despair, sadness, or anger, only a chilling resignation'.

The pitiless quality of *Sacre*, the impossibility of catharsis, is perhaps the main reason no one there that night quite knew what to make of it. As Prince Volkonsky, Diaghilev's friend and former colleague at the Imperial Theatres, said, 'Nothing could be less appropriate to prepare one for this spectacle than the word "ballet" and all the associations it carries with it.' Not only was there no demonstrable grace, virtuosity or eroticism, but there was also no narrative and none of the conventional devices that steered an audience towards a sense of unity and completion. 'This is not the usual spring sung by poets, with its breezes, its birdsong, its pale skies and tender greens. Here there is nothing but the harsh struggle of growth, the panic terror from the rising of the sap, the fearful regrouping of the cells,' wrote Jacques Rivière, hailing *Sacre* a masterpiece. 'Spring seen from inside, with its violence, its spasms and its fissions. We seem to be watching a drama through a microscope.'

The music and the choreography combined to create something simply breathtakingly new. If *Le Sacre du printemps* was for Roerich an attempt at reconstruction of an ancient ceremonial rite, for Stravinsky and Nijinsky the distant past was a metaphor for the tragedy of modern existence. Their *Sacre* – the music and the movement – was 'a bleak and intense celebration of the collective will' and its triumph over the individual. If audiences found it frightening, remorseless, inhuman, at times absurd – well, that was the point.

Grigoriev kept the curtain down for longer than usual before the next piece, *Le Spectre de la Rose*, in an attempt to restore order. Think of Vaslav in the crowded changing room while the wardrobe mistress stitched him into his pink body stocking, preparing himself after that tumult to dance a role which merely irritated him – one that he saw as cloyingly sentimental and outdated and by which he resented being defined.

After the final curtain, said Stravinsky, they were 'excited, angry, disgusted, and … happy'. He, Diaghilev, Nijinsky, Bakst, Cocteau and Kessler went off to dine. Diaghilev's only comment on the evening was,

'Exactly what I wanted.' After dinner, during which they agreed that it might take people years to understand what they had just shown them, they drove through the dark and empty city in a cab, Cocteau and Kessler perched on the roof, Bakst waving a handkerchief tied to his cane like a flag. Diaghilev was muffled up against the night air in his opossum coat; Vaslav sat in his 'dress coat and top hat, quietly contented, smiling to himself'.

Cocteau remembered their midnight ride taking them on to the Bois de Boulogne – where by coincidence Rambert and the rest of the company were also having a late supper, too excited to think of going to bed. The scent of acacia blossom hung in the air. When the coachman lit his lantern, Cocteau saw tears glistening on Diaghilev's face. He was reciting Pushkin under his breath, with Stravinsky and Nijinsky listening intently. Whatever happened later, Cocteau wrote, 'You cannot imagine the sweetness and nostalgia of those men.'

In June Nijinsky went on to London with Diaghilev and Walter Nouvel, his usual travelling companions. Also on their train was Romola de Pulszky, who had in Vienna some months earlier managed to persuade Diaghilev to allow her to follow the Ballet with the plan that if she carried on her training with Cecchetti she might one day dance with them. Nijinsky had been against the idea – what else could she be but a dilettante? – but Diaghilev, always aware of who people were, was happy to be able to please her mother, the great Emilia Márkus. Romola had managed to convince Diaghilev that it was Bolm, not Nijinsky, with whom she was in love; and so she had been accepted.

Since then, Romola had been tailing *le petit* (as she and her maid had codenamed Vaslav) with all the focus and guile of an international spy. The dresser at the Viennese Opera House, Mr Schweiner, fed her titbits of information; once a girlfriend entered Nijinsky's room at the Hotel Bristol while he was dressing 'as if she was making a mistake'; in Monaco Romola lay on a bench under a blossoming magnolia tree as Nijinsky, Diaghilev and their party had dinner on the terrace at the Hotel de Paris, 'and watched them for hours and hours'. Having exhausted Bolm and

Nijinsky in evening clothes by Valentin Sverov, head back and eyes half-closed, wearing the distant expression that fascinated Romola de Pulszky.

Cecchetti, she had moved on to Baron de Günzburg, one of Diaghilev's most important backers, and by his side had complete access to the Ballets. It was with Günzburg that she had watched the first night of *Sacre*, squashed in among the mob of dancers and friends watching from the wings, looking out for Nijinsky's pale, tense face in the crowd.

She was delighted to find herself on the same train as Vaslav – she always instructed her maid Anna to find out when he and Diaghilev were travelling, but this was the first time Anna's information had been accurate – and, hanging out smoking (at this time a very racy activity for a woman, especially an unmarried woman) in the corridor near his compartment, was overjoyed when he asked her in his broken French if she was looking forward to being in London. It was their first conversation. On the sea crossing to Dover they spoke again and Romola triumphantly told Anna, who took a dim view of her crush on Nijinsky, that flirting was a great cure for sea-sickness.

In London she tried as much as she could to be where Nijinsky and Diaghilev were, badgering her English relations to take her to dine at the Savoy, where they were staying. Nijinsky 'seemed now almost to take it for granted that I was here, there, and everywhere he appeared in public. He must have wondered how I managed it. I was really glad now that I had spent so much on my clothes in Paris,' Romola wrote. 'As I always went with some friends, it must have seemed natural to Diaghilev that I was present. He realised that I moved in the same society as he himself.' Nijinsky was unfazed by this pursuit; indeed, sometimes when he looked at her she noticed the shadow of a smile on his face.

One morning Nijinsky and Karsavina arrived early for their class with Cecchetti, before Romola's class had been dismissed. She took a long time to change so that she could watch them. Every day Cecchetti began with a little speech: 'Tamara Platonova, Vaslav Fomich. You may be celebrated, great artists, but here in my class you are my pupils. Please forget here all your crazy modern movements, all that Fokine, Nijinsky nonsense. Please, *ras, dva, tri, chetyre* …' They obeyed without question, helping sprinkle water on the floor, executing whatever he asked of them with the precision of clocks, listening to his criticism of the performances of the night before and his inexhaustible complaints about the terrible modern music they had to dance to. A few days earlier, for his birthday, Nijinsky had given Cecchetti a cane with a heavy gold top; Romola said she and the girls in her class wished there was less gold in it, because Cecchetti rapped them with it when they made mistakes.

The Opera House in Covent Garden was full every night for their season and again London surrendered for two weeks to the Ballets Russes's spell. Muriel Draper and her husband went to the first night of *Sacre* with the pianist Artur Rubinstein and marvelled at the sound Monteux extracted from the orchestra, 'a sound that is still sinking down through me with every blood-beat'. Nijinsky's geometrical, 'beyond-human' choreography, thought Draper, intensified the music's power. When the curtain fell, 'the house broke loose'. As they filed off to find their drinks at the bar, the audience was stunned, shaken, paralysed.

'You call that art, do you?'

'You call it *music*?'

'My God!'

Rubinstein saw it differently. He found the audience merely polite (this was also Monteux's view, though the fact that the English applauded wearing kid gloves made even enthusiasm sound no more than polite) and he left the theatre 'defeated and unhappy' on account of the difficulty of the music and the incomprehensibility of the action on stage. 'It took me weeks of study to understand the greatness of this work.'

Despite her loyalty to Vaslav, Lady Ottoline Morrell thought *Sacre* 'really *terrible* and intense. Too much of Idea in it to please the public. Too little grace.' Lytton Strachey, on the other hand (who had ordered a new suit for his first meeting with Nijinsky, deep purple, with an orange stock, and who had found him 'much more attractive than I'd expected' despite their lack of a common language) loathed it. He had not imagined, he told a friend, 'that boredom and sheer anguish could have been combined together at such a pitch'.

While the French critics had wittily dismissed *Sacre* as the *massacre du printemps*, the English were more measured. One journalist acknowledged that while many felt *Sacre* ridiculed the ideals of beauty, perhaps 'in a few years we shall have learned that there are other things in music and ballet than sweetness and sensuous beauty, just as there are other things in painting than domestic subjects'.

This was the way Nijinsky saw his work. In an interview published in the *Daily Mail* the day after *Sacre*'s premiere, he protested against forever being associated with *Armide*, *Spectre* and *Sylphides*. 'The fact is, I detest "nightingale and rose" poetry; my own inclinations are "primitive",' he told the interviewer. 'I eat my meat without *sauce Béarnaise*.' In painting and sculpture, once-great traditions became banal through repetition, familiarity and the inevitable debasement of being copied by inferior artists, he observed. 'Then there has always come a revolt. Perhaps something like this has happened in dancing.'

Meanwhile the shock of the new, the first experience of seeing and hearing *Sacre*, was easing and Nijinsky and Stravinsky's peers were beginning to form their judgement on the piece. Once Debussy had had time to digest its extraordinary wildness, he was less afraid, telling composer André Caplet dismissively that it was 'primitive music with all modern conveniences'. The influential editor Louis Laloy, who had been blown away by hearing Stravinsky and Debussy play the four-hand piano version of *Sacre*, described the score as being something people would not be ready for until 1940 and the dancing as epileptic and absurd. (In his diary Vaslav would write, 'An artist sacrifices his whole life for art. The critic inveighs against him because he does not like his picture.')

But Cocteau felt 'uprooted' by it: 'Beauty speaks to the guts. Genius cannot be analysed any better than electricity ... One has it, or one does not ... The Russian troupe has taught me that one must burn oneself up alive in order to be reborn.' The painter Sigismond Jeanès wrote to tell Stravinsky that *Sacre* had been 'one of the great emotional experiences of my life'.

Even though they had performed in front of full houses in Paris and London – the box office had taken 38,000 francs on the night of *Sacre*'s premiere – Diaghilev was still heavily in debt and Astruc was bankrupt. His beautiful new theatre would be closed down three months later. The contract he had signed, promising Diaghilev 25,000 francs a performance had been his 'death warrant ... But I do not regret my madness.'

Stravinsky had developed typhoid after *Sacre*'s Paris opening and he had remained there to convalesce while the others went to London. He and Diaghilev were arguing by telegram about cuts Diaghilev wanted to make to the score in an attempt to make it more palatable to audiences. Diaghilev told Misia Sert that Stravinsky was ungrateful, that their success had gone to his head. 'Where would he be without us, without Bakst and myself?' Relations between them were so strained that Sert had to intervene. She wrote to Stravinsky telling him of Diaghilev's troubles: Bakst, who thought *Sacre* dreadful, was about to quit because he thought Diaghilev should drop it from the programme; lawsuits over Diaghilev's debts loomed; and the rebellious orchestra did not even want to play *Sacre*. Worst of all was Nijinsky, 'intolerable and *mal elevé* ... [speaking] to Serge as if he were a dog'.

Occasionally Vaslav managed to give the ever-present Zuikov the slip. It was probably around this time that a curious incident occurred, recounted many years afterwards by the porter at the Friends of St Stephen's, a poorhouse on the Fulham Road. He remembered a young man being brought in late at night, unconscious. The man was given a bed in which to sleep off his excesses – nothing unusual in that – but when he awoke the following morning he astonished everyone by doing the splits over his own bed and then leaping over each of the twenty beds on either side of the ward. He spoke no English but somehow he must have managed to get out word of where he was, for a little while later Diaghilev appeared with some other people in a couple of cabs, thanked everyone profusely for looking after his young friend, tipped them lavishly in gold sovereigns, and bore him off.

During the summer of 1913, while he remained alone in Paris, Stravinsky continued to declare himself delighted with *Sacre* and its choreography. A few days after the premiere he gave an interview in which he called Nijinsky 'capable of giving life to the whole art of ballet.

Not for a moment have we ceased to think upon the same lines.' On 20 June he wrote to his friend Max Steinberg (Rimsky-Korsakov's son-in-law), calling Nijinsky's work superb: 'I am confident in what we have done'. Two weeks later, nearly recovered and about to leave Paris for the summer, he wrote again. 'Nijinsky's choreography is incomparable and, with a few exceptions, everything was as I wanted it. But we must wait a long time before the public becomes accustomed to our language.'

Diaghilev, though, was quick to dissociate himself from *Sacre*, which had not been as successful with the public as he had needed it to be. At the end of July he summoned Bronia to the Savoy to discuss her brother – since he had become impossible to deal with directly. 'I had to tell Nijinsky that his ballet *Jeux* was a complete failure, and since it has not had any success it will not be performed any more. The same also applies to *Sacre*. All the friends of the Ballets Russes – from Paris, or London, or St Petersburg – all agree that *Sacre* is not a ballet and it would be a mistake to follow this path of Nijinsky's. They say I am destroying my ballet company!'

Bronia tried to explain to Diaghilev how devoted Vaslav was to his art, and how well it had been received by the people they respected, but Diaghilev was unmovable: in other genres, like painting or literature, immediate commercial success was immaterial, but a ballet had to be loved by the public from the start to have any life at all. The theatres that wanted to present the Ballets Russes's programme did not want to sponsor Nijinsky's researches into the future of dance. Sir Thomas Beecham had already made Diaghilev promise that Fokine would create two new ballets if they were to play the Opera House in 1914, one of which would be Strauss's *La Légende de Joseph* – on which Nijinsky was already working. Baron de Günzburg, on whose financial support Diaghilev depended, had also made Fokine's return a condition of his continued investment in the company.

Nijinsky received the message with such fury that Bronia understood why Diaghilev had preferred to let her break the news to him. 'Let Diaghilev give it [*Joseph*] to whomever he wishes ... I do not care ... But it does matter to me that Diaghilev has become a servile follower, a theatrical lackey, and is destroying everything that is the heart of the Ballets Russes.'

When Bronia went back to see Diaghilev again, he urged her to sign her 1914 contract as soon as possible, obviously anticipating that a break with her brother would shake her commitment to him. He was honest with her when she asked him about the latest rumour flying around the company: that Fokine's price for returning to the Ballets Russes was dancing the lead roles – Nijinsky's roles – in all his ballets.

'It's a possibility.'

'But Nijinsky would have more to dance in the Imperial Theatres.'

'Well, something has to be arranged. Nijinsky cannot return to Russia. Perhaps he should simply leave the Ballets Russes and not dance for a year.'

If he would not accept his conditions, Diaghilev told Bronia, 'I shall have to part with Nijinsky'. This was when Bronia realised that their friendship was over, though despite all their differences she knew that her brother still saw himself very much as one of Diaghilev's artists.

Underlying the arguments about the creative direction of the Ballets Russes and Nijinsky's role within it was a longstanding and bitter debate over money. Vaslav had never received a regular salary and had never signed a contract. But as he became more important to the company he demanded to be paid like everyone else – if only as a mark of his independence. According to Bronia, he wanted several years' back salary, amounting to 200,000 francs per year for 1911, 1912 and 1913, minus expenses (four times what the opera superstar Fyodor Chaliapin had been paid for the month-long season of 1909). But Diaghilev, deeply in debt, didn't have the money – even if he had thought he owed it. After all, the old agreement had been that Diaghilev would look after Vaslav while Nijinsky danced. Both of them felt resentful and aggrieved.

When the London season ended in early August, the company was due to sail to South America for their first non-European tour, but although he had booked a stateroom Diaghilev had decided not to go with them; Günzburg would go in his place. He hated sea travel (whenever they went on a boat he made Zuikov pray for them both while he lay sick and groaning on his bunk, which was why Nijinsky had been free to flirt with Romola between Calais and Dover a few weeks earlier) and believed what a fortune-teller had once told him, that he would die on water. Instead he would have a holiday in Venice, pull himself together and plan for the future.

For the first time in his adult life, Vaslav was going to do something on his own. Before he left, Bronia, whose baby was expected in October and who was therefore remaining behind, urged Vaslav to remember that he was an artist and above such spats with Diaghilev. Instead, she said, he should look on the journey as a holiday: relax, enjoy himself, not work too hard and try to make friends.

CHAPTER 7

Roses
1913–1914

HAVING BID FAREWELL to Diaghilev, Benois and Nouvel, Vaslav boarded the SS *Avon* in Cherbourg on the afternoon of 15 August 1913. Except for Karsavina, who was travelling separately, the rest of the company had boarded earlier that morning in Southampton. Romola de Pulszky was with them. Without paying much attention to whether or not she could dance (her lessons with Cecchetti had been sporadic, consumed as she was with her pursuit of *le petit*), Diaghilev had engaged her for this tour as a member of the *corps*, providing that she could keep up with the routines. She had been lucky that not all the regular dancers wanted to go to South America and that Diaghilev was preoccupied by other matters.

Giving the second-class ticket bought for her by the company to her maid Anna, Romola had reserved a first-class cabin for herself, hoping it would be close to Nijinsky's. 'Twenty-one days of ocean and sky – no Diaghilev,' she told herself. 'He can't escape.'

The *Avon*'s passengers soon slipped into 'the agreeable routine of deck life'. Each morning before most of them were up, Vaslav, attended by his masseur and Zuikov, who stood beside the watering can and rosin box holding his towel, went through his daily class on deck, apparently unaffected by the motion of the sea. Sometimes a small crowd of curious admirers would gather, but he was relaxed and well rested, and for once he did not mind being observed. He would smile and occasionally explain a movement or answer a question. Then he would dress and take a stroll on deck before lunch, or read in a deck chair.

He spent the afternoons in a small hall with a piano off Deck C with the conductor, Rhené-Baton (Monteux's replacement for the South American tour). Baton played Bach, while Nijinsky was in the very early stage of creating something that was intended 'to be as pure dancing as his [Bach's] music is pure sound',* something he had been discussing with Diaghilev and the others in Baden-Baden. One afternoon Romola found them and sat down on a stair to watch before being ushered away by the chief steward. The next day she was there again and Baton asked her to leave. Then Vaslav looked up from his reverie and pantomimed to Baton that she could stay.

From then on, she was there every afternoon; and after rising unusually early one morning and noticing Nijinsky practising on deck, she was there every morning too. He noticed the awe with which she watched him and attributed it to her loving ballet, 'our art'. In his last letter before they began their crossing of the Atlantic, postmarked Madeira, Vaslav told Bronia and his mother about one of the other passengers, a beautiful blonde girl with blue eyes. 'She is also alone and we are often together.'

Romola, meanwhile, was making friends with Vaslav's masseur, cultivating the Batons, pumping the other dancers for information – Marie Rambert remembered having 'endless talks about Nijinsky, whom we both adored' – and in short finding out everything she could about him. She knew that 'he was only absorbed in one thing – his art. Society, success, wealth, fame, and flirtations did not seem to mean anything to him … [and] we had all heard that he had no interest for us women … But didn't I catch, in spite of this, here and there a smile, a glance which he threw to me? Where others had failed, why shouldn't I succeed?'

---

* Rudolf Nureyev also venerated Bach. 'When you listen to Bach you hear a part of God …When you watch me dance you see a part of God.' (J. Kavanagh, *Rudolf Nureyev*, 2008, p. 187.)

It is hard to describe Romola de Pulszky without slipping into the language of melodrama. Her parents were Emilia Márkus and Karoly, or Charlie, de Pulszky. The Pulszkys, though aristocratic, were liberal, artistic and above all political, prime movers in the struggle against the Austrian Empire for Hungarian autonomy. After the failed revolution of 1848, Romola's paternal grandparents fled to London, where Charlie was born (hence the nickname). One of his godfathers was Giuseppe Garibaldi. Neither the Pulszkys nor the Márkuses particularly approved of the marriage between Charlie and Emilia, and though Charlie doted on his beautiful, flirtatious wife, it was not an especially happy union. In 1896, while he was buying paintings for the National Gallery of Hungary, which he had co-founded, Charlie was accused of misappropriating state funds. He was disgraced and briefly imprisoned before fleeing to England and then travelling on to Australia, where three years later he committed suicide. It is possible that he had been framed, but the evidence even at the time was inconclusive. Romola was eight when her beloved 'Charlie-Papa' died.

She always blamed her mother for her father's tragic fate and throughout their lives the two women, mother and daughter, were entwined in the most destructive kind of filial relationship in which bonds of intense love and interdependence were joined on both sides by jealousy, competition, contempt and selfishness. From childhood, wrote her daughter, Romola 'harboured a burning ambition to prove to her father's memory that she, Romola de Pulszky, was *somebody* in her own right'. When she saw Nijinsky, she seems to have decided that capturing him would achieve this aim.

Evenings on board the *Avon* had a carnival atmosphere. As they neared the equator, Baron de Günzburg donned a white dinner jacket, wrapping a Bakstian shawl in wild colours, purple, green and orange, around his waist. He and his elegant mistress, Ekaterina Oblokova, had been charged by Romola's mother and stepfather with looking out for her on the voyage.

One night there was a fancy-dress ball. The Russian dancers, determined to have the best costumes, spent the afternoon racing between cabins, borrowing and lending clothes to one another. Romola put together a Hungarian gypsy outfit, but then Günzburg advised her – surely deliberately – to go as a boy, with her hair slicked back and wearing a pair of his tailored apple-green pyjamas. At the last minute she lost her nerve and came down to dinner in an evening gown. The only other person who had not worn fancy dress was Nijinsky, for whom costumes possessed a special magic: they were not something to be assumed and cast off on a whim. Besides, he didn't like parties. He had once been so nervous at an official reception that he began eating his glass. When he looked at Romola, she saw a sigh of relief in his eyes.

Still they had barely spoken. One evening soon after this, out on the moonlit deck, they were formally introduced by a Monsieur Chavez, an Argentinian couturier who had befriended the Russians. Josefina Kovaleska – the most chic of the dancers, who had been the Aga Khan's mistress, and the only one Romola considered her peer in looks and style – translated for them, telling Nijinsky how passionate Romola was about ballet. They talked, or rather Romola talked in the simplest French she could manage about music and dance and her passion for Wagner, for a long time as they watched the phosphorescence sparkling on the waves beneath them. She had no idea how much he understood, but she was so nervous she couldn't stop speaking.

It was perhaps on this night that Rambert saw Nijinsky lighting Romola's cigarette with a 'courteous, elegant gesture'. Once someone shook her hand too vigorously in greeting her and Vaslav cried out, '*Pas casser! Pas casser!*' Rambert also noticed Romola's glorious ash-blonde hair, which Anna brushed out every evening. When Vaslav told her he was in love with Romola, she asked him how he could speak to her, having no language in common. Smiling wistfully, Vaslav replied, 'Oh, she understands everything'. But Rambert consoled herself, certain it could not be serious. 'We all knew he was Diaghilev's lover.'

The next morning they sighted land, a long brown smudge on the horizon that was Brazil. But when Nijinsky saw Romola it was as if their conversation the previous evening had never taken place. Apart from a polite bow, he did not speak to her again until one evening a few days later when some passengers from first class went down to steerage to see the Italian and Spanish itinerant workers who helped bring in the Argentine harvests, playing, singing and dancing: boleros, tarantellas, real tango, flamenco. On the way back up to their cabins, using Kovaleska as her translator, Romola boldly asked Vaslav if he remembered having lost a little travelling pillow, or *dumka*, that his mother had given him, that she had heard he treasured. Would he like it back?

'Nijinsky gave me one long look and, mounting up the stairs, said to Kovaleska, "Tell her please to keep it." I could have choked him.' That night, when Anna tore another page off the calendar, she quoted a Hungarian proverb to her mistress: 'The sixteenth day. Really, Miss Romola. I wouldn't run after a hay-cart which refuses to give a lift.'

The following day Romola was sitting in the bar before lunch with the Batons, Kovaleska and a few others when Günzburg came up and asked to speak to her. Romola thought she was about to be sacked – that her dancing, which she knew to be not good enough, had been noticed. He took her out on deck and, very formally, said, 'Romola Carlovna, as Nijinsky cannot speak to you himself, he has requested me to ask you in marriage.' Thinking it a joke, a humiliated Romola burst into tears and fled to her cabin.

After dinner a note arrived from Günzburg, hoping she felt better and asking for a response as he could not keep Nijinsky waiting. Perhaps it was true. Romola got dressed and cautiously went out to find Günzburg. When she came out of her cabin, Nijinsky appeared and, pointing to her ring finger, said, *'Mademoiselle, voulez-vous, vous et moi?'* All she could reply was, *'Oui, oui, oui.'* It had been the missing *dumka* which convinced Vaslav: in his account of their meeting, he wrote that it showed him 'her affection was not just for my art, but also for me. Then and there I decided to marry her.' Evidently he never suspected she might have stolen the pillow, as I instantly did on reading this; Romola was as enthusiastic a Nijinsky fetishist as any of the fans who bought a discarded rose petal from Zuikov or crept into his dressing room to filch his underwear.

As they steamed towards land the next morning, an excited Kovaleska burst into Romola's cabin and threw her arms around her, kissing her three times in the Russian fashion. Vaslav had asked her to come with them into Rio when they docked there for the day, as chaperone and interpreter, to help buy their rings. 'This is indeed wonderful news. I congratulate you with all my heart. Unbelievable. But somehow I always knew Vaslav Fomich is not as people say.' Then she stopped, catching herself. 'I mean, I am glad for both of you … Oh, to see the faces of the others when they hear.' After choosing the rings they drove up into the mountains above Rio for lunch, meeting some other passengers from the *Avon*. It was the first time they had ever sat together at a table.

Back on board that evening, heading for Buenos Aires, Rambert heard Vaslav's news. She had to bury her face in her trunk, pretending she was looking for something, to hide her tears. 'I suddenly realised I was hopelessly in love with him, and had been for a long time.' She envied Romola so much, she thought she might throw herself overboard. That night after dinner, one of the girls (Romola does not say who) was in hysterics because of Nijinsky's engagement, and earned Madame Baton's ire by fainting in her husband's arms; probably it was Rambert.

That night Nijinsky and Romola sat together in the *Avon*'s dining room for the first time, with the Batons, Günzburg and Oblokova. Afterwards Adolph Bolm pulled Romola aside, asking her if the rumours were true. As a friend of her parents, he said, he had to warn her that Nijinsky would ruin her life. He was 'utterly heartless' and the friendship between him and Diaghilev was 'more than merely a friendship'. Romola told him stiffly that she would prefer to 'be unhappy serving Nijinsky's genius than be happy without him'. When Nijinsky left her at her cabin door that night, kissing her hand, Romola remembered Bolm's warning and was 'not quite sure if I should be flattered or offended'.

Vaslav refused the captain's offer to perform the ceremony on board; he wanted a real wedding in a church. They would marry when they landed in Buenos Aires. With Günzburg's help they sent a telegram to Romola's mother, formally requesting her permission, but they did not inform Eleonora or Diaghilev. As Romola would later say to Bronia, 'I am not stupid. To give advance notice of our wedding plans to Diaghilev or to Vaslav's family and risk you stopping us ...'

One great mystery remains: why Günzburg did not warn Diaghilev. There is no doubt that Diaghilev would have wanted to know about Nijinsky's blossoming romance long before any announcement was made; and that Günzburg, whose specified role was to keep Diaghilev fully informed about the company as a whole and Nijinsky in particular, had failed in this duty first by obviously encouraging them and second by not letting him know as soon as they were engaged. Perhaps he was simply swept away by the shipboard magic of it all, or perhaps for Nijinsky's sake he hoped to see him free of Diaghilev's influence. Benois and Grigoriev speculated afterwards that Günzburg was trying to separate Nijinsky from Diaghilev so that he could set up a rival company with Nijinsky, though since (according to Bronia) Günzburg had apparently already agreed to fund Diaghilev's new season with Fokine rather than Nijinsky, this is unlikely. Maybe, guessing that Nijinsky might not be dancing with the Ballets Russes the following year, Günzburg thought Romola would serve as a consolation.

Their first days in Buenos Aires were spent rehearsing frantically while Günzburg, still without contacting Diaghilev, arranged the wedding. When Romola made her confession before the service (as required by the Catholic Church), the priest made her promise that she would try to prevent Nijinsky from ever dancing in *Schéhérazade* again. Nijinsky's confession was short: thankfully the priest could speak neither Russian nor Polish. On the morning of Wednesday, 10 September, four days after arriving in Buenos Aires, Vaslav and Romola went through a civil ceremony at the city hall. He was twenty-four, she was twenty-one (though later, romanticising things, she claimed to have been under-age) and they had left Europe as virtual strangers less than a month earlier.

At the wedding breakfast Karsavina, who had joined them in Argentina, made a graceful speech and Bolm made a tactless one, 'saying that of all the great leaps Nijinsky had ever made this was the most prodigious one: the jump from his former life into marriage'. Lydia Sokolova thought the reception 'rather dreary'. Like most of the company, she was 'so shocked and so worried' about what Diaghilev would do when he found out. The dancers' accounts of the wedding, reported back to Bronia when they returned to St Petersburg, all carried a 'strong undercurrent of doom'. But neither the bride nor the groom noticed. Romola commented that 'they all seemed happy and Karsavina was constantly smiling at us'.

Afterwards Romola asked Rambert to take her upstairs to wait for Vaslav, who followed with a piece of wedding cake for his bride. If Romola had guessed Rambert's feelings, it was the cruellest of digs at her vanquished rival. She sat in bed eating her cake while Vaslav kissed the crumbs off her fingers and poor Mim, as Rambert was known, looked on hopelessly.

The ceremony took place in the Iglesia San Miguel that evening. Anna refused to allow Romola to marry in pale blue, instead making her buy a heavy ivory dress. At the last minute they couldn't find orange-blossom anywhere, so Romola wore a white turban. Zuikov, loyal to Diaghilev (though strangely, he had not contacted him), was the only member of the company who did not attend. The Latin and Spanish service was long and almost incomprehensible to them both. From the church they went on to the Teatro Colon for the company's dress rehearsal where Romola was to dance as part of the company for the first time.

After the rehearsal the newlyweds met in the drawing room of Romola's little suite, where a cold supper had been laid out for them. Romola was desperately frightened. She had wanted Nijinsky so much for so long – and here he was; but she barely knew him and she knew nothing about love or sex. They ate in embarrassed silence and afterwards Vaslav kissed her hand and left. Romola was so relieved she almost cried. In the morning – and every morning thereafter – she received a large bunch of white roses from her husband, 'handed to Anna by Vassily [Zuikov] with a furious look'.

Each day they got to know each other better. Mornings were spent practising and in the afternoons they would go out driving or walking. Nijinsky 'made me notice everything lovely around us. It seemed to me that life began to have a new meaning. Suddenly I realised that so much beauty surrounds us which, before, I had failed to observe.' Before they left Buenos Aires, where they stayed for a month, Nijinsky asked Romola – formally, through Günzburg – to move down to his suite in the hotel. 'The charm of his personality, the tenderness of his whole being, radiated so much goodness, such beauty, that the evening he chose to remain [in her room] I felt I was making an offering on the altar of happiness.'

Bronia was in St Petersburg with Eleonora, weeks away from her baby's arrival, when they opened the newspapers and saw the headline: 'NIJIN-SKY MARRIED'. Although, as Romola had discovered, Vaslav wrote to his mother every night, the last letter she had received from him was postmarked Madeira.

Eleonora was devastated to think that he could have married without discussing it with her, and to someone she had never met. They struggled to think of who the beautiful Hungarian socialite described in the papers might be. Bronia thought she remembered a girl in a train station sitting on one of the big wicker baskets in which the costumes were transported, smoking a cigarette and chatting to Bolm; at performances in Paris and in London, Eleonora had been shocked to find herself sitting next to a girl who tried to talk to her, and had had to ask Günzburg not to place her next to her again (Romola had evidently asked him to do it): the common thread was the boldness of the girl. Then a telegram signed Vaslav and Romushka arrived, asking for Eleonora's blessing.

Meanwhile, after being told by the Imperial War Ministry that Vaslav's petition to be exempt from military service needed only a signature to be confirmed, the news came that it had been denied, on the grounds that he was very wealthy and had ample means to support his mother without dancing. Someone, Bronia was certain, had given new 'information' to the Minister. Although she did not accuse Diaghilev directly, she made it clear in her memoirs that she did not think his return to Russia, having heard the news of Vaslav's marriage at the same time as the exemption was denied, was a coincidence.

Diaghilev was in Venice in early September 1913. Misia Sert

remembered going up to his room one morning to play something for him on the piano. She was wearing a white muslin dress and he was still in his nightshirt and Turkish slippers when she knocked at the door. In high spirits, he seized her parasol, opening it up and dancing with it across the room, while Misia urged him to close it – both of them were 'madly superstitious' and thought opening an umbrella inside would bring bad luck. Just then a telegram arrived. It was from Nijinsky, announcing that he had married.

Diaghilev fell apart, crying, screaming, swearing and sobbing shamelessly. 'He had entirely formed and fashioned him [Vaslav], moulded him, led him to his glory. He was his work of art and his beloved child.' Later a sort of council of war was held, an alternate version of Diaghilev's committee meetings. Irreverently, Bakst wondered whether Nijinsky had bought new underclothes before leaving, which would be certain proof he had intended to elope. 'Diaghilev burst out again: To hell with their talk of underpants when he was in the depths of despair!'

It was in effect a divorce, and a divorce complicated by a shared business interest, a company created and made valuable by both parties separately as well as together. Diaghilev had made Nijinsky a star, but Nijinsky was Diaghilev's main box-office draw. How lawyers would rub their hands over that prospect today. Then there was no method of arranging a split in a civilised way – because theoretically nothing had existed to be split. Except for the first season in 1909, Nijinsky had never signed a contract with the Ballets Russes. Besides, though Diaghilev had threatened to sack Nijinsky for defying him, he had never expected to be dumped himself. He wanted revenge. He told Bakst, 'As high as Nijinsky stands now – so low am I going to thrust him.'

Walter Nouvel told Arnold Haskell, one of Diaghilev's early biographers, that though Nijinsky's desire to marry was understandable, it should not be seen as 'an escape from some ogre'. At the start of their relationship Nijinsky had pursued Diaghilev; there could be 'no suggestion that Diaghilev seduced him. Nijinsky was not a child' (though they all treated him as one, and he had been a teenager, half Diaghilev's age, when they met). Throughout their time together, Nijinsky 'had an enormous respect and admiration for Diaghilev and [had] profited both materially and as an artist from the friendship'. All this was true, and later Vaslav would tell Romola that he would never regret his friendship with Diaghilev, 'for I believe that all experience in life, if made with the aim of truth, is uplifting'.

However Nouvel also told Haskell that Nijinsky, during his years with Diaghilev, was 'a being never fully sexually awake ... someone who poured all his emotions into his work, and to whom the active adventures of love meant absolutely nothing'. I think Nouvel intended this statement to mean that Nijinsky never returned Diaghilev's love, and was therefore calculating in his relations with him; my interpretation of it would be that he was trapped and immature, utterly in thrall to the older man's intelligence, worldliness and domineering personality, but not physically attracted to him.

Nijinsky's diary corroborates this idea of him being sexually immature during his relationship with Diaghilev – the only times he mentions Diaghilev in connection with sex is with a sense of repulsion at what Diaghilev 'taught' him – and makes clear that with Romola he woke up. Though occasionally he continued using prostitutes in secret (because, he says, he had so much semen he 'had to ejaculate'), their sex life was satisfactory: he writes of screwing her, of licking her, of having sex five times a day, of her liking 'experiencing a feeling of lust for me'.

It is possible – I believe likely – that Diaghilev had not minded Nijinsky remaining asleep, an adolescent *beau aux bois dormant*, channelling all his creative energy into his work and expending whatever was left over on prostitutes (I find it hard to fathom that Diaghilev didn't know anything about this aspect of Nijinsky's life, regardless of how well Vaslav thought he was keeping it secret). Even he could not have believed that their constant arguing and sexual incompatibility was domestic bliss, but he had his own distractions, and he was perhaps content to adore Nijinsky from a distance – from the stalls, so to speak – as long as he knew he 'possessed' him.

There was a quality in Nijinsky that permitted this sense of ownership. After all, despite his creative independence, he was used to being looked at and admired. The stage somehow makes performers passive, screens for whatever the audience wants to project onto them; Diaghilev (and Romola too in her own way) was just the audience magnified. And Vaslav recognised that he 'was not mature enough for life': he needed a protector so that he could concentrate on his art. It is speculation, but maybe, just as Romola believed his fame and glamour would be more than enough for both of them, Vaslav assumed that she was an heiress – who else, after all, would have been able to pursue him as she did? Benois was just one of their circle who believed she was very rich – and would thus be able to look after him. On a practical level she would be a replacement for Diaghilev, but one who would facilitate his creative endeavours rather than secretly compete with or stifle them.

Misia Sert's memoirs provide us with another angle on Diaghilev's view of the break-up. In her view, Diaghilev had provided Vaslav with 'the background best fitted to bring out his exceptional gifts' and without that he was 'a lost child ... insecure, unsure of himself ... profoundly miserable'. His dependence on Diaghilev, what Misia described pointedly as 'a flaccid will', made him refuse to condemn to Romola his relationship with Diaghilev and refuse to accept that they could not work together in the future, despite her opposition to it.

Misia and her lover, José-Maria Sert, took the grieving, angry Diaghilev to Florence and Naples where, beyond consolation, he surrendered to 'a wild orgy of dissipation'. The plans to replace Nijinsky with Fokine were finalised. On the way back to Russia, Diaghilev stopped in Clarens to see Stravinsky and break the news to him that *Sacre* – the work he considered his best – would not be performed as a ballet again. Diaghilev blamed it on Nijinsky's running away with Romola and thus, perhaps inadvertently, leaving the Ballet, but in reality the decision had been taken before Vaslav ever set foot on the *Avon*.

One of the Ballets Russes's dancers, Anna Fyodorova (whose sister Olga had run off with Aleksey Mavrin in 1909), saw Diaghilev by chance in Montreux. 'He was sitting alone, at a café table on the terrace of the hotel on the shore of the lake. The table in front of him was empty. Diaghilev appeared deep in thought, his chin resting on his hands folded on top of his cane. "When I approached to greet him ... he lifted his head and I was frightened to see his face so distorted by grief ... he did not say a word, he did not answer me.'"

In October Diaghilev was back in Russia where, possibly, he interfered with Nijinsky's application for exemption from military service and instructed Grigoriev to telegram Nijinsky informing him he was fired. He sent him no word directly himself. Grigoriev brooded over the situation, unable to influence Diaghilev but blaming him 'for treating Nijinsky so harshly. For, after all, Nijinsky had spent years in his company and had perhaps done more than anyone else to win it fame.' Despite their longstanding friendship, Diaghilev was treating Nijinsky no better than he had treated Fokine eighteen months earlier. Grigoriev decided that the violence of Diaghilev's attitude must be in part a reaction to the failure of *Jeux* and *Sacre*: commercial considerations made the break easier for him.

Benois, who had been through his own ruptures with Diaghilev, wrote to Stravinsky with almost audible glee: 'Be kind and tell me one thing: was it a complete surprise for Serge, or was he prepared for it? How deep was his shock? Their romance was coming to an end, and I doubt that he was really heartbroken, but if he did suffer I hope it was not too terrible for him. However I imagine he must be completely bewildered in his position as head of the company. But why can't Nijinsky be both a ballet-master and a Hungarian millionaire?' Later he would write that Diaghilev, evidently needing someone to blame, told him Günzburg had pushed Vaslav and Romola together, hoping to steal Nijinsky away from him, and that he was more angry because he had been deceived than because he had been abandoned.

Stravinsky's response to Benois was more considered, though typically more concerned with the impact of events on him than on anyone else. 'Of course, this turns everything upside down – literally everything we've been doing – and you yourself can foresee all the consequences: for him [Nijinsky] it's all over, I too may long be deprived of the possibility of doing something valuable in choreography, and, even more important, of seeing my creation which had been made flesh, choreographically speaking, with such incredible efforts. Ah, my friend, this creation gives me not a minute's rest. It's surrounded by a dreadful din, like devils gnashing their teeth.' He went on to complain that Diaghilev had surrendered to commercial concerns, just as Nijinsky had railed against Diaghilev to Bronia in London earlier in the year. 'Very simply I fear he has come under bad influences, ones that I think are strong in a material rather than a moral sense.'

For Stravinsky, Nijinsky's leaving the Ballets Russes meant the end of a hugely productive and exciting working relationship. It could not be replicated. Spoilt and stubborn though he may sometimes have been, difficult though he found it to articulate his ideas – there simply was no one else around who combined Nijinsky's classical technique and iconoclastic creativity. After four years of seeing each other almost daily, once Diaghilev broke with Nijinsky he and Stravinsky would scarcely meet again.

Diaghilev's first priority was to find – or make – a new *premier danseur*, the star of his upcoming season. He saw what he wanted when a handsome eighteen-year-old boy, dark-haired and dark-eyed, carried a ham on a platter on stage in a feast scene at the Bolshoy in Moscow. This was the young Léonide Massine, who had just given up ballet to concentrate on acting. Diaghilev took him to St Petersburg to audition for Fokine, then to the Hermitage, and then (presumably; this would become Diaghilev's standard seduction routine) to bed. Grigoriev said those winter months of 1913–14 were similar to the spring of 1909, with an infatuated Diaghilev infecting the entire company with his energy and high spirits. Nijinsky had been replaced.

The Ballets Russes tour of South America progressed after their month in Buenos Aires to Montevideo, briefly, and on to Rio de Janeiro. Marie Rambert suffered her broken heart in silence. She was one of the swans in the *corps de ballet* of *Swan Lake*. At one point Nijinsky had to go down the line, scrutinising each face as he searched for Odette. 'There was a heavenly moment of waiting for him to approach, and then for one second he looked into my face before passing on.'

At one performance in Rio, apparently trying to compel Günzburg to pay him some of the back salary he was claiming, and urged on by Romola, Nijinsky refused to perform. He was presumably hoping to prove that without him the Ballets Russes was nothing – an attempt to force Günzburg's hand. The plan backfired spectacularly. Not appearing for a scheduled performance, without a doctor's note, was a sackable offence. Günzburg – so remiss in this duty just a few weeks earlier – telegraphed Diaghilev immediately and it was this incident that Diaghilev later used when he ordered Grigoriev to inform Nijinsky that he had been dismissed from the Ballet.

Until they returned to Europe, Vaslav hoped that Diaghilev would accept his marriage. One cannot read Romola's version of any event without bearing in mind her carefree relationship with the truth, but she insisted that he believed Diaghilev would be happy for them, writing from Buenos Aires to ask for his blessing, and that he assumed – at this stage he had not been told otherwise – that despite their arguments the previous spring he would be dancing for the Ballets Russes in the 1914 season.

Day by day they were able to communicate better, speaking in pidgin French and Russian, but the insights they revealed were not always welcome. Romola found that there was a total separation between Nijinsky the artist and Vaslav the man. The first time she tried to go into his dressing room – as a child she had always loved watching her mother while she made up for a role – he gently asked her to leave. At rehearsals he helped her with her steps but the expression on his face was impersonal, that of a master to his pupil; and he was marvellously patient and polite, but unsparing. When he told her that she could never be a top-flight ballerina because she hadn't trained as a child, she decided to stop dancing. But she misunderstood him; he wanted to share his art with her. Although he said nothing, he was disappointed. 'I asked her to learn dancing because for me dancing was the highest thing in the world after her. I wanted to teach her ... I wept bitterly.'

Romola 'began to rave about all the Callot dresses, Reboux hats and Cartier jewels, and all of the *mondaine* life I was going to lead'. This was what she had been brought up to believe marriage meant, especially marriage to a great and successful artist. All her life, as her daughter would confirm, she thirsted 'for material things that were the most luxurious, the most exquisite': some kind of physical validation of her worth. Vaslav smiled and said that of course he would try and give her those things but, 'I am only an artist, not a prince'. Later, he would write that it was then that he knew he had made a mistake: 'she loved me for my success and the beauty of my body'; she wanted 'a young, good-looking and rich husband'. The side of her he distrusted – what he called 'the intelligent Romola' – was this aspect of her character. Her concern with the material world, with practicalities like social success and smart hotels, would, he feared, 'prevent her from understanding me'.

In Rio, Romola learned that she was pregnant and she spent the entire voyage back to Europe in her cabin, morning sickness compounded by the movement of the sea. Jealous of her happiness with Vaslav, eager to enjoy to the full her glamorous new life, she did not want the baby. They landed in Cadiz in late November and took the train to Paris where Vaslav hoped to meet Diaghilev, who was not there. From Paris they travelled to Budapest so Vaslav could pay his respects to Emilia Márkus. In both places they were greeted by banks of reporters and cameramen waiting to capture for the papers the *dieu de la danse* and his pretty bride. Pleading delicate health, Romola had planned to have an abortion in Budapest. On the night she was due to enter the sanatorium, to Vaslav's delight and relief, she changed her mind.

Two days before they were due to leave Budapest for St Petersburg, Grigoriev's telegram arrived, informing Nijinsky that his services were no longer required by the Ballets Russes. 'I was petrified ... This was Diaghilev's revenge,' wrote Romola. 'Now, for the first time, it dawned on me that perhaps I had made a mistake; I had destroyed, where I wanted to be helpful.' With a wife to provide for and a baby on the way, and nowhere to work or even live, Nijinsky's 'whole world had collapsed around him'.

I keep thinking of what Nijinsky would have owned, what the few trunks and suitcases he had taken to South America (and which followed him back to Paris and thence to Budapest) might have contained as he embarked on his new life: practice clothes and shoes; suits for day and evening, but not many – Romola said he only had two when they met and he had travelled to Europe with two in 1909, one brown and one blue; shirts, underwear – though probably not the new underwear Bakst had speculated about; and his new gold watch. Even in the Lvov days he had had well-made shoes; after all, his feet were essential to his work. He kept everything immaculately clean and perfectly in order.

Reynaldo Hahn had given him a letter signed by the great eighteenth-century dancer Auguste Vestris. Several times Diaghilev had given him sapphire rings and Cocteau had presented him with a gold pencil studded with a sapphire. The emerald girdle Ottoline Morrell had heard about must have been an exaggeration, but anyway it would soon have been pawned. Perhaps there was the camera Cocteau remembered them bickering about, if it had been saved from the hockshop this long. As a perpetual traveller – he often referred to himself as a gypsy or a wanderer – he might have had things he used to make his hotel rooms feel like home: books, a photograph or two. He liked reading (Tolstoy and Dostoyevsky were favourites) and when he was creating *Sacre* he showed Bronia books containing Gauguin reproductions. But his possessions were few, especially compared to the weight of belongings we consider normal today.

One thing he did not possess was a passport. After three years' absence, Russia – war-torn and on the edge of revolution – was closed to him. The only thing he could be was an exile. The dancer Li Cunxin has written about the heartbreaking homesickness he suffered after his defection from China to the United States in 1981, the grief he stored inside himself while he concentrated on ballet to fill the hole being away from his home and family left in him; and the way the wealth and luxury with which he was surrounded in his new life never compensated for his feelings of loss, isolation and guilt.

Despite having no papers, immediately – predictably – the offers began flooding in. The incredible success of the Ballets Russes had made all dancers, let alone one of Nijinsky's status, into hot commodities.

For the past few years, according to one Parisian theatrical agent, dancers had been offered 'engagements on golden trays'. Nijinsky had been rejecting lucrative offers for years. Now Jacques Rouché, newly appointed director of the Paris Opéra, wanted him for a four-month season of thirty performances from May 1914, for 90,000 francs. A rich German was offering him 'something like a million francs' to set up a new company to rival the Ballets Russes.

But Vaslav still hoped he could repair things with Diaghilev, writing affectionately to Stravinsky within days of receiving Grigoriev's telegram to try and find out what had gone so wrong. Naively he asked Stravinsky to tell him if it was true that Diaghilev really meant to dismiss him. 'I can't believe that Seryozha would behave so badly to me. Seryozha owes me a lot of money. For two years I wasn't paid anything at all for my dancing or for the new productions of *Faune* and *Jeux* and *Sacre*. I was working without a contract. If it's true that Seryozha doesn't want to work with me any more, I have lost everything … I can't understand why Seryozha's behaved like this. Ask him what the matter is, and write to me.' As Stravinsky would later comment, the letter was so unworldly that if Vaslav hadn't written it, only a character from Dostoyevsky could have: 'It seems incredible to me … that he was so unaware of the politics and sexual jealousies and motives within the Ballet.' But Diaghilev was unmoved and Vaslav's initial disbelief crystallised into resentment.

Both Bronia and her husband had already signed contracts with Diaghilev for the 1914 season. Understanding her position, Diaghilev invited her and Kochetovsky to dinner in St Petersburg in December to persuade them to stay with the Ballets Russes. Never, before or afterwards, did she see him display 'his legendary irresistible charm' as on that snowy night. They ate lobster and strawberries and drank champagne while Diaghilev told Bronia that he loved her as a daughter and respected her as an artist. He told her how hurt he had been, how insulted he had felt by the break with Vaslav; and together they discussed Günzburg's role in Vaslav's marriage with bitterness. She saw something new in his attitude to her, as if losing her brother had made her dearer to him.

Then Diaghilev turned to business, promising Bronia that all her earlier roles would still be hers if she stayed. Bronia knew that Fokine had tried to demand her dismissal as well as Vaslav's as a condition of his return (as well as being an unwelcome reminder of her brother, Vera Fokina liked dancing Bronia's parts), but Diaghilev had refused. Again and again he asked her to promise she would join the company in Prague for the start of the season, but he never reminded her that she had signed a contract to be there.

'When we parted he embraced me several times, and as he helped me on with my fur coat he looked deep in my eyes. Suddenly he took my *valenki* [felt overboots] from the hall porter, and as gallantly as a youth he bent on one knee to help me put them on. That was too much for me. I took my *valenki* from him and gave them to Sasha. I hugged Sergey Pavlovich and said, "All right, I shall come to Prague!" And so we parted that evening, but were not to meet again for many years.'

When Bronia and Kochetovsky got to Prague, Diaghilev was in Paris, having left Günzburg behind as acting director. The other dancers were unfriendly to them and Grigoriev informed Bronia that Fokina would be dancing her roles. Then a telegram from Vaslav arrived saying that he had agreed to put on a season in London: would Bronia and Sasha come and dance for him? Günzburg asked them to speak to Diaghilev, who would be returning later that day, before deciding, but their minds were made up. As their train waited on the platform in Berlin, Bronia caught sight of Diaghilev staring at her out of his window on another train heading east as their carriages pulled away in opposite directions.

Vaslav had turned down Jacques Rouché's offer because it did not offer him creative control. Instead he signed a contract with Alfred Butt, a successful vaudeville impresario and director of the Palace Theatre, a music hall on Cambridge Circus in London, for an eight-week season for which he would receive a thousand pounds a week.

Bronia was astonished to discover that Vaslav had agreed to dance at the Palace. For several years Pavlova had performed there, preferring her own name in lights than Diaghilev's (and the money that went with it), and she and Vaslav had argued passionately about it. At dinner at the Savoy in 1911, while Diaghilev tried to persuade Pavlova to come back to the Ballets Russes, Vaslav insisted that it was beneath her dignity as an artist to perform 'sandwiched between performing dogs and acrobats'. An artist's one goal was 'to perfect himself', he said and at the Palace Theatre Pavlova's art would be destroyed. Pavlova had not spoken to him since.

Bronia was also surprised to find that Vaslav would be dancing some roles choreographed by Fokine, most of which were still in the Ballets Russes repertoire; but Butt had specified that he had to dance at least some of the roles which had made him famous. Vaslav insisted they would be his own versions of *Le Spectre de la Rose*, of Harlequin in *Carnaval*, of the poet in *Les Sylphides*, which, as he said to Bronia, were his creations, and the creations of Bakst or Benois, as much as Fokine's. They would re-orchestrate them and create new scenery and costumes and *Faune* and *Jeux* would also be performed.

The season was to begin on 2 March 1914 after only a month of preparation. Bronia and Sasha went to Russia to recruit dancers while Vaslav went to Paris to ask Bakst, whom he still believed to be his friend, to design the new scenery. Romola waited in the carriage when Vaslav went into his studio. He came down some time later with tears in his eyes. Bakst had told him that Diaghilev had made him promise that he would not work for Nijinsky. 'He also felt it was his duty to tell Vaslav the truth, that his dismissal from the ballet was not the end, it was the beginning, of a state of war which Diaghilev had declared against Nijinsky.'

Rehearsals began in Paris, with both Vaslav and Bronia working so hard they barely slept or ate. Under these strains there was no time for pleasantries. Bronia did not bother to hide her dislike of Romola, blaming her for what had befallen her brother. 'I was the intruder in the Russian ballet, in the family. She isolated herself behind a screen of ice which I could never penetrate. At Laroux's [sic], or at Viel's, I used to await them for lunch sometimes until four or five o'clock in the afternoon. But they worked and danced all the time.' Despite following the ballet for all those months, Romola had not grasped the fact that this was what they had always done. The work of art came first: lunch, even with her, was just a distraction. Now, with a wife and expecting a baby, there was more pressure than ever on Vaslav; and no Diaghilev to wave his magic wand and make sure that the show would go on in the end.

As the opening night approached, it was evident that Vaslav had taken on too much. The administrative demands of running a company and managing the dancers were overwhelming, despite all the help Bronia could give him. On the day of the dress rehearsal, probably not coincidentally, Bronia received a summons to appear in court to answer charges of breaking her contract with Diaghilev. She missed the rehearsal, but the next day, by explaining that by allowing Fokina to dance her roles Diaghilev in fact had broken his contract with her, she won her case and was released. When she got to the theatre to dress for their first performance, Bronia found Vaslav dreadfully upset, having received an unexpected telegram: 'CONGRATULATIONS BEST WISHES TO MUSIC HALL ARTIST. ANNA PAVLOVA.'

Their programme began after the comic singer, Wilkie Bard, whose most popular piece was performed in drag. Bronia and Vaslav stood on the darkened stage waiting for the music to begin; Maurice Ravel had reorchestrated Chopin's music for Vaslav's version of *Les Sylphides*. Bronia looked out over the audience and saw Diaghilev sprawled nonchalantly immediately to the left of the conductor. It was a deliberately conspicuous seat, intended to be noticed from stage. While they were dancing, Bronia's eyes kept flickering back to Diaghilev, whose gaze never left Vaslav. *Les Sylphides* had always been his favourite ballet. The sardonic smile he had been wearing before they started had disappeared and he seemed 'to shrink in his seat and his arms were tightly crossed' over his body, pudgy fingers tucked into his fists. 'I do not believe that he applauded once, not during *Les Sylphides* and not at the end.' Their act was followed by the Bioscope, an early cinema.

Cyril Beaumont was in the audience as well, watching 'with a pang of disappointment'. Although Nijinsky danced with the same style and elevation, 'he no longer danced like a god. Something of that mystic fragrance which previously surrounded his dancing in *Les Sylphides* had vanished.' Beaumont knew Diaghilev, but he did not notice him at the Palace Theatre that night and nor did Romola; Bronia's is the only account that puts him there.

Alfred Butt was pleased with the nine encores Nijinsky received on the first night, the huge audiences he initially drew and the positive critical reception, which he reprinted in the Palace's advertisements, but Nijinsky was oppressed by having to shoehorn his soul into a vaudeville show. Almost worse was 'the responsibility and the necessity for constant supervision of details … He became subject to moods of intense irritability and depression, and he flew into a rage over the most trivial incident.' On one night it was the house lights being turned on while the sets were changed; on another it was a stagehand trying to flirt with Romola.

One afternoon Bronia and Vaslav walked out of the Savoy together, following a business meeting with Romola's mother and stepfather, Oskar Padany, who were trying to help plan the future of their son-in-law's small company. They almost collided with Bakst, who simply looked at them and walked quickly away. Both Bronia and Vaslav were devastated by his behaviour. 'It was as if our friend had lashed us with a whip.'

By the start of the second week disaster loomed. Vaslav's relations with Butt had already been soured by Butt's businesslike approach to his art, which he considered disrespectful – in Russia, tsars bowed to artists – and when Butt suggested that slowing ticket sales might be improved by adding a Russian number to his programme of Russian ballet he was irrationally furious, squatting down in Butt's office and angrily lashing out his legs in a few steps of the *prisyadka*, shouting, 'Is this what you want to see from Nijinsky?'

On Saturday, 14 March, Vaslav and his company danced matinee and evening performances, although Bronia had to persuade an enraged Vaslav to go on stage as the Rose because the orchestra had played Tchaikovsky – 'a wretched choice of music' – during the pause before *Spectre* began. This may have been the incident Cyril Beaumont heard about, in which Vaslav became uncontrollably angry, rolling on the floor of his dressing room, refusing to get into his costume, with his dresser and some others wringing their hands and weeping. The theatre's manager Maurice Volny thought he was about to have a fit. He threw a jug of water over him and shouted at him to get up and get dressed, which Vaslav did. This was by no means Nijinsky's first backstage tantrum but it was the first without Zuikov to guard him inside his dressing room and Diaghilev to defend him outside it. It did not augur well.

She could not know it then, but that was the last time Bronia would ever dance with her brother or see him perform onstage. The next morning Romola telephoned Bronia to say that Vaslav was running a high fever. He was unable to dance for three consecutive performances – a breach of contract – and the season was cancelled. The Saison Nijinsky was replaced by (among others) the ballad singer and actress Evie Greene and Hetty King, a comic singer who performed dressed as a man.

Although she thought it was probably a relief for Vaslav – an end to the practical worries of trying to organise a company and, more importantly, an end to the effort of putting commerce before art – Bronia blamed Romola for not protecting Vaslav better in this, his first formally negotiated engagement. Since she knew so much about money and business, Bronia observed tartly, and spoke perfect English, she might have read the complicated document her inexperienced husband had signed.

While Vaslav recuperated from flu and what was perhaps his first nervous breakdown, preparations were in course for the first concert performance of *Le Sacre du printemps* in Paris. It had already been played once in St Petersburg, in February, and on 14 April at the Casino de Paris Pierre Monteux conducted it before an audience for the second time. Camille Saint-Saëns, who sat with Monteux's mother, was no more convinced by a second hearing – he kept repeating, '*Mais, il est fou, il est fou!*' – but others were. Stravinsky was carried out of the theatre on the shoulders of cheering fans. He never looked back.

It was after this triumph that Stravinsky began, as one historian has phrased it, 'busily revising his past'. His autobiography, ghost-written in the 1930s by Walter Nouvel, describes *Sacre* as having been a task too great for Nijinsky's capabilities. He had apparently had misgivings about working with Nijinsky from the start, Stravinsky wrote, because 'his ignorance of the most elementary notions of music was flagrant. The poor boy knew nothing of music'.

Perhaps he hoped that belittling his collaborator would mean he could take all the credit for *Sacre*'s revolutionary impact: though Nijinsky's *Sacre* was not danced again after its nine performances in 1913 until revivals in the 1980s, at the time many believed his work was more radical than Stravinsky's. Perhaps Diaghilev exerted pressure on him to cut ties with Nijinsky as he had done with Bakst, or persuaded him that the radical choreography had made *Sacre* unpopular (he told Massine it had failed as a ballet because Nijinsky 'had attempted to do too much ... He had not realised that the eye and the ear cannot absorb simultaneously as much as the ear alone'). Almost certainly Stravinsky hoped that if he could persuade people to think of *Sacre* as concert music rather than a ballet it would be accepted as great more quickly. He was always, as Bronia put it, 'very sensitive to applause'. Only many years later, long after Nijinsky's death, did Stravinsky admit that he had been 'unjust' to Nijinsky and that his was 'by far the best' version of *Sacre*.

In May 1914 Nijinsky went to Spain to perform for King Alfonso at the wedding of Belle, the daughter of the American Ambassador to Spain, to Kermit Roosevelt, son of the former President. On his way back to a heavily pregnant Romola in London, he stopped in Paris to see the premiere of *Le Legende de Joseph* – the Strauss ballet that was to have been his. He took an unobtrusive seat in the stalls, but during the interval went up to Misia Sert's usual box. A frozen silence greeted him, and then Cocteau said, 'This year, your creation is a child. The Spectre de la Rose chooses the part of a father. How utterly disgusting is birth.' Vaslav replied, 'The entrance of the Spectre de la Rose's child will be quite as beautiful as his own, which you always admired'. He bowed and left.

Following several months' intensive tuition with Cecchetti, Léonide Massine was dancing the part of Joseph. He was so gorgeous, and he wore such a skimpy sheepskin tunic (designed in part by Diaghilev), that wits called the ballet *Les Jambes de Joseph*. Vaslav saw straight through him: 'Massine's aim is simple. He wants to become rich and learn everything that Diaghilev knows.' Elsewhere he would write that Diaghilev had given Aleksey Mavrin 'a taste for *objets d'art*' to make him love him, and 'Massine a taste for fame. I did not take to objects and fame'.

Harry Kessler had tried and failed to persuade Diaghilev to retain Nijinsky as choreographer for *Joseph*. He and Strauss thought Nijinsky the only person capable of communicating Joseph's 'terrible beauty', which contained within its perfection a destructive element – Mephisto and God in one; but Diaghilev, still smarting, could not be convinced and had used Fokine. *Joseph* was one of the least successful of his ballets and would not be performed again after the 1914 season. 'Everything goes much *deeper* than I thought,' Kessler wrote. 'Diaghilev is mortified in his vanity, in his *sentiment*, in his pocket, in *everything*.'

The critics were divided about *Joseph*. One congratulated Fokine for bringing back to the Ballets Russes 'all the graceful attitudes and harmonious gestures which M. Nijinsky, with his grotesque ideas, sought to abolish'. Jacques Rivière remained loyal: without Nijinsky the Ballets Russes were nothing. 'He alone gave life to the whole company.'

Lady Ripon also made several unsuccessful attempts to bring Nijinsky and Diaghilev back together. But although she persuaded the Drury Lane Theatre (today the Theatre Royal) to make Nijinsky's dancing with the Ballets Russes for three nights a condition of their appearance there that summer, she could not make the dancers welcome him back. The reception he received was glacial – they simply turned their backs on him when he arrived – and Diaghilev refused to see him at all. He lasted 'one single excruciating and humiliating rehearsal' before leaving London and returning to Vienna where Romola and their newborn baby were waiting for him.* 'Now I am beginning to think that it was Diag. [sic] who suggested to Fokine that he should refuse to return to the Ballet if Nijinsky was there,' a disappointed Lady Ripon wrote

---

* Grigoriev told Walter Nouvel that Romola had entirely made up the rehearsal; Nijinsky had gone to London on the hope, rather than a promise, of reconciliation. (A. L. D. Haskell, *Ballet Russes: The Age of Diaghilev*, 1968, p. 259.)

to Misia Sert, 'or that anyway he has done nothing to make the thing possible.'

While Lady Ripon continued to consider Nijinsky her friend and had sympathised with his desire to marry, she found Romola 'avaricious [and] anaemic'. Ottoline Morrell, on the other hand, thought Romola delightful and pitied 'the little dancer and his pregnant wife. In 1913, everybody had wanted to know him, now nobody did.' To Lytton Strachey in the summer of 1914 Vaslav was no longer an idol but – perhaps partly because of his marriage, a betrayal of Strachey's homosexual creed – 'that cretinous lackey'.

Vaslav returned to Vienna where Romola and their newborn daughter were waiting for him. When the baby was overdue and Romola and Vaslav were anxious for her arrival, a friend suggested they attend a performance of Richard Strauss's complex opera, *Elektra*: Kyra was born later that night. Despite having longed for a boy during Romola's pregnancy, Vaslav was so happy to be with his wife and baby that all their recent difficulties were forgotten; and when news came of the assassination of an archduke and his wife in far-off Sarajevo it seemed at first a distant and irrelevant tragedy.

CHAPTER 8

Mephisto Valse
1914–1918

IN LATE JULY 1914 they went to Budapest to introduce Kyra to her grandmother. From there they planned to travel to St Petersburg to see Eleonora and meet Bronia's little girl, Irina, but Russia declared war on Austria-Hungary on 29 July in response to the Empire's invasion of Serbia. All trains going east were suspended and it was impossible to find another way out of the city. There was nothing the Russian consul could do to help; he was trying to flee too. After a few days, a shy police officer, dressed in civilian clothes, came to Emilia's house and told Vaslav and Romola that as enemy subjects they were prisoners of war and would have to remain for the foreseeable future in Budapest under house arrest.

No one was happy about this turn of events. Emilia Márkus did not want a Russian living in her house and urged her daughter to divorce Vaslav so that she could be Hungarian again. Romola, however, did not want to live with her mother. Nijinsky was miserable because there was nowhere for him to practise; and the war troubled him deeply, as all around them euphoric soldiers with soft cheeks went off singing to the front. 'All these young men marching off to their death,' he said, 'and for what?'

The servants distrusted their Russian house-guest and Vaslav did not endear himself to anyone by refusing to dance a benefit for the Hungarian soldiers who were going off to kill his countrymen. His consolation for being in Budapest – hot chocolate layered with cream and Dobos torta at the old-fashioned Ruszwurm Patisserie near the Coronation Church – was soon curtailed by wartime rationing. Everything that went wrong was blamed on him: when the boiler broke down or when the unused parts of the house became damp. When Emilia's cat – a very ordinary sort of cat, Romola commented crossly – went missing, she accused Vaslav of killing it. What Vaslav later remembered of this period was being depressed; he and Emilia 'quarrelled for eighteen months on end'.

Thrown together in a hostile atmosphere, Vaslav and Romola learned to lean on one another: their relationship, their young family, was all they had. Though in some places in his diary he wrote of hating Romola, particularly her obsession with money, other memories make clear that they did love each other. 'I loved her terribly. I gave her everything I could. She loved me.' Living with the Márkus family (it has to be said, including Romola) was like inhabiting a den of snakes; Sigmund Freud, who published *On Narcissism* the year war broke out, would have had a field day with them. Romola believed her mother and stepfather were informing on Vaslav to the authorities; her sister, Tessa, charming but too heavy a drinker, tried to seduce Vaslav, inviting him into her room while she was undressed, deliberately lying on the bed in front of him, wearing 'small silk panties and thin camisoles'; if Emilia thought Oskar was looking at the servants, she would slap their faces.

When the wet nurse refused to feed Kyra any more because she was Russian, Vaslav took over her care, learning how to sterilise and prepare the bottles, and fed her himself. He painted her little nursery and its furniture in bright colours so that it looked like 'an enchanted habitation of a Russian fairy-tale'. Unlike his own father, Vaslav was tenderly devoted to Kyra, determined she would love him as he had not loved Foma. He spent hours with her, playfully childlike once again; she called him Tataka and no one else interested her.

Vaslav spent much of his time working on a system of dance notation, a concept to which he had been devoted since his time at the

Imperial Theatre School; he hoped to 'invent signs which will enable the gestures [of dance] to be fixed for all time' – and he was also thinking about future ballets. One was set to Richard Strauss's tone-poem, *Till Eulenspiegel*, about a Puck or Robin Hood figure, the irrepressible 'merry prankster' of German folklore; another was set to Franz Liszt's *Mephisto Valse*. Sometimes for fun he would dance for Romola and her cousin Lily or her sister – wild gypsy dances he remembered from his youth, or imitations of the great ballerinas with whom he had danced (his parody of Kshesinskaya was their favourite). 'But we loved it most when he showed us how the peasant women flirt whilst dancing. He had an inimitable way of throwing inviting glances, and undulating in such a lascivious manner as to stir up the senses of the spectator almost to frenzy.'

In 1915 Lady Ripon managed to get word to them that she was trying to obtain their release and then, after a year, help came from an unexpected source. Diaghilev, who needed Nijinsky to star in a Ballets Russes tour of the United States that he hoped would pay off all his debts, had begun to agitate on their behalf.

As early as the summer of 1914 he had been making noises about one day working with Nijinsky again, whether to pacify Stravinsky and Harry Kessler, who still valued him, or because it was simply his pattern to fall out spectacularly with collaborators who questioned his authority and then readmit them, chastened, to the fold, is not clear. In June 1914 Diaghilev had suggested Kessler write a libretto for a ballet Nijinsky would dance with Karsavina and Massine; that November he had told Stravinsky that despite how stupidly he was behaving, Nijinsky should choreograph *Les Noces* – though he was not prepared to discuss it with him yet. At this stage, the gravity of Nijinsky's position in Budapest had not sunk in.

Throughout 1915 Vaslav's friends – including Diaghilev, Lady Ripon, the duke of Alba, the king of Spain, Otto Kahn of the Metropolitan Opera House in New York and the Comtesse Greffulhe – lobbied the American ambassador in Vienna and the US Secretary of State on his and Romola's behalf, and by early 1916 the pressure they had exerted on the Hungarian government had secured their release. With Kyra, a nanny, a maid and sixteen trunks that Romola (with the help of Madame Greffulhe) had managed to fill on their twenty-four-hour stop in Paris, they arrived in New York in April. Diaghilev, who had travelled out to New York in January with the rest of the company for a preliminary tour, was waiting for them on the dock with Massine, holding a large bunch of 'American Beauty' roses for Romola. But there would be no real reconciliation.

The deal was that Nijinsky would be the star of the Ballets Russes's autumn season at the Metropolitan Opera House in New York and then their extended tour around the United States in the winter. When they met Otto Kahn a few days after their arrival, Romola told him that Vaslav was only willing to dance if Diaghilev paid him the money he owed him from past seasons. After intense negotiations, it was agreed that Diaghilev would repay Nijinsky part of a total of $24,000 each week along with his salary – dashing Diaghilev's hopes that the American tour would make him financially independent.

A few days later, Diaghilev invited them to lunch. He was alone when they arrived at Sherry's, Massine having remained behind at the Ritz. At first he tried to speak to Vaslav in Russian, reproaching him for his demands for money; Vaslav spoke in French and insisted that Romola should be party to any business discussion they had. Romola recounted the conversation:

'I now have a family to support, but I am willing to do now, as in the past, my utmost for the Russian Ballet. I am the same; I have not changed towards you. I am grateful for your past friendship, and it only depends upon you for us to be united again in our common aim. My wife is part of me, and she understands this, and wants, as much as I do, to further the cause of the Russian Ballet. Please, please understand me.'

'We never had any contract; there was never any question of money between us. What has happened to you, Vaslav?'

'But, Sergey Pavlovich, you take money from the theatres, and you make them pay it in advance, too. Be just,' interrupted Romola.

'No, it will become impossible for me to run the Russian Ballet. Fokina wants to manage Fokine and dance all the leading roles. You, Madame, are mercenary. How do you expect the Russian Ballet to exist under such conditions?'

By this time, Diaghilev had been in the US four months, and he was persuaded by Kahn to return to Europe leaving Nijinsky in charge of the company as artistic director. Kahn hoped that Diaghilev's absence would ease the pressure on Nijinsky; he was prepared for a small loss in return for the glory of having brought the Ballets Russes to the United States. 'Everyone but Kahn, Nijinsky and Romola realised this was madness,' wrote Sokolova.

Diaghilev left in early May with Massine and Grigoriev. Vaslav would spend the summer in the US and most of the rest of the company – minus Diaghilev, Massine, Grigoriev and the dancers trapped in war-torn Russia, including Bronia, Karsavina and Fokine – would regroup to begin their New York season and fifty-two-city tour of the United States in September, while Diaghilev would maintain a small experimental troupe in Europe.

At first New York was as exciting and new as Paris had been in 1909. Late at night Vaslav and Romola would sneak out to soda fountains for ice-creams, sitting on high stools at the counter, and he loved jazz, tapping out what he had heard with his hands and feet. Romola blossomed: living in New York as the wife of a feted artist was just what she had always believed life should be. But her desire for money, luxury and social success blinded her to the fact that her worldly goals 'harmed rather than abetted her husband'. Little by little the intimacy they had created and relied upon in Budapest began to wear away.

As soon as they were settled, Vaslav began working on *Till Eulenspiegel* and *Mephisto Valse*, which he planned to premiere that autumn. The young artist he chose to create *Till*'s sets and costumes, Robert Edmond Jones, left an evocative account of working with Nijinsky over the summer of 1916. They met for the first time in a darkened New York drawing room on a stifling afternoon. Romola entered first, 'extremely pretty' and stylishly dressed in black. Vaslav followed, small and stocky, with a delicate, precise dancer's walk. 'He is very nervous. His eyes are troubled. He looks eager, anxious, excessively intelligent. He seems tired, bored, excited, all at once.' His manner was direct and simple, but when he smiled – which was not often, and never for long – his smile was dazzling.

'I like him at once ... I realise at once that I am in the presence of a genius.' What Jones meant by this was, he said, 'a continual preoccupation with standards of excellence so high that they are really not of this world ... incredible perfections'. He was struck, too, by Vaslav's 'extraordinary nervous energy ... an impression of something too eager, too brilliant, a quickening of the nerves, a nature wracked to dislocation by a merciless creative urge'. It may have been hindsight but he also noticed an atmosphere of something like oppression that Vaslav carried with him.

Nijinsky, Romola and Kyra decamped to Bar Harbor, Maine, with Jones in their wake. 'I am quartered in a huge old-fashioned summer hotel, all piazzas and towers, with curving driveways and mammoth beds of angry red cannas on the lawns. Nijinsky lives there, too, with his pretty wife – always a little *souffrante* from the heat – and an enchanting baby girl with oblique Mongolian eyes like her father's. He practises long and hard during the day with his accompanist in the lovely little Greek temple set among the pines by the shore of the bay. In the evenings we work together until far into the night.' As they created *Till*, Jones was astonished and delighted by Vaslav's 'energy, his ardour, his daring, his blazing imagination, by turns fantastic, gorgeous, grotesque' and by his ability to change in an instant from a wide-eyed, mischievous child to a demonic figure to a jeering clown to a tender, imploring lover.

He was constantly reminded what a surreal world Nijinsky inhabited. One afternoon they were invited to a club for a swim. Vaslav and Jones were dressing in adjacent cabanas after swimming when Jones answered a tap at his door. A tall man, exquisitely dressed in pearl-grey, with a silvery, scented moustache, was standing there. Without saying anything, he took a pearl-grey leather case from his pocket and opened it, holding it out to Jones. A tangle of cabochon rubies, emeralds, black pearls and diamonds lay glittering in the sunlight on a bed of pearl-grey velvet. Jones heard Nijinsky putting on his shoes next door and burst out laughing at the situation in which he found himself. The pearl-grey stranger closed his case and silently walked away.

This strange idyll came to an end when they returned to New York at the beginning of September. The conductor Pierre Monteux met them there and found everyone in the company on edge. Vaslav, in particular, was 'suspicious of everyone and hostile'. Anatole Bourman, who had called Nijinsky 'universally loved despite the occasional fits of temperament which marked his genius' when he left the Ballet in 1913, said that in New York three years later he was conceited, 'pompous [and] ... totally devoid of sincerity or naturalness'. Diaghilev had known how to manage Nijinsky, commented Lydia Lopokova, who danced opposite him during this period, and 'when he came on stage he was a god to all of us, but on tour he was rather tiresome'. She and Vaslav never gelled as a partnership and their offstage relationship remained uneasy.

The Met's young press agent, Edward Bernays (Sigmund Freud's nephew, who would go on to become a public relations legend), marvelled at the way the company lived and worked: 'I had never imagined that the interpersonal relations of the members of a group could be so involved and complex, full of medieval intrigue, illicit love, misdirected passion and aggression.'

Lydia Lopokova was just one of the dancers who had joined the Ballet Russes for this tour. Dmitry Kostrovsky had been in the Bolshoy's *corps de ballet* in Moscow with Massine. Kostrovsky was an ardent disciple of Tolstoy; Romola often noticed him preaching to the other dancers Tolstoy's rational gospel of vegetarianism and pacifism. Along with his friend from the Bolshoy, Nicholas Zverev,* who had been a member of the company since 1913, he focused on Vaslav at once. Vaslav, whose

---

* Zverev was known to his fellow dancers as Percy Greensocks because he always wore green practice clothes, and he was painted several times by Picasso in late 1922.

hunger for a spiritual life was not answered by the mundanity of his work – all the art having been removed by the need to administrate – nor by his sophisticated, selfish wife, responded eagerly.

Lydia Sokolova said Vaslav made no effort to run the company at all: he didn't organise the rehearsals properly, so no one knew what was going on from day to day, and he wouldn't turn up for anything unless he was fetched. Romola's account of the period in her 1932 biography of her husband, in which she describes him as the innocent victim of malign circumstance, was, according to Sokolova, pure fiction. 'She puts into his mouth long speeches which would have taken him a whole week to say, as he always spoke in monosyllables. Reading her descriptions, one would think that poor Nijinsky conversed and behaved as a normal person, which was quite untrue.' The only time Vaslav was not lost for words, apparently, was when he was angry.

Till Eulenspeigel was proving a challenge. Monteux, who had fought in the trenches, refused to conduct music by a living German, so another conductor had to be found. When Vaslav first saw Jones's finished sets, he was furious. They were not as he had imagined them – 'not high enough to give the effect of crazy exaggeration the maestro had visualised'. He summoned Jones to the theatre in a fury and screamed at him in Russian and broken French, before beginning a rehearsal in which he fell and sprained an ankle with a week to go before opening. 'Your scenery is so bad that when our maestro saw it he fell down,' the dancers chorused bleakly to Jones. When Jones visited Nijinsky at the Biltmore Hotel, he found him in bed, 'drenched in pathos, sad as a dying prince out of a drama by Maeterlinck', but still quite capable of haranguing and insulting him.

Mephisto Valse had to be abandoned, there wasn't enough time to finish *Till* even though its premiere was postponed for a week, and the season had to open without Nijinsky dancing. After the abuse Nijinsky had hurled his way, Jones remembered standing with him hand in hand for curtain call after curtain call on *Till*'s triumphant first night, with Nijinsky smiling and saying how happy he was, but privately Nijinsky was dissatisfied with the ballet. Despite working so hard, needing the money for his new life, *Till* ended up 'taken out of the oven too soon'. All the same, the American critics acclaimed it a masterpiece.

What we know of *Till* and *Mephisto Valse* suggests that Vaslav was retreating 'from the front lines of experiment represented by *Sacre*'. His return to a style of ballet that in theme and setting was more like *Petrushka* than any of his own ballets, and to which dancing as audiences would recognise it was central once again, implies that he may have come to agree with Osbert Sitwell that *Sacre* was 'the most magnificent and living of dead ends'.

By late December, halfway through their four-month tour, they had reached the West Coast, playing to half-empty theatres, and Vaslav was desperate, unable to pay the dancers and musicians and begging Diaghilev by telegram to come to America or send him Grigoriev. The Met, sponsoring the tour, would eventually lose $250,000 and Diaghilev was paid $75,000 less than he had been anticipating. The audiences of Wichita, Spokane and Tallahassee were not ready for the Ballets Russes; one critic wrote of having to suppress his urge to leap on stage and thrash the repulsive 'negro who makes love to the princess' in *Schéhérazade*.

In Los Angeles, though, Vaslav found an admirer: Charlie Chaplin. He described Nijinsky as 'a serious man, beautiful looking, with high cheekbones and sad eyes, who gave the impression of a monk in civilian clothes … The moment he appeared [on stage] I was electrified,' wrote Chaplin. 'I have seen few geniuses in this world, and Nijinsky was one of them. He was hypnotic, god-like, his sombreness suggesting moods of other worlds; every movement was poetry, every leap was a flight into strange fancy.' He was most impressed by *Faune* (in fact, three years later it would inspire a scene in *Sunnyside*): 'The mystic world he created, the tragic unseen lurking in the shadows of pastoral loveliness as he moved through its mystery, a god of passionate sadness – all this he conveyed in a few simple gestures without apparent effort.'

Vaslav took to Chaplin, inviting him into his dressing room to watch him make up – a privilege he never accorded his wife – and making gauche attempts at conversation. Chaplin invited him to come and watch him filming *The Cure* in a Hollywood that was still little more than a desert dotted with pepper trees and wooden shacks. For three days Vaslav sat on set, never smiling, looking sadder and sadder, as Chaplin created sequence after sequence of marvellously funny slapstick comedy. At the end of each day he would compliment Chaplin warmly on his 'balletique' comedy.

Despite his unwillingness to perform in music halls, Nijinsky had never looked down on popular entertainers. When asked in 1911 what was his favourite thing in London, he had unhesitatingly replied 'Little Tich' (Harry Relph), the music-hall comic whose most celebrated piece was a dance in which he wore twenty-eight-inch-long boots. Whenever he performed, Vaslav and Diaghilev watched utterly spellbound: Littler, as Vaslav called him, was, '*un très grand artiste*'.

Chaplin and Nijinsky seem to have responded to something similar in one another – it is not hard to imagine the critics Gilbert Seldes or Edmund Wilson describing Chaplin as 'a god of passionate sadness' and Ottoline Morrell thought the two men shared a quality of 'intense poignancy'. Both had grown up in the circus; both could look anonymous in person, but had a highly recognisable stage or screen persona by which their audiences became obsessed; both used their bodies as their primary vehicle for communication, expressing complex emotions and vulnerability with an extraordinary economy of gesture. For Morrell, although Nijinsky was 'far more impersonal than Chaplin, freer from temperament and freer from himself', what they shared was an 'intensity of passion and absorption in the ideas they express'.

In some ways Nijinsky had as much in common with the movie stars of 1910s and 1920s Hollywood as with the modernist artists by whom he was surrounded in Europe. The icons of the era – Chaplin, Mary Pickford, Valentino, Jack Dempsey and many others – tended to come from impoverished backgrounds and were often immigrants, with a position in American society not unlike that of Poles in Russia. They were possessed of driving ambition, but many found it hard to learn to live with their fame, adulation and newfound riches – drugs and insanity claimed more than their fair share. Nijinsky's story, like so many of these lives, was helping to create the narrative for what would become an established trajectory of twentieth-century celebrity.

They saw in the New Year for 1917 in San Francisco. Lydia Lopokova's first husband, who claimed to be clairvoyant, told everyone's fortune. For Romola he predicted health and a long life, but in five years' time a separation from Vaslav: 'I see a divorce, but not exactly.' Romola was shaken, but laughed it off.

Then he looked at Vaslav's palm and, as if he had been hit, staggered back, covering his hands with his own. 'I don't know, I can't say ... sorry, it is strange ...'

'Am I going to die? Come on, say it.'

'No, no, certainly not, but ... but this is worse ... worse.'

As the tour went on, Kostrovsky and Zverev's hold over Nijinsky grew stronger. Romola regularly came upon the leeches, as she called them, in her and Vaslav's train compartment, reading and talking in Russian (which she could not understand) for hours. Vaslav was becoming ever more silent and morose, contemplating giving up dancing altogether and living on the land in Russia as a kind of Tolstoyan peasant-monk. He began wearing rough cotton shirts and refusing to eat meat.

Even in their worst days in Budapest, or during the unhappiest moments of their dispute with Diaghilev, Romola had not seen him so withdrawn. When she tried to discourage them, Zverev reacted with open hostility. The other members of the company called him Rasputin because he was so manipulative, suggesting to Nijinsky that he run the Ballet in a more democratic way by allowing less experienced dancers to perform the central roles. In practice this meant Zverev dancing the part of the Golden Slave in *Schéhérazade* while Nijinsky, unrecognised, played the Eunuch; the audiences, who had paid to see Nijinsky, were not impressed by seeing Zverev in his roles.

Finally Romola snapped. She told Vaslav that he had to choose between them and her and that, while he thought about it, she would go back to New York, where Kyra had been living with a nanny. Six weeks later, when the company reached New York, Vaslav was wearing his silk shirts again and eating normal food, though he was lost, with no idea what to do or where to go next. Romola 'felt as if [she] was abandoning a child'; she promised him she would not leave him, whatever happened, until the war was over. Diaghilev had invited him to Madrid to join his smaller company there and perhaps travel to South America that autumn. Vaslav allowed himself to hope, according to Grigoriev as well as Romola, that this meant Diaghilev wanted to work with him again, rather than just send him out on tour as his golden goose. He cabled Diaghilev that he would come to Spain to discuss his offer.

They made wills before setting sail into the torpedo-filled waters of the Atlantic and, one evening as they dined together, Vaslav slipped a cheque under Romola's napkin: it was made out for the amount of his American earnings.

Vaslav, Romola and Kyra waited for Diaghilev in Madrid while spring came. Diaghilev had been with Massine in Italy during the winter of 1916–17, while Nijinsky led his faltering circus around the States. In Rome Diaghilev heard the news of the collapse of the tsarist regime in Russia and turned down a request to return to his homeland as the new Minister of Culture.

The young Sergey Prokofiev – who hoped to interest Diaghilev in his work – observed Diaghilev and Massine acting like lovebirds in Rome, even though Massine refused to share Diaghilev's rooms in the Grand Hotel de Russie. As Picasso's biographer John Richardson so neatly put it, Massine was a 'hot blooded heterosexual [and a] … cold blooded operator', and from the start of their relationship he spent his time surreptitiously making eyes at the other dancers in the company – who all knew better than to bat their eyelashes back – and chasing prostitutes with Picasso, Diaghilev's latest discovery. They were in Paris in May premiering Massine's first ballet, *Les Femmes de bonne humeur*, followed by the avant-garde Picasso-Cocteau-Erik Satie collaboration *Parade* a few weeks later.

The other dancers had been amused to note that while the sapphires Diaghilev had given Vaslav had been set in gold, the rings he gave Massine were platinum. The sign that a fundraising trip to Paris had been successful was a new jewel gleaming on Massine's little finger. Sinking into his mid-forties, Diaghilev was no longer the imposing, infallible creature he had once been, though his tyrannical tendencies remained unabated. He was eating and drinking to excess. One young visitor to the house he rented briefly outside Lausanne in 1917 noted that on his arrival Diaghilev called imperiously for Burgundy and crystallised cherries – 'lots of cherries and lots of Burgundy'. Even his friends had begun to poke fun at him. Before he went to New York, Misia had written to Cocteau that Serge was getting 'fatter and fatter, his clothes tighter and his hat smaller, rather "circus director" as Igor says ...'

When he and Massine arrived in Madrid, Diaghilev 'burst into the lobby of the Ritz and embraced Vaslav passionately ... It was the Sergey Pavlovich of the old days.' Diaghilev was even prepared to charm Romola. Vaslav's happiness was matched only by his relief and he would not allow his wife to bring up the old matter of the contract. 'Sergey Pavlovich is the same as ever; there is no need of discussion; he will be fair to me – let us give him the chance to prove it.' Along with Picasso, Massine and Stravinsky, once again they talked of art and their ambitions through long lunches and dinners, and afterwards, late at night, they ventured out to dance halls to marvel at flamenco.

Vaslav gave an interview in June in which he described how with *Sacre* 'the music and the ballet were composed together: they were born at the same time'. Though he had great affection and admiration for the older musicians whose work he danced to, like Chopin and Schumann, he said, he saw them more as parents he respected than contemporary inspirations. His real passion was for modern music which had a different spirit, closer to his own, and what he was aiming for when he choreographed a ballet was for the dancing to be not 'stuck on to the music but, instead' propelled by it.

The young pianist Artur Rubinstein, whom they knew from London, was also in Madrid. He took Vaslav to watch *jai alai* games 'where the violent leaping and running of the players excited him so much that once he actually fell off his chair. "They are the most perfect dancers," he screamed. "I would like to jump down there and dance with them straight away."' Rubinstein held him back. He also tried to take him to a bullfight, but at the gates Vaslav stopped. He turned to Rubinstein, ashen, and whispered, 'Let's go back. I couldn't stand that.'

Then their Madrid season began, watched every night by the King,*, a devotee of the Ballets Russes, who had been part of the diplomatic efforts to obtain the Nijinskys' release from Hungary. Though Massine had met Vaslav in New York, these performances were the first time he saw him on stage. He marvelled at Nijinsky's transformation from the quiet, reserved man he was offstage. 'He had an instinctive effortless control of his body; every gesture expressed the most tender and complex emotions. His movements were never broken off abruptly, but merged into one.'

Their holidays over, the rest of the dancers had also come to Madrid for the start of the season – including Kostrovsky and Zverev, who quickly reasserted their influence over Vaslav. One day, she wrote, Romola saw Diaghilev deep in conversation with Zverev, not as a director 'but like two accomplices'. She became convinced that Diaghilev was using him and Kostrovsky to separate her and Vaslav, deliberately appealing to his altruism, his peaceful, spiritual, innocent nature, to make him reject marriage, family, and what Romola called normal life. 'I sensed now that Sergey Pavlovich would rather annihilate Vaslav completely if he could not own him both as an artist and as a man.' (I have to add here that though I agree that Diaghilev was determined to use Nijinsky to his own purposes, regardless of Romola, I think it was highly unlikely that he was manipulating him through Zverev.)

Romola was determined to win back her husband. When he tried to suggest that sex even in marriage was only virtuous if performed with the aim of producing a baby, Romola was so desperate (their intimate

---

* He teased Diaghilev. 'You don't direct, you don't dance, you don't play the piano, what is it you do?' Diaghilev replied, 'Your Majesty, I am like you: I don't do anything, but I am indispensable.' (R. Davenport-Hine, *A Night at the Majestic*, 2006, pp. 17–18.)

life, she wrote, had been perfect, ideal, ecstatic) she was willing to encourage a friend who had been pursuing Vaslav since their arrival in Spain, the Duchesse de Durcal. Despite Vaslav entreating Romola not to leave him alone with her, she made every effort to throw them together, reasoning somewhat spuriously that the love of two women would be more effective in saving him from a monastic life than that of one. When Vaslav did eventually succumb to the Duchesse's advances he was miserable. He returned to her saying, '*Femmka* [little wife; Nijinsky has added the Russian diminutive -ka to the French femme], I am sorry for what I did. It was unfair to her … and the added experience, that perhaps you wanted me to have, is unworthy of us.'

Despite these preliminary skirmishes between Romola and Diaghilev, it was not until they were in Barcelona and Vaslav told Diaghilev that he had decided he did not want to return to South America for another tour that the gloves came off. Diaghilev told them that, according to Spanish law, Vaslav's telegram from New York agreeing to the tour in principle was a binding contract. That afternoon, after an argument, Vaslav and Romola were arrested as they boarded the Madrid train and informed that Nijinsky would have to honour his contract by dancing that night in Barcelona and that he would have to go to South America. Diaghilev was determined to have his money's worth from him. No theatre in South America would take the Ballets Russes without Nijinsky and so he would go. Submission was their only option, but Romola insisted that a clause be put in the contract that Vaslav be paid in gold in full an hour before every performance.

They left for South America in July. Vaslav was devastated. Finally he had realised that no reconciliation with Diaghilev would be possible. The promise Massine was showing as a choreographer meant that Diaghilev no longer needed Nijinsky as a creative artist; he was content simply to milk him as a performer. Someone told Vaslav how sorry they were that he and Diaghilev had not been able to make up: 'I wanted to, I did everything, I am heartbroken about it.' He must have understood that without Diaghilev's encouragement his genius might never flourish again.

At first, Vaslav seemed himself. In Rio, their first long engagement, he and Romola made friends with the French ambassador and through him, with Darius Milhaud (later to compose *Le Train Bleu* for Diaghilev). Milhaud noticed 'how beautiful he was when he turned to speak to someone behind his chair. He turned his head, but his head alone, so precisely and rapidly that he seemed not to have moved a muscle.'

Another young composer they met in Rio, Oswald d'Estrade Guerra, thought his inclination towards mysticism was merely Slavic and his highly strung temperament and intelligence artistic. 'One of the most endearing aspects of his character was the rather childlike, natural side of his character, without the slightest pretension. He was certainly conscious of his worth and knew quite well what he was about, but he was totally without vanity. Neither in private life nor on the stage was there anything effeminate in his behaviour… When I heard subsequently that Nijinsky had become insane, I was unable to believe it. Nothing in our meetings in Brazil could have led me to foresee that.'

But as the tour went on Nijinsky's deteriorating mental state became increasingly obvious. Romola arranged everything for him, even writing up his interviews with the press, while Vaslav was more absent, more erratic and more irritable than ever. According to André Oliveroff, a dancer with Pavlova's troupe, which was touring South America at the same time, his usual silence was broken only during rehearsals when he would rage at the dancers, especially the women. He treated them 'as so many vermin' and if a dress or a step was wrong he would scream violent and obscene insults at them. Afterwards, blankly, he would say, 'But I meant nothing by it, nothing at all. I spoke the truth, didn't I? She is a whore, as you know.' All the dancers 'hated him bitterly'.

Oliveroff used to practise with Vaslav in Buenos Aires, the last stop of their tour. Vaslav worked in the darkest corner of the stage and was 'feverishly concerned' with small technical exercises, repeating them constantly. To Oliveroff his work was perfect, but Vaslav was never satisfied. Almost certainly benefiting from hindsight, Oliveroff also noticed his arresting eyes, brooding but full of life, and the perpetual, expressive use of his hands and fingers. You felt, he wrote, that only a thread connected Nijinsky to this world; and it might snap at any moment. Normal life seemed, to him, an 'utterly foreign world to which he was forced to adapt himself'. Even with his wife it was as if he were wearing a mask.

Sometimes he would walk round Buenos Aires with Oliveroff late at night, raging against the war, incoherent with despair at the killing and the meaninglessness of it all, the seas of blood; and he would talk too of his fears that Diaghilev and the other members of the company were secretly working to destroy him. His paranoia, in which Romola was an eager participant, led them to hire bodyguards and to believe any accident – a fire at the theatre, a nail left on the stage, a falling counter-weight near him, collapsing sets – was an attempt on his life.

He dreaded going to the theatre; he began to hate performing. One night at the Teatro Colón, Artur Rubinstein – another artist escaping war-torn Europe with a tour around the theatres of South America – saw Vaslav refusing to go on stage. The police were called (in South America, as in Spain, performers were legally required to perform if they were not ill) and Nijinsky, terrified of being arrested, ran on stage and danced 'better than ever'.

In her account of this period, Romola claimed that rumours were flying around Buenos Aires about both of them having affairs with dubious people (Vaslav was barely capable of speaking to someone, let alone conducting an affair, but Romola introduced the subject to defend herself against the accusations; she had been discovered in her hotel room one afternoon with a man wearing Vaslav's dressing gown, but it was – apparently – entirely innocent); about money being extorted from them and her fears of being accused of being a German spy.

Vaslav was distraught about the break with Diaghilev and by Romola's role in it, the lawsuits she had taken out in his name against Diaghilev and Butt and her continual demands for money, insisting in his diary that he had never wanted anything he had not earned. 'She was cunning and made me keen on money ... I withdrew into myself. I withdrew so deep into myself that I could not understand people. I wept and wept ...'

Before returning to Europe, they made a brief stop in Montevideo where Vaslav was to dance a gala performance for a Red Cross benefit. For some reason, according to Artur Rubinstein, whom Romola had persuaded to form part of the programme, they hoped this would make them eligible for British passports. After their experience in Budapest at the start of the war they were desperate to belong somewhere, to be citizens of some state, and Russia was no longer an option.

As the performance was about to begin, Vaslav was in a highly nervous, agitated state, complaining that his feet were wet or sore, and refusing to come out. Rubinstein alternated with the Red Cross band playing national anthems and popular arias until past midnight when finally Vaslav appeared. Another accompanist – not Rubinstein, who was exhausted after hours of playing for time – played three Chopin dances so Vaslav could perform the poet's sequences from *Les Sylphides*.

'Nijinsky gave a few of his incomparable jumps, which raised such dust from the stage that the people in the first rows were choking … To me he looked even sadder than when he danced the death of Petrushka.' Rubinstein began crying. 'The horrible mixture of a seemingly endless farce with one of the most heartbreaking tragedies was more than one could bear.' It was clear that everyone in the room understood what they were witnessing. 'We gave him an endless ovation.'

CHAPTER 9

Spectre
1918–1950

VASLAV AND ROMOLA sailed back to Europe in the late autumn of 1917. They knew that Vaslav would never work with Diaghilev again; and though Romola wrote of Vaslav's hopes of continuing to dance and create ballets and perhaps, one day, of establishing a school, it must have been clear to her that he might never work with anyone again: a complete mental breakdown was a very real possibility. For the time being, the most important thing was to see out the war as quietly as possible and this they decided to do in Switzerland. They rented a chalet in St Moritz, the Villa Guardamunt, and three-year-old Kyra joined them from the children's home where she had been living in Lausanne.

After such a long time living out of suitcases, Romola noted with pleased surprise that 'our house looked like a real home'. The winter of 1917–18 was 'a very happy one' in which she skied and skated enthusiastically and they all tobogganed and went on long sleigh-rides with Vaslav driving. When spring came, the winter visitors left and St Moritz became again a quiet Alpine village. Vaslav practised daily on the chalet's sunny balcony, with Kyra watching her Tataka-boy delightedly, and he continued to work on his system of notation and to sketch out choreographic works. He loved domestic life – playing with Kyra, chopping wood for the winter, scraping out the mixing bowl when a cake was being made. 'I like family life ... I like playing with children. I understand children. I am a father. I am a married man.'

A Swiss-English girl, Marta Grant, came out to live with Vaslav and Romola as Kyra's nanny. They were, she said many years later, 'a very happy yet serious married couple' and 'Romola was the most wonderful, kind, patient and loving wife any man could ever wish for.'

She noticed, though, that Vaslav, who had nowhere except the balcony to dance, 'looked like a caged animal at times'. It was an isolated life and in retrospect, said Grant, 'I suppose I should have realised his loneliness.' He had no one to talk to about his ideas but Romola and Grant, and 'he was ages ahead of us ... [he needed] someone who spoke his own language ... [But] there were very few who understood.' Sometimes he would tell her about his mother and brother – 'It was evidently a sad life' – and at others he would talk of his fear of being made to fight in the war, because he knew he would not be able to kill. Grant had spent some time in India, and she and Vaslav discussed yoga and Indian spirituality, in which he was interested. She thought him enlightened. Just as 'coming generations will have a different level of consciousness, Nijinsky had it already'; for her it was evident in his dancing.

Winter arrived early in 1918 with days and nights of continuous snow blanketing them in sleepy whiteness, far away from the rest of the world. A letter came from Bronia and Eleonora – the first for a long time – saying that after the Bolsheviks seized power the previous autumn they had fled to Kiev, but that they were well, and together. They had received the money Vaslav had sent them. A separate letter was enclosed for Romola, asking her to tell Vaslav that Stassik had died in the chaos after the Bolsheviks had opened all the prisons and asylums (later Bronia would tell Richard Buckle that Stassik had died in bed of a liver complaint after contracting pneumonia). Vaslav had last seen Stassik over a decade before, and Bronia and Eleonora four years earlier.

Then came the news that the Armistice had been signed. 'We decided to make our first Christmas in our own home and in peacetime a cheerful one, and we were convinced that after the sad, stormy years we were sailing at last towards a calm and happy future.' But Romola had noticed that Vaslav had begun taking long, silent walks through the woods, during which he seemed to be meditating. He did not tell her – perhaps even at this stage he could not distinguish between what was real and what was not – that he was hallucinating violently too.

In his diary he described a terrible walk through trails of blood in the snow. God began speaking to him, telling him to jump into the abyss; he fell and was stopped by a tree in his path. This, he was sure, was a miracle. 'God said to me, "Go home and tell your wife you are mad." I realised that God wished me well.' He continued through the trees, seeing more blood-trails and imagining someone had been killed, and God gave him more and more instructions – to lie down in the snow, to run, to go and come back, and go again. Eventually he saw that what he had thought was blood was just urine, a yellow stain in the snow, and he was able to collect himself enough to go home.

There were other signs of things not being right, but one of the tragic elements of Vaslav's mental illness was that he 'did not slip or "descend" into madness … he leapt in and out of it with a ferocity that bewildered those who had to witness the resulting chaos'. One day, for no reason, Vaslav suddenly attacked their nanny, Marta Grant, trying to strangle her. Romola appeared and he let her go, but Grant – traumatised – fled home to London.

He took up skeleton-running, hurtling wildly head-first, face-down on a small sled down what was called the 'village run'; he took Romola down with him sometimes, and, to Romola's terror, Kyra too. When they went out in the sleigh he would drive recklessly fast, occasionally into the paths of other sleighs. He began drawing strange insects with human faces and staring eyes and weird circular rhythmic patterns. At night Romola would wake to find Vaslav staring at her. Once, very deliberately, he pushed her and Kyra down the stairs. Just as when he was under the influence of Kostrovsky, he refused to eat meat, and he tried to prevent Kyra eating it too. He took to wearing a large gold cross given to Kyra by Emilia over his clothes and trying to engage strangers in religious conversations. Sometimes he would go into the village and spend thousands of francs on paints, scents, shoes, presents, a rainbow-coloured pile of sweaters.

But at the same time, he also had moments – even days – of lucidity. Romola's sister Tessa and brother-in-law came to stay. At Christmas, he and Romola wrapped all the presents for their household and took packages to the children in the village. They decorated a Christmas tree with sweets, toys, silver nuts, garlands and a silver star at the top, but when they awoke on Christmas morning the tree had fallen. The decorations were scattered all over the floor and the silver star lay in two pieces. Trembling, the maid managed to stammer out that a fallen Christmas tree was bad luck.

Their young stoker, who as a child had run errands for Friedrich Nietzsche further down the valley while he was going mad during the 1890s, hesitantly told Romola that he had acted and looked as Vaslav did just before he was taken away. Romola consulted a local doctor, Hans Frenkel, who had studied under Eugen Bleuler, the psychiatrist who eight years earlier had invented the term 'schizophrenia'. Frenkel gave Vaslav word-association tests and prescribed chloral hydrate as a sedative, which may have made his already wandering attention worse, and recommended to Romola that she take Vaslav to see Bleuler. He also embarked upon an affair with Romola. It is not known whether Vaslav knew about this affair. Joan Acocella, the dance critic and editor of the first complete English translation of Nijinsky's diary, has argued, I think convincingly, that he did not.

The young French writer Maurice Sandoz met Vaslav at this time, watching a figure-skating competition. He was wearing black sports clothes with the gold cross prominently displayed on his chest, and he was pulling a toboggan on which sat 'an exquisite little girl', Kyra. They fell into conversation about the skaters.

'He skates with his heart. That's the right way.' Sandoz agreed that the skater was the most graceful of the competitors. 'Grace comes from God. Everything else can be acquired by study.'

'But grace too can be acquired by study, can't it?'

'The kind that can be learnt stops short; grace that is innate never ceases to grow.'

Sandoz asked if Vaslav's little girl would follow in his footsteps. 'Oh no! Her grandfather could only walk, her father can only dance. She'll have to fly! You'll fly, won't you?' Kyra clapped her hands and laughed as he threw her high up over his head.

In early January 1919 Vaslav decided to give a recital in the village at the Suvretta House Hotel. He told Romola a few days before, when they were discussing his costume with the dressmaker, that he wanted to 'show how dances are created. I will compose them there before the audience. I want the public to see the work. They always get everything ready-made. I want to show them the pangs of creation, the agony an artist has to go through when composing, so I will even make the costumes in front of them.'

On the afternoon of the performance, Vaslav, Romola and the dressmaker drove over to the Suvretta House. As always before dancing, Vaslav was silent, his face pale and intense between the dark fur collar of his coat and the fur of his Russian hat. When they arrived, Romola asked what time she should ask the Hungarian accompanist, Bertha Asseo, a friend of her sister's, to begin playing.

'I will tell her at the time. Do not speak. *Silence!*' he thundered. 'This is my marriage with God.'

About two hundred people were waiting in the hotel's ballroom. Vaslav came in in his practice clothes. According to Sandoz, who was one of the guests, Nijinsky was in good humour, greeting people easily, while, despite her slender elegance, Romola looked worried.

In Romola's account of the evening, which differs from Sandoz's, Vaslav ignored the guests. Instead of dancing, he picked up a chair and sat facing the audience for what felt like half an hour, staring at them as if he wanted to read their minds. Then, hoping to prompt Vaslav into action, Bertha Asseo began playing some Chopin. Still he didn't move. Romola went up to him and urged him to begin dancing.

'How dare you disturb me! I am not a machine. I will dance when

I feel like it.' Close to tears, Romola fled the room. When she returned Vaslav was dancing.

Sandoz did not notice this delay. What he noticed was the precision with which, when Vaslav did start dancing, each movement corresponded exactly to each chord, emphasising the fragmentary quality of the music (it was Chopin's Prelude No. 20 in C Minor). Sandoz was surprised at the time but, over the years, thinking about it again, he realised how right Vaslav had been, how intuitive and full of musical understanding. After a brief rest, Nijinsky stood up and shouted, 'We're at war.' He laid out the fabric he had brought with him – long rolls of black and white velvet – on the floor in the shape of a cross.

Romola remembered him saying, 'Now I will dance you the war, with its suffering, with its destruction, with its death. The war which you did not prevent and so you are also responsible for,' and standing with open arms at the head of the velvet cross, his body forming another cross above it.

'And we saw Nijinsky [continued Sandoz], his face ravaged with fright and horror, walking to the sound of a funeral march on a field of battle, striding over a rotting corpse, avoiding a shell, defending a shallow trench which was soaked in blood that clung to his feet, attacking an enemy, running from a tank, coming back on his steps, wounded, dying, tearing, with hands that spoke volumes, the clothes which covered him and were now becoming rags and tatters.

'Nijinsky, barely covered with the shreds of his tunic and gasping for breath was panting hard. A feeling of oppression came over the room, grew tense and seemed to fill it. Another moment and the audience would have cried out: "Enough!"

'One last spasm shook his body which seems riddled with bullets, and another dead man was added to the victims of the Great War.

'This time we felt too much overwhelmed to applaud. We were looking at a pitiful corpse and our silence was the silence that enfolds the dead.

'If Nijinsky had stopped there, our memories of him would have been perfect.'

Romola said that he had danced at once gloriously and terrifyingly: 'it was the dance for life against death'. She did not mention the last sequence of the evening, in which according to Sandoz, Vaslav turned to the wall while the accompanist played a Bach fugue and, half-listening, made strange manic movements like some kind of mad magician. 'A shiver of fear passed through the room.' Asseo stopped. 'What are you doing? That's not dancing.' A rigid, haughty expression came over Vaslav's face, 'the mask of an offended idol': 'I am an artist.' There was a moment of embarrassed silence and then Asseo began playing a Chopin Ballade. 'No, I don't want to hear that music,' shouted Vaslav. 'I know it. I want some music that I don't know, some music that nobody knows.' Asseo played something else and he danced, briefly, with 'delicious grace'. Then she got up and the performance was over.

Afterwards Asseo had tea with Romola and said to her kindly, 'It must be very, very difficult to be married to a genius like Nijinsky. I almost wish you could be free to marry one of our nice, charming, inoffensive compatriots.'

When they got home, Vaslav retreated to his room and carried on feverishly writing in the diary he had begun earlier that day. 'The audience came to be amused … [but] I danced frightening things. They were frightened of me and therefore thought that I wanted to kill them. I do not want to kill anyone. I loved everyone, but no one loved me, and therefore I became nervous,' he wrote. 'I felt God throughout the evening. He loved me. I loved Him. Our marriage was solemnised. In the carriage I told my wife that today was the day of my marriage with God.' It was also the day that Romola realised that there was nothing she could do to stop her husband's psychological collapse.

Nijinsky's diary is an extraordinary document. Written during a period of forty-five days between 19 January and 4 March 1919 in Russian (very bad Russian, according to his translator Kyril FitzLyon, but perhaps that is not surprising for a man who had done as little schoolwork as possible) with tremendous speed, it was, said Romola, almost illegible except for the fact that 'the sentences repeated themselves continuously and that the two names Diaghilev and God dominated' the pages. 'To my knowledge,' writes Joan Acocella in her introduction to its first full English translation, published in 1999, 'it is the only sustained, on-the-spot (not retrospective) written account, by a major artist, of the experience of entering psychosis.'

He began writing to express, describe and justify what he thought he was going through. Knowing Romola was worried about him and fearing, because of the hallucinations he was at this stage only experiencing intermittently, that he might be going mad – he wanted to show that what seemed (even to him) to be madness was in fact an ascent to a higher plane, a mystical union with God in which he would translate God's message to the world. The message was simple, heavily reliant on Tolstoy, and throughout he never deviated from it, wherever his free-falling mind took him: materialism and opportunism were destroying the world and the remedy was not thinking, but feeling. FitzLyon notes that feeling as Nijinsky used the word 'means intuitive perception, the ability to understand something – a person, a situation – by merging with it emotionally … akin to a spiritual experience'.

Several themes recur amid the rambling repeated phrases, disjointed memories and associations, wild swings in mood, back-to-front arguments ('I am afraid of death and therefore I love life'), apparent contradictions and cries of existential anguish. The first is God, the closeness Vaslav feels and longs to feel to Him, and the torment he suffers when he feels detached from Him. He has no time for the Church as an institution or for the Pope; his spirituality is based on an intense personal association with the divine, through Christ in particular. 'I am God in man. I am what Christ felt. I am Buddha. I am a Buddhist and every kind of God. I know everyone. I am acquainted with everything. I pretend to be mad for my own purposes. I know that if everyone thinks I am a harmless madman, they will not be afraid of me. I do not like people who think that I am a madman who would harm people. I am a madman who loves people.' (This passage gives a good indication of the style of the diary. As one critic has written, 'Reading it is like watching an autistic child rocking back and forth, back and forth, absorbed in the patterns of a speeding universe but unable to waylay them long enough to process into purposeful action. It's a terrible sight. We want to stop him, comfort him. But we know he's doomed.')

His ideas recall the sense of oneness for which Buddhists strive, and remind me of *The Way of a Pilgrim*, a classic of Russian mysticism, about an itinerant peasant trying 'to find out what it means in the Bible when it says you should pray incessantly'; it is the book J. D. Salinger's Franny Glass (in *Franny and Zooey*) can't let go of. Sometimes he verges on delusions of grandeur that make him think he might actually be an omnipotent deity; most of the time he seems to mean, when he says he is God, that he sometimes feels attuned to a communion with the divine in which anyone could participate. 'I am not a magician, I am God within the body,' he writes. 'Everyone has this feeling, only no one uses it.'

But then he is overtaken by torturous doubts: he is evil, he does not love anyone; he is an animal, a predator, a masturbator. He is the angriest man in the world. The very worst things he can contemplate he will do: 'I will eat everyone I can get hold of. I will stop at nothing. I will make love to my wife's mother and my child. I will weep, but I will do everything God commands me to. I know that everyone will be afraid of me and will commit me to a lunatic asylum. But I don't care. I am not afraid of anything. I want death. I will blow my brains out if God wants it. I will be ready for anything.'

And just as he does not flinch from the darkness in his own soul, so too does he seek to understand the baser instincts that animate the world around him. The stock market is a brothel, he writes; men become rich by fraud; politics is death. Lloyd George, whom he blames for the war, is as aggressive and power-hungry as Diaghilev. They are both eagles 'who prevent small birds from living'. Amid the flashes of insight are moments of wild delusion: he will gamble on the stock exchange to make money to give to the poor, he will invent pencils that never go blunt, he will ask Gabriel Astruc to arrange for him to dance for the poor artists of Paris, and if they understand him he will be saved.

He can comprehend everything spoken in front of him, no matter what language it is. 'To understand does not mean to know all the words,' he writes, referring to Romola and her sister Tessa speaking Hungarian in front of him. 'I know few words, but my hearing is very well developed.' This delusion is less odd than it might sound: Vaslav must have been extraordinarily good at picking up on non-verbal communication. He had spent most of his adult life speaking and listening to languages in which he was not fluent, saying little but understanding a lot. I think of those endless champagne-drenched dinners in mirrored private dining rooms, with everyone but him fighting to make their voice heard and Vaslav just listening; and of the way he could express so much on stage with a glance or a gesture.

Later he writes that he can do everything, be anyone: 'I am an Egyptian. I am an Indian. I am a Red Indian. I am a Negro. I am a Chinese. I am a Japanese. I am a foreigner and a stranger. I am a seabird'; and later, 'I am a peasant. I am a factory worker. I am a servant. I am a gentleman. I am an aristocrat. I am a tsar. I am an Emperor. I am God. I am God. I am Everything.' One must bear in mind, reading these lists, that he had played almost all these roles on stage. His professional life had been made up in large part by inhabiting skins other than his own, by observing people's actions, understanding what they revealed about their interior states, and using that in his work.

Diaghilev appears again and again in Vaslav's writing, viewed at times with bitterness, at times with respect, and at times with compassion. He describes their meeting and his feelings for him in searing detail; he blames him for the 'terrible things' he taught him sexually ('Diaghilev taught me everything'), because now he fears lust and its power over him and does not want to feel it. He gave up meat because it made him lustful. 'Lust is a terrible thing.' At the same time, he does 'not want people to think Diaghilev is a scoundrel and that he must be put in prison. I will weep if he is hurt. I do not like him, but he is a human being.'

Towards the end of the diary, Vaslav addresses to Diaghilev a long letter in verse, a strange and moving poem containing snatches of half-remembered conversations or arguments, a reference to Diaghilev's well-known preference for communicating by telegram and telephone rather than by letter, and increasingly compulsive repetitions and word associations.

'You do not want to live with me.

I wish you well.

You are mine, you are mine.

I am yours, I am yours.

I love writing with a pen.

I write, I write.

You do not write. You tele-write.

You are a telegram, I am a letter … You are not my king, but I am your king. You wish me harm, I do not wish harm. You are a spiteful man, but I am a lullabyer. Rockabye, bye, bye, bye. Sleep in peace, rockabye, bye.

Bye. Bye. Bye.

Man to man

Vaslav Nijinsky'

I find that 'Man to man' heartbreakingly poignant: an insistence that, *au fond*, however Diaghilev may have treated him, they are equals – not adult and child, not patron and protégé, not powerful impresario and puppet-performer.

The other person who features prominently in the diary is Romola and, as with Diaghilev, Vaslav's responses to her are not straightforward. He respects her for engaging in battle with Diaghilev and he likes the fact that Diaghilev is scared of her intelligence. He bemoans the fact that she is not careful with his money, even though he has given her everything he had. He will not go to cocktail parties with her because he has 'had enough of this kind of jollity to last me a lifetime'. He knows they disagree: 'You think I am stupid, and I think you are a fool.' But despite her flinty materialism, her craving for things he considers unimportant, he feels compassion and affection for her; he loves her 'more than anyone else in the world'. Beneath it all, the deep connection between them endures. 'I do not like the intelligent Romola. I want her to leave you. I want you to be mine.'

Although the diary's erratic style makes it appear unreliable, I trust much of what Vaslav is saying in it. He might have been hallucinating (those dreadful trails of blood in the snow), but he was not fantasising (I believe him when he says Romola's sister flitted around in front of him in her underwear). If cubism was a way of trying to express a three-dimensional experience of the world in two dimensions, then what Nijinsky is doing in his diary is expressing the quicksilver multiplicity of emotions people simultaneously contain about events, past and future, and about one another – fragmentary, shifting, hard to pin down, very often contradictory – but no less authentic for that. We are 'splinters and mosaics', wrote Virginia Woolf; 'not, as they used to hold, immaculate, monolithic, consistent wholes'.

He can be startlingly observant. Stravinsky seeks fame and riches; he 'loves me in his heart because he feels, but he considers me his enemy because I am in his way'. Diaghilev smokes to appear impressive. 'He is a tidy man and likes museums. I consider museums to be graveyards.' Emilia gives presents to Vaslav and Kyra: 'She thinks that love is expressed in presents. I believe that presents are not love.' Romola 'wants money because she is afraid of life' (a very Tolstoyan phrase). He is even able to shine this spotlight on himself: 'I am an unthinking philosopher.'

Another striking aspect of the diary is how it illuminates the way he thought and worked. Like Woolf, another modernist artist whose fractured mental state granted her extraordinary insights, the 'whirring of wings in the brain' she described may have stimulated Nijinsky's creativity in indefinable ways. 'The quality of abstraction that made his acting so remarkable may have been rooted in the same traits of mind as his communication problems,' writes Acocella. Similarly, his willingness to experiment, the radical way he viewed and analysed movement, 'may have been connected to some neurological idiosyncrasy ... Why should he worry about being understood? He was seldom understood.'

Taking risks, being obsessive and self-obsessed, being drawn to new and extreme experiences – these were traits people had been remarking about him for years. 'Later, too, I came to understand the absences [in Vaslav's personality] as a kind of stigmata,' wrote Stravinsky. The tragedy was that Vaslav's spiritual insights and soaring creativity came in parallel with a paralysing inability to cope with the everyday world. Inarticulate and shy in normal life, achingly conscious of his inexperience, repeatedly told by people he admired that he was their intellectual inferior, he knew 'he had no reason to credit himself with unusual spiritual maturity'.

Many of the diary's characteristics are qualities of early modernist art. Repetition, elision and odd juxtapositions are hallmarks of visual artists like Picasso, of writers like Joyce and Eliot, who created stream-of-consciousness narratives akin to Nijinsky's. He revels in complex rhymes and puns like a rapper or a scat singer, moving between Russian, Polish and French, for example linking Massine with *singe* and associating the fabulously rich Misia Sert repeatedly with gold and silver. The insistently rhythmic quality of much of his writing may be 'a verbal expression of his experience as a dancer'. Vaslav's preoccupation with the visceral was also part of being a professional athlete: the minute details of what he ate and excreted or ejaculated, when he slept and how his body felt were all vitally important to his work.

Throughout he struggles to express and understand what is happening to him. 'I am standing in front of a precipice into which I may fall,' he writes. 'He knows,' comments Acocella, 'that something extraordinary is going on in his brain, but he does not know if this means that he is God or that he is a madman, abandoned by God.' Repeatedly he refers to artists who, like him, suffered from mental illness: Gogol, Maupassant, Nietzsche. 'I feel so much pain in my soul that I am afraid for myself. I feel pain. My soul is sick. My sickness is of the soul and not of the mind.' In Russia the insane are called 'soul-sick', FitzLyon notes. 'I have been told that I am mad. I thought that I was alive,' he writes, six pages later. 'I am Nijinsky. I want to tell you, humans, that I am God. I am the God who dies when he is not loved.'

There is an electric connection between the God with whom Vaslav identifies himself and the *dieu de la danse* he had been acclaimed as by audiences ever since his professional debut ten years earlier. The sense of the dancer-artist as a semi-divine figure, capable of attaining what Erik Bruhn called 'something *total* – a sense of total being', has been beautifully expressed by Rudolf Nureyev, and I imagine that something like this is also what Nijinsky felt when he performed. 'There have been certain moments on the stage – four or five times – when I have suddenly felt a feeling of "I am!" A moment that feels as though it's forever. An indescribable feeling of being everywhere and nowhere.' This zen-like transcendence, a route into what Colin Wilson describes as 'more abundant life', was something to which Nijinsky was exquisitely attuned but could not translate into his day-to-day experience. He could not communicate it to Romola; even he could not always grasp it. It was no wonder people had always thought of him as inhabiting a different plane. Perhaps only Diaghilev had understood, in part at any rate.

And without being a performer – a future he was forced to contemplate without Diaghilev in his life – without being loved by his audience, which in many ways Diaghilev had come to represent, what would Nijinsky be? Repeatedly he refers to living as working and death as not-working, conflating the meanings of the words. For him 'the working life was the only real life': human relations were fraught with pitfalls, 'probably pointless, possibly dangerous, and in the end entirely destructive'. When he describes the first time he made love to Diaghilev, he writes that he needed to live – to *work* – and was therefore willing to make any sacrifice. Now that there was no sacrifice he could make, he could feel his art slipping away from him. 'I want to dance because I feel,' he wrote, immediately after the Suvretta House performance, 'and not because people are waiting for me.'

Yet another layer of the diary is the events being played out as Vaslav writes. All around him the noises of their domestic life intrude on his frenzied attempts to write out his soul: Romola calls for him to answer a ringing telephone; Kyra sings outside his room; he can hear Oskar Padany carefully enunciating his name to someone in Zurich on the other end of the telephone or the maid answering the telephone 'with tears in her voice'; Romola talking to the servants in another part of the house, or crying and being comforted by Frenkel. 'Before us we have the man, and, in the background, the muffled sounds of his fate being decided.'

The night of the Suvretta House performance they are in their bedroom when the telephone rings and he won't answer it. Romola is in her pyjamas. 'I am afraid of people because they want me to lead the same kind of life as they do. They want me to dance jolly and cheerful things. I do not like jollity. I love life. My wife sleeps next to me, and I am writing. My wife is not asleep, because her eyes are open. I stroked her. She feels things well. I am writing badly because I find it difficult. My wife is sighing … She asked me what I was writing. I closed the notebook in her face because she wants to read what I am writing. She feels that I am writing about her, but she does not understand. She is afraid for me and therefore does not want me to write.'

At the end of the first notebook he can hear Romola speaking in another room. 'I do not know what they are telephoning about now. I think they want to put me in prison. I am weeping because I love life … My little girl is singing: Ah! Ah! Ah! Ah! I do not understand the meaning of this, but I feel its meaning. She wants to say that everything Ah! Ah! is not horror but joy.'

The narrative comes to a desperate crescendo as Vaslav prepares for a journey to Zurich, half-understanding that he will be hospitalised there. Romola tells him to say good-bye to Kyra because he won't be coming back and then, weeping, tells him they will never leave him. 'Come on out!' he writes in despair, a last gasp of defiance as the waters close over his head. 'Come on out and fight with me. I will defeat everyone. I am not afraid of bullets and prison. I am afraid of spiritual death. I will not go insane, but I will weep and weep.'

In March 1919 they went to the state asylum in Zurich, with its iron-barred windows, to consult Dr Bleuler. Vaslav seemed to accept Romola's story that they were visiting him to discuss whether she could have another child. Romola waited while Vaslav went obediently into his study. Then Bleuler invited her in while Vaslav waited outside, and he told her that her husband was incurably insane. She raced out to the ante-room where Vaslav stood flipping absently through the magazines, his face pale and sad. He said, '*Femmka*, you are bringing me my death-warrant.'

Diaghilev had managed to hold the Ballets Russes together all through the war, taking them on ramshackle tours of provincial Spain, even accepting a season for them at a London music hall. His efforts just staved off extinction: he and his dancers lived in hotel rooms for which they could not pay, ate as little as possible and dipped into the wicker costume baskets when their own clothes wore out. When Lydia Sokolova's little girl was ill Diaghilev found an old purse full of foreign coins, tipped it out on the bed and gave her his last silver and coppers to pay the doctor.

Following their long stay in Spain, Massine worked with a flamenco dancer called Félix Fernández García (his day job was as a printer) on a flamenco ballet, *Le Tricorne*, which premiered in London in 1919. Before its first night Fernández García was found naked on the altar of the church of St Martin in the Fields, having forced his way in through a locked door after being heard lamenting that the Lord was reduced to living in a brothel. He was taken to an asylum where he lived until his death in 1941. He was the Ballets Russes's second casualty in six months. Years later, weighed down by the fates of Vaslav and Fernández García, Diaghilev would tell Ottoline Morrell sadly that his company had left 'a trail of madness behind it'.*

Muriel Draper, meeting Diaghilev again in London after the war, found him 'a shade worn and tired'. There was 'no conscious nobility of purpose in life and therefore no great living. No great living, and therefore less and less great art.' He was preoccupied by events in Russia,

---

* Olga Spessivtzeva, one of Diaghilev's five Auroras in the ill-fated 1921 production of *The Sleeping Princess*, was the last of the original Ballets Russes dancers to succumb to mental illness, in the United States in the 1950s. See Anton Dolin's 1966 biography, *The Sleeping Ballerina*.

from where he had had news that his beloved stepmother had died and that friends like Walter Nouvel, who had burned all his furniture as firewood, were barely surviving. He was disappointed that the new generation of artists and set designers in whose hands he had hoped to place the Ballets Russes's future, like Picasso and André Derain, were only using the company to promote their own interests. He was missing the creative companionship of Bakst and Stravinsky, both of whom he had alienated with his tyrannical management style and insulted by trying to pay too little. Finally, with Massine scarcely bothering to conceal his disdain for him, he was lonely too. He told the conductor Ernest Ansermet that he had been 'living in a dream world and not in reality, in an empty bubble of prosperity and success. It was all just masturbation, and he didn't want any part in it any more.'

In 1920, reconciled with Stravinsky, Diaghilev asked Massine to choreograph a new version of *Le Sacre du printemps*. When Lydia Sokolova (who had danced as a maiden in Nijinsky's version of the ballet seven years earlier) was told that she was to dance the Chosen Maiden, she was so excited she threw her arms around Sergey Grigoriev's neck – earning the highest fine ever paid by a member of the Ballets Russes (£5 for 'assault' as noted in Grigoriev's little book). After her first performance, Diaghilev and Massine gave Sokolova their eczema-ridden lapdog, Mickey, which (perhaps because she was English) she had always pitied because they treated it so badly, letting it eat pots of make-up remover and getting it drunk and laughing at it.

During the rehearsals for *Sacre*, Diaghilev heard that Massine was having an affair with one of the dancers, Vera Clark, an English recruit to the company whom Diaghilev had given a Russian stage name, Savina. Desperate not to lose another lover-protégé, Diaghilev had the couple followed by private detectives to find out if the rumours were true and, when he was convinced it was, had Massine beaten up by hired thugs. Varying accounts of the fall-out described Massine ordering Diaghilev in front of the company to tie his shoelaces and Diaghilev lumbering down onto his knees to obey; and Diaghilev getting Savina drunk, telling her to strip, and then throwing her into Massine's bedroom, saying,

'If that's what you want, take her now.' Massine and Savina quit and started their own company and married the following year.

Once again Diaghilev was heartbroken and humiliated, complaining to Grigoriev that Massine had been nothing when they met. And once again he lost no time looking for a replacement. A young man hoping to find a position as a secretary was ushered into Diaghilev's hotel room at about this time. Diaghilev was sitting at his desk writing. He did not look up. The young man cleared his throat, and still not looking at him, Diaghilev said, 'Take off your clothes.' When he had done so, the young man cleared his throat again. Diaghilev screwed in his monocle, looked at the man, said, 'Put your clothes on,' and went back to his work. The young man understood he had been dismissed; his hairiness was not to Diaghilev's taste. The successful applicant for the position, who later added the role of librettist to his responsibilities, was Boris Kochno, a darkly handsome Russian émigré of seventeen with a thing for older men.

Although the Ballets Russes continued to attract and incubate the best talents of the era,* no great creative or commercial triumphs consoled Diaghilev for his unsatisfactory private life during the 1920s. Stout, bored and diabetic – though characteristically he refused the insulin injections that, from 1921, would have relieved his condition – he survived on a diet largely of champagne, chocolate and cocaine, keeping a posse of fresh young men around him and compulsively touching his wooden cane to stave off bad luck.

In 1921, hoping to create a modern classic that would bring in audiences for years to come, Diaghilev decided to mount an ambitious and eye-wateringly expensive revival of Tchaikovsky's 1890 full-length ballet, *La Belle au bois dormant*. Renamed *The Sleeping Princess* by Diaghilev, it was to be shown in London that winter. Calling on all his powers of persuasion, Diaghilev gathered together his old guard: Stravinsky would

---

*The roll call of artists and composers with whom he worked during this period is astonishing and included (apart from those mentioned in the text) Poulenc, Auric, Milhaud, Berners, Laurencin, Braque, Gris, de Chirico and Utrillo.

orchestrate the music, Bakst (after both André Derain and Benois had turned him down) would design the costumes and sets, and Bronia Nijinska – back in Paris and an established ballet mistress in her own right – would refresh Petipa's old-fashioned choreography.

Despite their combined talents, the ballet was not right for the time. Audiences of the 1920s wanted to be modern, and did not share Bakst's and Diaghilev's passionate nostalgia for the St Petersburg of the 1890s, a quality that had been absent from their previous, pre-revolutionary productions. *The Sleeping Princess* closed early with Diaghilev owing impresario Sir Oswald Stoll £11,000. Fleeing London to avoid his creditors, Diaghilev arrived in Paris to find that Bakst was suing him because, after having dropped everything to help with *The Sleeping Princess*, Diaghilev had rewarded him by giving Stravinsky's short opera *Mavra*, which he had promised Bakst, to a rival artist. Bakst won the lawsuit (for compensation for lost income). He and Diaghilev never spoke again and he died in December 1924.

Bronia and Stravinsky worked together again the following year with Natalia Goncharova as designer on *Les Noces*, which premiered in Paris in June 1923.* It was a ballet Diaghilev had originally intended for Vaslav and he would surely have been delighted by the way in which Bronia made the dancers, male and female, perform the same steps. In all her ballets Bronia worked on and expanded themes her brother had established, using the same modernist aesthetic. This is especially evident in the detached playfulness with which she dealt with the representation of gender on stage, recalling the ambiguity and fluidity of *Jeux*. In *Les*

---

* After the preview at Winnie de Polignac's, in an evening that exemplified Paris in the 1920s for a certain set, the glamorous American exiles Gerald and Sara Murphy – who, through their friendship with Goncharova, and along with the unlikely figure of their shy and bespectacled friend John Dos Passos, had helped paint the sets for *Les Noces* – threw a party for the company and its friends on a barge in the Seine. Sara Murphy had decorated the boat with piles of cheap children's toys from a Montparnasse bazaar, which delighted Picasso; Goncharova read the guests' palms; Cocteau stole the captain's dress uniform from his cabin and kept putting his head through the porthole to announce they were sinking; as the sun rose, Stravinsky jétéd down the centre of the cabin.

Fâcheux (1924) she danced a male role and put Dolin *en pointe*; in *Les Biches* the Girl in Blue is dressed as a pageboy. She would later write that *Jeux* and *Sacre* had been more influential on her work as a choreographer than *Faune* as the starting points for modern and neoclassical ballet.*

---

* All through the writing of this book, I have been conscious of the presence of Bronia Nijinska at my shoulder, like the sister of Shakespeare whom Virginia Woolf imagined for her 1929 essay 'A Room of One's Own'. (Irina Nijinska, Bronia's daughter, told Millicent Hodson that her mother always loved Woolf's books – perhaps because, as Hodson speculated, the role Nijinsky had conceived for Nijinska in *Jeux* was based on Woolf.)

In her wonderful memoir of their early life, Bronia focused on her brother, seeking to understand the marvels of his art and how he so captured the imaginations of those who saw him dance, but occasionally she could not help making a point about her own achievements, almost as if to say, I know you are reading this book about him – and that is of course why I have written it – but you must understand that I have my own story, and I possessed greatness too. At school Vaslav was always top of the dancing classes, but lagged behind in academic subjects; Bronia was top in every subject. When she remembers the circuses of their childhood, she cannot resist adding proudly how much they influenced her own choreographic work, too: *Le Renard* (1922), *Le Train Bleu* (1924), *Impressions de Music Hall* (1927) …

The theme of gender recurs throughout Nijinsky's story, a subtext running in silent parallel to the more obvious discussions of sexuality. For the most part, ballerinas were exalted and adored on stage, but were seldom given control over their careers offstage or admitted to the creative process, though three notable exceptions in their different ways were the trail-blazers Kshesinskaya (post-feminist before her time), Pavlova and Duncan. Karsavina described longing to penetrate Diaghilev's 'mysterious forge where creative minds worked a new armour of art' and wondered if it would 'ever be open' (Karsavina, *Theatre Street*, 1948, p. 192) to her. When Romola saw her husband with Stravinsky for the first time after their marriage she had to acknowledge to herself that along with Diaghilev they inhabited a world to which she could never hope to be admitted. 'I felt so crushed. What did I have to do among those men – those gifted initiates of God?' (Romola Nijinsky, *Nijinsky; and, The last years of Nijinsky*, London, 1980).

Despite her evident talent, Bronia struggled against Diaghilev's misogyny. Her unconventional looks were given as the reason she would never be a star in her own right; when he told her to dye her hair and dress more like a ballerina off-stage, she was appalled. Besides, he had chosen Nijinsky, not her. 'I cannot have two geniuses of the dance from one family!' (Nijinska, *Early Memoirs*, p. 326.) When she married, Vaslav was her best man but Diaghilev gave her away, and he gave her her wedding ring, set with sapphires and brilliants, which he declared, in a tone rather contrary to the spirit of the occasion, was 'to wed her to her art' (Buckle, *Nijinsky*, p. 263). (cont.)

Very soon after he was admitted, the writer Robert Walser saw Vaslav at Bellevue, the comfortable Kreuzlingen sanatorium to which he had been taken in 1919 and where he lived until 1923, and again in the 1930s. He was still dancing, in a limited way, for visitors to the asylum: 'his dancing is like a fairy tale,' Walser wrote, as if he never would – perhaps never could – stop.

Vaslav found being institutionalised severely traumatic. Despite the humanitarian principles (for its time) by which Bellevue was run, the level of understanding of mental illness was so low that Vaslav was not assigned a Russian-speaking psychiatrist until his third stay there. At his worst moments, according to their records, he refused to eat, masturbated in public, harmed himself, begged for poison so he could commit suicide, hallucinated wildly, attacked his attendants and had to be restrained by straitjackets on iron beds; when he was lucid, he could be heard crying out, 'Why am I locked up? Why are the windows closed, why am I never alone?'

In 1921, Eleonora, Bronia and Bronia's two children, Irina, aged seven, and two-year-old Leo, managed to escape Russia and meet Romola in Vienna. She took them to see Vaslav in the Steinhof Sanatorium there. He sat, withdrawn and unemotional, throughout their visit. The next day Bronia returned and sat with him, telling him about her work. 'Would you believe, Vatsa, that ... I have already devised two ballets?' He looked straight at her, saying firmly, 'The *ballet* is never devised. The *ballet* must be created.' But that was all; once more he sat as if he had never spoken, indifferent and unmoved, and she could not reach him again.

Perhaps hoping that making him part of their normal life might prompt a recovery, in 1923 Romola brought Vaslav to Paris where they lived with their two daughters – Kyra, aged seven, and another girl, whom

---

Bronia would become one of Diaghilev's most important collaborators of the 1920s – significantly, unlike her brother, one who could provide him with a steady stream of successes – though in the same breath as admiring her he could not stop himself belittling her. 'The choreography [of *Les Biches*, 1924] has delighted and astonished me,' he told Boris Kochno. 'But then, this good woman, intemperate and anti-social as she is, does belong to the Nijinsky family' (Burt, *The Male Dancer*, p. 95).

Romola did not publicly acknowledge until 1971. She was rumoured to have been Frenkel's child, but she was born in September 1920, nine months after Vaslav returned to the Villa Guardamunt (against doctors' orders) from Bellevue for a few months, conceived when Romola still hoped a child might bring him back to himself. Although she was not christened Tamara, Vaslav always called her that – a silent homage to Tamara Karsavina.

Though she never knew her father as a sane man, Tamara worshipped him just as Kyra did. When she climbed onto his lap it was 'as though an unspoken conspiracy had developed between us. We did not need words to communicate with each other. We were so different, his two daughters, the embodiment of his own split personality: Kyra, the explosive, colourful artist already as a child and I, shy, withdrawn, peace-seeking.' Romola – highly critical and quick to lash out in anger – made Tamara nervous; only with Tataka-boy did she feel at ease.

She remembered a dinner Romola gave during these unhappy years in Paris. Afterwards Romola gave Tamara a lump of sugar dipped in coffee. When another guest gave her one, Tamara, in her eagerness to take it, jogged the spoon and dropped the morsel. Romola was furious and sent the mortified little girl out of the room. As she reached the door Vaslav called her name. He was standing by his chair holding a huge, dripping sugar-lump between his fingers. 'I can still taste the warm, sweet coffee in my mouth and recall wistfully Tataka-boy's gentle, understanding face.'

Vaslav was a ghost; the children were lonely and scared, and very worried about their father; Romola was desperate to find a way to make a living to support them all (during this period she started nine different businesses, including a pastry-shop, a taxi company and a remedy for toothache, none of which came to anything) and pay Vaslav's medical bills. She spent an hour a day with Vaslav and the rest of the time she was out, frantically networking, determined to live. Diaghilev came to visit him. 'Vatsa, you are being lazy. Come, I need you. You must dance again for the Russian Ballet and for me.' But Vaslav shook his head. 'I cannot because I am mad.'

In 1923 Vaslav was taken to the premiere of his sister's ballet, *Les Noces*, which he watched blankly. On seeing him Bronia burst into tears, crying, 'I can't take it, I can't take it.' Lydia Lopokova wrote to her lover (later her husband) John Maynard Keynes that she had gone up to the box to see him, 'but he did not know me, nor anybody, he does not recognise anyone, but being in a quiet state the doctors want to give him a thrill, so as to move him, and then perhaps he might be cured. His wife is with him. Who is so cruel to him? Terrible, terrible ...'

Anton Dolin, who danced for Diaghilev during the early 1920s, asked his mentor to take him to meet Vaslav – neither the first nor the last of Diaghilev's lovers to have a fascination with Nijinsky. He described him living in an 'almost suburban' third- or fourth-floor apartment (in the avenue de la Bourdonnais, near the École Militaire in the Septième) with lace curtains hanging in the windows and photographs in frames propped on every surface. Vaslav was 'like a convalescent invalid ... but somehow in this man's face there was something more expressive than a volume of words'. Dolin noticed also his 'beautiful mouth' and 'hands that were never still' and could not help wondering what the imperturbable Diaghilev felt on seeing him.

Ottoline Morrell visited too. She found Vaslav fat and silent. 'I had the impression that he knew what was going on, but was unable to break down his prison walls – Petrushka again.' His hands were the same, always in motion, the thumbs clenched into his fists; and his dark eyes were just 'more haunted ... I thought he knew me, but was not sure'.

Others have agreed with this assessment, suggesting that Vaslav's breakdown was somehow voluntary – a retreat from the struggles that had conquered him, a surrender to forces he could no longer resist. In the mid-twentieth century the maverick psychiatrist Ronald Laing posited the theory that psychotic behaviour may be an unconscious strategy enabling sufferers to shed the 'false self' that an uncaring society has forced them to adopt. Laing liked to say that the word schizophrenia, usually translated as split personality, can also be read as broken-hearted.

When he read Vaslav's (admittedly heavily edited) diary in 1953, Cocteau compared his idealism to that of Einstein and Chaplin, insisting, 'Nijinsky is not mad'. Suffering from and revolting against the dry hearts of Diaghilev and Stravinsky, diminished by his marriage to Romola, thought Cocteau, he had turned to mysticism and humanitarianism, taking a vow of solitude, a marriage with himself. Later in life Stravinsky said he often thought of Vaslav, 'captive in his own mind, his most perfect gift of expression in movement stricken, immobile'.

Roy Porter, reviewing a 1991 psychiatric analysis of Nijinsky's life, agreed with Peter Ostwald's thesis that Nijinsky's mutism 'was to some degree a deliberate acting out of despair by one of the supremely gifted actors of modern times: playing parts was all Nijinsky had ever learned to do'. Ostwald broke Vaslav's behaviour down into three dominant modes: the dancer, his core identity since childhood; the lunatic, a violent, moody, destructive role he took on in times of crisis, such as when his father was leaving his mother, when he was struggling to escape Diaghilev and later, when he was grappling with his declining mental health; and the patient, the gentle, passive obedient boy his mother and Romola adored. By this analysis the patient simply stepped into the foreground, gradually edging out the dancer and the lunatic.

The diagnosis was that Nijinsky was suffering from what we would today call schizophrenic disorders: hallucinations, delusions of many kinds (persecution, grandeur, control), distracted thoughts, disorganised language and behaviour, a loosening of connections and associations. Ostwald adds that he was probably bipolar too.* Although his psychosis was partly 'biologically based', writes Joan Acocella (his brother's illness, though it too ostensibly sprang from an external source, cannot be discounted not only as a stress factor but also as an indication of a troubling shared genetic inheritance), 'constitutional vulnerability must be combined with some potent psychological stress in order for the illness to develop'. She believes this stress was his inability to work, to dance and more specifically to choreograph – on a general level, to create.

---

* Professor Josh Miller, who read this in draft, suggested to me that Nijinsky may also have been diagnosed as being on the autism spectrum today.

Diaghilev, meanwhile, had replaced Anton Dolin with a new protégé, Serge Lifar, a dancer who had arrived in Paris in 1922, aged seventeen, on Bronia Nijinska's recommendation. It took Lifar two years to persuade Diaghilev to take an interest in him but when he describes in his memoirs Diaghilev taking him off to the museums of Italy in the summer of 1924 we know a romance has begun. Diaghilev commended his young friend to Sacheverell Sitwell, their host in Florence, for reading his Baedeker at lunch – on closer inspection Sitwell found Lifar had tucked into the pages photographs of himself.

Cyril Beaumont described Lifar as lacking only pointed ears to be a faun and he embraced Nijinsky's roles with alacrity. After dinner at Coco Chanel's, Misia Sert would play the prelude to Debussy's *L'Après-midi d'un faune* while Lifar reclined on the piano. Then, languorously, he would stretch and get up to dance a one-man version of *Faune*: the sexiest of drawing-room entertainments. (Bronia also danced the role of the Faun for Diaghilev during this period but Ninette de Valois thought that, danced by a woman, it took on a sinister quality. Was Diaghilev hoping that through half-closed eyes he might catch a glimpse of his lost love?)

For Lifar, Diaghilev was an idol, a mentor and his 'spiritual father' – 'our two souls met together in an upsurge towards the Beautiful' – and Lifar's influence on Diaghilev, for example persuading him to give up cocaine, was sometimes beneficent. The life of an artist was Diaghilev's great gift to Lifar – the same gift he had given Nijinsky, Massine and Dolin. 'I was enraptured with my life in the Theatre, my dancing, my appearances in front of the footlights ...' he wrote. But their relationship was a tempestuous one, marked by Lifar's jostling for position with the equally possessive and adoring Boris Kochno and by Diaghilev's obsessive desire for control. He was jealous of 'everything and everyone – about my childhood dreams, girl dancers, my partners, people I met casually ... and even my success as an artist'.

In late December 1928 Diaghilev brought Lifar to see Vaslav, who was living in a flat in Passy on the outskirts of Paris with Tessa de Pulszky – separated from her husband, still charming but increasingly alcoholic – his negligent guardian. The sad little group in the avenue de la Bourdonnais apartment had been disbanded three years earlier, with Emilia Márkus paying off the back rent and servants' wages, long-owed, and Romola's debts. Romola had fled to the United States to make her fortune; eleven-year-old Kyra was sent to a boarding school in Switzerland (again) and three years later went to live with a young American woman, Natalie Rodgers, who wanted to pay for her dance lessons and be her mentor, but soon abandoned her; Tamara, then five, was taken to Budapest where she was loved and looked after by her grandmother, the two of them forming an alliance against an increasingly defensive and distant Romola.

The Passy apartment smelt of chemicals and Nijinsky was looked after by male attendants of whom he was obviously frightened. It was clear that he had few visitors; Romola had not seen him since leaving Paris in 1925. When they came in he was lying in a dressing gown on a mattress, his legs stretched out in front of him. He was flabby and his nerves showed in the way he was playing with his hands, biting at his bleeding nails or making affected gestures with his wrists.

Diaghilev told Vaslav that Lifar was a dancer too and that he loved Nijinsky. 'Loves me?' asked Vaslav in Russian. 'Yes, Vatsa, he loves you and so do I, and all of us, as ever.' *C'est adorable!* said Vaslav and laughed. His speech was mostly in French and it was vague and indifferent, occasionally betraying a hint of lucidity; he giggled at inappropriate moments.

That night, having helped bathe and shave and dress him, Lifar and Diaghilev took Vaslav to the Opéra to watch *Petrushka*. When Karsavina kissed him backstage, before the performance, she thought he knew her and was afraid to speak in case she interrupted a coalescing memory. A group photograph was taken – Vaslav smiled obediently, emptily; it is a photograph with 'all the tragedy and horror' of one of Goya's Los Caprichos etchings, which Vaslav had loved. Vaslav leant forward to look into Karsavina's eyes, but when she turned to face him, 'he again turned his head like a child that wants to hide tears. And that pathetic, shy, helpless movement went through my heart.' Harry Kessler saw him too. 'With his big eyes, like a sick animal, he gave me a look that was uncomprehending and yet deeply moving.' Throughout the evening he refused to take off his heavy overcoat. He showed no emotion during the evening except when Lifar came on stage as Petrushka. 'Who is that?' And then, 'Can he jump?'

Marie Rambert heard he was there and rushed upstairs to catch him before he left, racing through a maze of passages and staircases. At the top of the last flight of stairs she saw Diaghilev holding Vaslav's hand to lead him away; his anxious, hesitant shuffle. 'Then I saw that absolutely blank face, and I thought, "No, I'm not going to try to talk to him or touch his hand." It hurt me bitterly to see what had become of that marvellous human being.' It is interesting that of all the comments on Vaslav after 1919 only Rambert mourned the man, while everyone else (even Bronia, I think, was guilty of this at times) regretted the loss of the artist. Lydia Sokolova, who had shared Rambert's cabin on that fateful voyage on the Avon, would later write that she had often thought that if Rambert had been given the chance 'she could have done more than anyone else to keep him sane and happy'; perhaps she was right.

Both Diaghilev (to Harry Kessler) and Lifar said that Vaslav hadn't wanted to go home that night, saying firmly, '*Je ne veux pas!*' They had to take him back to Passy by force.

Diaghilev died in Venice six months later. That spring he had acquired another protégé, the sixteen-year-old piano prodigy Igor Markevitch (who was perhaps the 'modest, self-effacing, and utterly ruthless careerist who was about as fond of Diaghilev as Herod was of children' to whom Stravinsky referred), but it was Boris Kochno and Serge Lifar who nursed him through his last illness. At the end he was a very sad and world-weary man. Among his papers Lifar later found a phrase Diaghilev had jotted down on an article he had written about the Ballets Russes earlier that year: 'The longer the earth turns, the deader it gets.'

Misia Sert and Coco Chanel arrived in Venice to find their old friend shivering in bed in an old dinner jacket, despite the August heat. He was suffering from blood poisoning as a result of infected abscesses and it was obvious to them all how ill he was. He begged to be moved to a bed in another room, but Lifar refused to do it because of a superstition that to change beds meant death was near; then, horrified, they found him on the floor trying to crawl from one bed to the other.

Diaghilev died at dawn on 19 August 1929 after Misia forced a reluctant Catholic priest to give him the last rites (though lapsed, Diaghilev was Russian Orthodox) and then the pent-up jealousy between Lifar and Kochno exploded: they fought each other, rolling on the floor, tearing and biting at each other, 'like two mad dogs fighting over the body of their master'. At the funeral, both of them crawled to his grave on their knees and then Lifar tried to throw himself in after the coffin.

It was to Walter Nouvel, his friend for forty years, rather than Kochno or Lifar, that Diaghilev's old associates chose to express their grief at his death. Benois wrote to say that even though Diaghilev had played only a small part in his life in recent years and he had become used to feeling he no longer needed him, 'now, suddenly, it seems as if I'm still to a very great extent "filled with him"; he occupies a unique place in my spirit, in my mind and in my heart; he continues to be there and by old habit I continue to turn to him constantly, to ask his opinion and at the same time to worry about him and to live for his interest.'

And it was Nouvel, too, who best summed up Diaghilev, replying to Stravinsky's letter of heartfelt condolence. 'Many things united us, many things kept us apart. I often suffered because of him, I often got angry. But now, when he is in the grave, all is forgotten, all is forgiven, and I understood that one can't apply the normal measure of human relationships to this exceptional man.

'He lived and died "a favourite of the gods". For he was a pagan, and a Dionysian pagan – not an Apollonian. He loved everything earthly – earthly love, earthly passions, earthly beauty. Heaven for him was just a lovely dome above the lovely earth … He died in love and beauty, under the tender smile of those gods whom all his life he passionately served and worshipped.'

Although it is likely that Romola's first affair after marrying Vaslav was with Dr Frenkel in 1919–20 (he wanted to leave his wife for her and, when Romola refused him, developed a life-long addiction to morphine), the first time she lost her heart after losing it to Vaslav was to the glamorous, fast-living Hungarian silent movie star Lya de Putti whom she met in the United States in the late 1920s. De Putti had made it big as a vamp in the mould of Louise Brooks and Pola Negri, but her heavy accent hindered her transition to the stage or talkies. By the time she met Romola she was trying in vain to revive her career and drinking too much; their relationship was a savagely tempestuous one.

In April 1929 Romola wrote to the Binswangers (directors of the first Swiss clinic in which Nijinsky had stayed after being diagnosed) from the Savoy in London, asking them to collect Vaslav from Paris and take him back to Bellevue. The nurses they sent found him in a cell in Tessa's apartment, neglected, raving and smeared in faeces. At Bellevue throughout the 1930s his condition was stable but not easy to deal with, consisting of long periods of catatonia interspersed with states of frenzied excitement and regular masturbation. Romola gave orders that he should have no visitors.

Distracted by her new life, Romola visited him for the first time in three years in December 1929, and then again in 1934. By the time Kyra was eighteen, in 1932, Romola was bemoaning the fact that she could not yet hand over to her 'the burden of taking care of her father, [because] that would be asking too much'; previously she had complained that neither Bronia nor Diaghilev wanted to help her with his care. Despite having been dropped by the American ballet-lover who had taken her out of boarding school, Kyra had persevered with her dance-training and in 1931, at the age of seventeen, was living alone in Berlin before beginning to dance for her aunt Bronia, then directing a company for Ida Rubinstein. Bronia treated Kyra badly, according to another dancer, because she 'tries to act like she is somebody'.

Although de Putti had promised Romola she would pay Vaslav's hospital bills (and would have been able to, five years earlier), she died in 1931 from complications after having a chicken bone removed from her throat. Romola's next lover was a cross-dressing Dutchwoman,

Frederika Dezentje. When Kyra found the two women in bed together, Romola told her that she had chosen Dezentje because she did not want to betray her father's memory: 'the only man in this world I will ever love is Vaslav'.

Encouraged by Dezentje, Romola decided to write Vaslav's biography, hoping that book sales – and perhaps a movie biopic – would fund Vaslav's care and the extravagant lifestyle to which she felt entitled. The young Lincoln Kirstein, later founder (with George Balanchine) and director for over forty years of the New York City Ballet, agreed to help her write it. As 'supervisor cum ghostwriter', twenty-six-year-old Kirstein accompanied Romola to London in the summer of 1933 to begin the research. Dezentje had died suddenly the previous year and Romola wanted the book they had dreamt up together to be her memorial.

In Paris, Kirstein wrote on 3 June, Serge Lifar and George Balanchine, supported by Boris Kochno, were competing for the post of *maître de ballet* at the Opéra, a position controlled by Misia Sert (Lifar eventually prevailed). Bitter differences continued to divide the ballet community. Marie Rambert, Ninette de Valois and Lydia Lopokova were all ranged against one another. Sergey Grigoriev hated Lifar; Bronia hated Romola; Colonel de Basil, who had taken on the Ballets Russes after Diaghilev died, was falling out with Léonide Massine, his star. Only Karsavina managed to remain on good terms with everyone. These long-standing rivalries, dating back to Diaghilev's time, made Kirstein wonder how it would be possible to enlist the old members of Nijinsky's circle in Romola's project without antagonising anyone; hardly any of them were willing even to dance in a benefit to raise money for Nijinsky if the others were involved.

A month later a heavily powdered Ottoline Morrell told Kirstein that Vaslav had trusted her because they shared the same religious ideals, but then cancelled the appointment at which she had promised to elaborate further. Romola was desperate for money – partly to pay a medium, Ma Garrett, on whom she was dependent – and came up with increasingly wild schemes to raise funds. On 15 July she slid an astonishing note under Kirstein's hotel room door, telling him that she was divorcing

Vaslav to marry Lifar, who had agreed to dance in Nijinsky's gala. 'Long talk later,' noted Kirstein. 'Difficulty of obtaining a divorce, since they were married in Argentina. None of this is a caprice; it is a means of getting back into the big world; ultimately of supporting Vaslav.' For all his sympathy for Romola, Kirstein added an incredulous '(?!)' on this page.

Romola's myth-making *Nijinsky*, edited in part by critic and writer Arnold Haskell and dedicated to Dezentje, was published in 1934 and became a bestseller. But while it eased Romola's financial worries, the portrait she unwittingly painted of herself was of a manipulative, selfish and superficial woman and the book turned both her daughters against her (there was no mention of Tamara at all) and made public her old rift with Bronia. The following year, Stravinsky (aided by Nouvel) published the first volume of his autobiography in which he was bitingly derogatory about Nijinsky's choreography for *Sacre*. By then his masterpiece had already been hailed (possibly initially by Diaghilev) as being what, for the twentieth century, Beethoven's Ninth Symphony was for the nineteenth.

Hoping to capitalise on the interest in his old schoolmate, in 1937 Anatole Bourman brought out *The Tragedy of Nijinsky*. Aggressively ghostwritten by Miss D. Lyman, it placed Bourman at the heart of Vaslav's story for almost fifteen years and present at every important event in his life. Although Bourman had been Vaslav's contemporary at the Imperial Theatre School and had danced in the Ballets Russes's *corps*, and so cannot be discounted, many of the scenes he and Lyman described, especially later in Nijinsky's life, were entirely invented. But, as Kirstein would observe, 'sometimes one can snatch the residue of Bourman's actual reminiscences from the airy lies of his collaborator'.

The same year Romola published a severely cut (by almost half) and edited version of Vaslav's diary. The polished result was intended to make Nijinsky sound like a noble, romantic, tormented genius, so she removed all references to defecation and most references to sex and rearranged the structure to make it more coherent. Any unflattering descriptions of her – for example, 'My wife is an untwinkling star' – were left out.

She had asked Sigmund Freud's advice about Vaslav, but he bluntly told her analysis was no use in dealing with schizophrenia; Carl Jung (another friend of Binswanger's) also refused to get involved. When she approached Alfred Adler, he was willing to look at Vaslav's case – and at her request wrote a piece intended to be the introduction to the published diary – but she disagreed with his conclusions and did not use his article. Adler theorised that Vaslav suffered from an inferiority complex. His life had been a series of punishments: 'punishment at school for being a prodigy; from Diaghilev, his surrogate father, for creating masterpieces, as a god might challenge his creator; punishment for marrying Romola'. Adler recommended greater understanding of his problems; Romola just thought he needed better – or more – medicine.

The drama critic John Heilpern, whose 1982 article in *The Times* revealed Adler's suppressed work on Nijinsky, agreed with many of Vaslav's friends that Romola was more a part of his problem than its cure. Having trapped him into marriage, and into a cycle of needing to dance for money, he 'fought back ... finding cover from her domination behind his illness while enslaving her with his dependency'. Tamara Nijinsky could not argue with this assessment of their destructive interdependence. While her mother was fond of 'this exceptional, gentle human being, guilt and anger must have entered her soul for maybe ruining his life', and – though Tamara did not say this – quite possibly also for Vaslav ruining hers.

In 1937 Nijinsky's family gathered for the first and only time at Kreuzlingen. Tamara came from Budapest with Emilia and Oskar Padany and Tessa, her aunt; and Kyra joined them with her new husband – not by coincidence, Igor Markevitch, Diaghilev's last protégé – and their baby son, Vaslav. Although Romola had barely seen Vaslav for over a decade she still 'complained about everything' to the doctors at Bellevue and was as negligent about paying her bills as Diaghilev. Tamara said that when Romola was with Vaslav, 'she was every inch the gentle, devoted and understanding wife ... And then, the incredible metamorphosis – the moment he was out of sight the poised, cold, elusive Romola was back.' She was, Tamara wrote elsewhere, 'incapable of showing unfeigning warmth and tenderness toward a child'.

Romola would not allow anyone else, even the nurses, to be alone with Vaslav. Once when she was called to the telephone, Tamara, aged seventeen, was left with her father for a few minutes. Nervously she picked him a bunch of flowers. 'Silently, he gazed at the daisies, lifted them upward to the sky ... like an offering, then sank back in his chair, shut his eyes, and pressed the flowers to his heart.' Even behind the veil of madness Nijinsky's eloquence as an actor was unmistakable.

Later that year Anton Dolin organised a charity gala to raise funds for Nijinsky's care, at which he danced with Margot Fonteyn and, in the most beautiful moment of the evening (for Dolin), Tamara Karsavina talked about her memories of Vaslav. Ottoline and Philip Morrell were members of the committee of the new Nijinsky Foundation, formed with the proceeds. The money was desperately needed because Romola had decided – against the wishes of the Binswangers – to have Vaslav treated with insulin shock therapy. These massive (and expensive) injections were designed by Dr Manfred Sakel (now discredited) to provoke severe hypoglycaemic shock that would jolt the patient's system out of insanity.

By modern standards, the amount of medication Vaslav was given was staggering – insulin, bromides, barbiturates, morphine, neuroleptics, scopolamine, opium – but Romola was determined to believe he would recover. After his insulin cure began, she let it be known that soon Nijinsky would be dancing once again and in 1940 she released a photograph of them, their faces strained in rictuses of optimism.

In about 1939 Lifar visited him for the third time, with Romola, his brother Leonid Lifar and some press photographers; another gala was planned and they wanted to promote it. After the shock therapy, he found Vaslav more sociable and less obviously anguished – his nail beds were no longer torn and bloody – but the shy, childlike, confiding smile was gone. He talked to himself constantly, mostly unintelligibly, in a mixture of languages. When he was offered strawberries, he ate them with exquisite delicacy, exclaiming, 'How good! How good!'

Lifar wanted to dance for Vaslav (and the photographers) and he changed into practice clothes and began warming up at a barre which had been installed for him. Behind him Vaslav said, 'You might fall into the air.' Romola and Leonid Lifar were astonished when, after Lifar had performed *Faune* with Vaslav correcting his steps, Vaslav joined in as Lifar danced *Le Spectre de la Rose*, executing an *entrechat-six*, a *bourrée* and some *cabrioles*. When they had finished, Vaslav giggled and retreated back into his private world.

Convinced that Vaslav was better in her care than at Kreuzlingen, and with nowhere else to go and no way of obtaining papers or passports in wartime (a particularly difficult task because most countries, including Britain and the United States, were reluctant to admit someone with a mental illness, even if he was Nijinsky), Romola took Vaslav to Budapest when war broke out.

They arrived in 1940 to find Emilia and Oskar had left the city rather than being there to welcome them home. Though family tensions again ran nearly as high as international ones, Tamara was overjoyed to be with her father for the second time in her life. Torn between her warring grandmother and mother, aware of the violence simmering inside her father – once she watched him smash Emilia's favourite chair to splinters – most of the time she 'simply relished being in his presence because there he always radiated serenity and love'.

When life in Budapest became too dangerous for Vaslav and Romola, as well as for Emilia and Oskar (though he had converted to marry Emilia, he had been born Jewish and they were sheltering Jews in their house), the Nijinskys moved for a few months to Lake Balaton before receiving a visit from the local police who suspected them of being Russian agents. They returned to Budapest and then found a rented house outside the capital. In 1943 they moved closer to the Austrian border to await the longed-for German retreat, living very humbly in a tiny hamlet in the woods.

They survived desperate living conditions and heavy American bombing throughout 1944 and into 1945. One day Romola arrived home to find a dust-covered Vaslav standing silently in a roofless room. Sometimes he stayed at the local hospital, where she hoped he might be safer, until the afternoon when he was brought home by a nurse who told her they had received orders to exterminate their mental patients the following morning. In March 1945 the Western press reported that the Nazis had killed Nijinsky, but that August he was seen alive again. Because they were using false papers there was no way of looking for or identifying them.

The war brought out Romola's best qualities: charm, resourcefulness, energy and devotion. Mr Quand, the ballet-loving young general manager of the National Bank of Hungary, whom Romola had invited herself to meet when she and Vaslav needed money, always magically managed to replenish their account when it looked as though it might be empty. For five years she managed to keep them both fed, clothed and alive, while she looked after a seriously ill man in the most challenging of conditions.

The Russian soldiers who occupied their part of Hungary near Sopron once peace was declared gave Vaslav a new lease of life. For the first time for many years he could speak Russian once again, and shyly he began to engage with them, listening to their folk songs and stories, even dancing with them as they sat around their campfires.

With peacetime came their first move, along with Romola's devoted cousin Paul, to Vienna where the manager of the Sacher Hotel agreed to allow them to stay. While they were in Vienna they were 'found' by Margaret Power, a ballet-loving widow of thirty-seven who worked for the Allied Commission in Vienna. Before she left London, Cyril Beaumont had told her to try and look out for the Nijinskys, as they would almost certainly be in need of money and help. She brought them a parcel of tea, biscuits, chocolate and toothpaste and became very close to Vaslav. Although he barely spoke, he expressed his affection for her in gentle patting. 'I fell in love with him with Vienna,' Power told biographer Richard Buckle, 'and have remained so ever since.'

In Vienna, the Russians made a bid to woo Vaslav back home, putting on a performance in his honour at the Ronacher Theatre by the company which was the descendant of the old Mariinsky, inheritors of the traditions with which he had grown up. It began with a piece from the *Nutcracker Suite* and went on to include Russian and Polish national dances and a gypsy *divertissement*, before ending with *Les Sylphides*. Vaslav followed the dancers with perceptible movements of his own body and at the end applauded with all the abandon of a student.

Romola was increasingly obsessed by the hope that Vaslav might return to sanity, issuing reports in 1945 of his 'complete recovery' and proposing to the Met in New York that he might even be well enough to dance *Petrushka* for them. But her ideas were roundly condemned in a *News Review* article of October that year: Lydia Lopokova declared her sadness at the prospect and cabled Vaslav not to make the attempt; the Met was accused of 'sensation mongering and bad taste' and Tamara Karsavina was provoked to an outspoken 'cruel, very cruel'.

In the summer of 1946, helped by the money left over in the Nijinsky Foundation's account and by Margaret Power and Anton Dolin, who had been raising money for Vaslav in America during the war, Vaslav and Romola went to Switzerland again. Power visited occasionally from Vienna and played table tennis with Vaslav. 'Sometimes he would kiss my cheek, always quite unexpectedly – not in greeting or farewell, but just out of affection.'

Late the following year Romola obtained her British passport and permission for Vaslav to live in England too. After spending Christmas of 1948 in a hotel courtesy of Romola's friend Alexander Korda, they rented a house near Windsor. Still focused on his recovery, Romola hoped to take Vaslav to America to consult doctors there. She and Lifar paraded Vaslav in front of press cameras to publicise a gala performance in November to raise money for the trip, but it brought in an inadequate £132 rather than the £1,000 they had been expecting; grandly Romola refused the money, donating it instead to the Sadler's Wells Benevolent Fund.

Encountering him at the BBC in 1950, Arnold Haskell thought Vaslav looked like 'a plump and well-contented suburban commercial traveller. He watched the proceedings [a reheasal of a Lifar ballet] with no interest and the only reaction I saw was one of pleasure when the tea was brought in.' A journalist who met him during this period described him as being 'like a docile child until he flashed an eternally-wise smile that made everybody else in the room seem a thousand years behind him'.

In early 1950 they moved to a house in Sussex. 'Like gypsies,' Vaslav said sadly as Romola packed their things again. Despite living a more normal life than he had done for decades, Vaslav's physical health was declining and on 8 April 1950 he died quietly of kidney failure after a short illness, with Romola at his side. He only had £30 to leave to her. Although, because of the rift with Romola, Vaslav had barely seen her in recent years, Kyra was named as his daughter in the obituaries; there was no mention of a second child.

His first funeral was held at the Catholic Church in Spanish Place, St James's, on 14 April. At the last minute George Balanchine could not come, so the pall-bearers were Serge Lifar, Anton Dolin, Frederick Ashton, Richard Buckle, Michael Somes and Cyril Beaumont. Of these, Buckle noted, only Beaumont had seen Nijinsky 'in his glory'. Lifar laid a wreath of primroses by the grave. It was a beautiful spring day; the buds on the trees were about to burst into leaf. The mourners at the burial at the Marylebone cemetery in Finchley Road included Marie Rambert, Tamara Karsavina and Lydia Sokolova, as well as Margaret Power and the Indian dancer, Ram Gopal.

His second funeral was held in Paris at the Russian Church in the rue Daru on 16 June 1953. Three years after Nijinsky's death, Serge Lifar had arranged for his body to be reinterred in the cemetery at Montmartre near Auguste Vestris's grave – and perhaps more significantly, beside Lifar's own plot. Margaret Power accompanied the coffin to Paris because Romola was in America. Bronia was there, and Mathilde Kshesinskaya, and Tamara Nijinsky. She remembered the 'saintly' priest in white by the grave, who 'spoke of the beauty of Vaslav's life, of the talent given to him by God and of the wonderful beauty and pleasure he was able to give to the people who saw him. He said that the joy which Vaslav gave to us was still with us, held in precious memory in our hearts.'

A libretto for a ballet based on Nijinsky's life (*with apologies*)

ACT ONE

St Petersburg. A window- and mirror-lined
classroom at the Imperial Theatre School.

A teacher (Fokine) is leading a class of six young ballet students in their barre exercises. Gradually, as the class becomes more challenging, it becomes clear that one of the boys (Nijinsky) is far more accomplished than his peers. One by one they fall back, leaving Nijinsky dancing in a competition of leaping and turning virtuosity with his closest rival (Georgy Rozai). Once Rozai has reluctantly admitted defeat, Nijinsky dances alone with Fokine, following but exceeding him. Even Fokine stops dancing to marvel at him and when Nijinsky finally comes to a standstill after a dazzling solo they rush to congratulate him.

As Fokine is shaking Nijinsky's hand, an imposing dark man (Diaghilev) with a silver streak in his hair, wearing a black cape, enters the classroom. (Mitsouko wafts out over the audience.) He is attended by two followers (Bakst, small and fiery, with a dapper ginger moustache; and Benois, dark and heavily bearded). Fokine invites them to watch Nijinsky dance. He performs part of *Le Spectre de la Rose*, with

Diaghilev, whom Fokine has solicitously seated in a wooden classroom chair, inadvertently acting the part of the girl. Diaghilev is cynical at first and then won over. As the curtain falls and the music dies away, he is standing, his clapping the only sound in the theatre.

ACT TWO

Paris. A theatre presented side on with the curtain running perpendicular to the stage, so that the left side of the stage is backstage and the right faces an invisible audience.

Nijinsky, still in his practice clothes, and Diaghilev in white tie, are backstage as, amid the intermittent flurry of stage-setting onstage, other Nijinskys dance solos from his celebrated roles – Armida's Slave, Zobéïde's Slave and Petrushka. At first they are clearly together, very much a couple, but by the time Petrushka is dancing his tragic piece backstage Nijinsky is isolated, dreamily practising steps alone or sometimes with a girl (Karsavina) in a white practice tutu and pink tights, while Diaghilev is surrounded by a fawning, bickering entourage of Fokine, Benois, Bakst, Stravinsky and Misia Sert, costumed almost as caricatures of themselves (Misia, for example, very buxom, glittering with jewels and with a feather almost as tall as her sprouting from her headband; Igor, bald, bespectacled and fussy).

During Petrushka's solo a young blonde girl (Romola) in street clothes drags a wicker costume basket from backstage closer to where Petrushka is dancing. At first she sits on it smoking and swinging her legs, occasionally examining her nails and making eyes at backstage Nijinsky, who appears not to notice. Sometimes she jumps down and rummages through the basket, holding costumes up to herself; or smiles and waves over-animatedly to one of the other people backstage; increasingly she stares at Petrushka and then the Faun, her chin propped on her hand.

Midway through the Faun's piece, he notices that Diaghilev, Bakst,

Fokine and backstage Nijinsky are arguing backstage. He comes back-stage and dances around them, as if trying to distract them, but they do not notice him and he comes to centre-stage to finish his piece. Romola jumps up and watches him from uncomfortably close range, amazed by his performance; the others, storming off after their argument, have not seen it.

Backstage Nijinsky sits alone in a corner at the front left of the stage, his head in his hands, while the Tennis Player from *Jeux* comes out and dances with Romola and Diaghilev centre-stage (an echo of Wayne Eagling's recent version of *Jeux* for the English National Ballet). The curtain falls as Romola triumphantly whirls into the wings with the Tennis Player.

ACT THREE

New York. A studio.

Nijinsky is rehearsing a group of dancers for *Till Eulenspiegel*. As he fin-ishes demonstrating his final solo, Diaghilev, Bakst and Stravinsky walk in and begin moving the other dancers around, instructing the pianist how to play, discussing the set among themselves. Every time Nijinsky tries to contribute they wave him away like an annoying child; eventu-ally he just continues practising alone on the side of the stage while the others carry on talking and gesticulating without him.

Romola sweeps in, wearing a fur coat and showing off a sparkling ring. Diaghilev and his friends ignore her. She rushes up to Nijinsky and urges him to challenge Diaghilev for insulting her. They end up fighting over Nijinsky, who is trying to intervene. In a scene reminiscent of the final act of *Petrushka*, Diaghilev accidentally knocks Nijinsky down as he tries to hit Romola and then Romola drags Nijinsky's limp, twitching body away.

The stage empties and darkens. A metal bed is wheeled onto the stage, with a straitjacketed figure lying on it. As the figure rises, we see that it is Nijinsky. He struggles against his bonds and then falls back exhausted. Then, as if by magic, on his third effort he extracts himself from the constraints and comes to the front of the stage where he dances alone. At first his dancing is strange and fragmented, like the descriptions of the Montenegro or Suvretta House performances; then it becomes something else entirely. Like Petrushka's or Till Eulenspiegel's ghost, Nijinsky seems to be dancing as himself for the first time – perhaps something from Russell Maliphant's *AfterLight*. The curtain falls.

CHAPTER 10

The Chosen One

LONG BEFORE HE DIED, Nijinsky's legend was being written. Even when she no longer needed, as she saw it, to promote her husband's memory in order to raise funds for his care, the indomitable Romola 'refused to accept that his name' – and her importance as his wife – 'might fade into oblivion'. Without her, it is almost possible to imagine that Nijinsky might live on today in nothing more than old press cuttings and photographs and in the memories of a handful of artists who danced with someone who once danced with him.

Until she died in 1978, Romola controlled the myth she had in large part created. Richard Buckle, author of the only major English biography of Nijinsky, published in 1971, was scrupulously careful to satisfy her demands when his book came out, but after her death he issued an addendum saying that she had deliberately sensationalised and in places falsified her account of Nijinsky's life to make money. 'And who could blame her?' he asked. 'She had to look after her sick husband.' Her daughter Tamara described her mother as imperious and self-assured, which was 'both her strength and her weakness. Did she know when she crossed the borderline between fact and fiction?'

This is the most generous interpretation of her actions. Others – like the psychiatrist Peter Ostwald, whose 1991 account of Nijinsky's life focused on his mental health – have portrayed her as a villainess. Reviewing Ostwald, Roy Porter described Romola as 'truly awful ... a hysterical egotist, greedy for fame but talentless', who confined Vaslav to a series of uncaring asylums which she then blamed for his failure to recover and, when she was not looking after him – which was most of the time – swanned around the world living off his name and milking the role of martyr to art and love.

In the last decades of her life, Romola lived between Switzerland, Japan and the States, jealously guarding the manuscript of Nijinsky's diaries (it was sold to a private collector the year after her death for £45,000 and is now in the New York Public Library), bickering with Serge Lifar over which of them would lie next to Nijinsky's grave in Montparnasse Cemetary (Lifar had not mentioned to her when he moved Nijinsky's body that he planned to lie beside it) and following the spectacular racehorse named after her husband wherever he was running.

Both Karsavina and Rambert tried desperately to avoid her on her flying visits to London. The producer John Drummond encountered her in an office at the BBC in the 1960s. Her hair was dyed a brassy red and she wore a moth-eaten fur coat. She was saying, 'You know, they all got it wrong; I was the only woman Diaghilev liked ...' – rather a bold statement, even for her.

Romola had become alienated from both her children and they barely spoke to one another (she told Kyra's son that Tamara was not Nijinsky's daughter). In 1960, at the age of forty-seven, Kyra entered a Franciscan order as a lay sister. She believed her father had not been mentally ill but broken by the brutality of his surroundings and she found consolation – as he had tried to – in an intense spirituality. In 1991 Tamara wrote a brave and compassionate book about her parents' relationship which she dedicated to her grandson – the child of a daughter from whom she in turn was estranged – so that he could 'feel pride in the past'.

Kyra, who danced several of his roles for Marie Rambert, among others, in the 1930s, was astonishingly like her father physically, with the same powerful, compact body and the same compelling expression of feline grace in her slanted eyes. In the late 1940s Igor Markevitch, by then separated from Kyra, was in Venice with their teenage son Vaslav. An elderly man approached them. 'Very strange. There was a Russian dancer who used to come here before the First War. He was very famous. The boy reminds me of him.' The boy would grow up to be a painter, Vaslav Markevitch.

The other great moulder of Nijinsky's legend was Diaghilev, Svengali to his Trilby and, in the mythology of the Ballets Russes, somehow almost his rival. In the early, first-hand literature about the Ballets Russes – the accounts of Benois and Nouvel (through Arnold Haskell), of Lifar and Massine, Stravinsky and Cocteau, Fokine and Monteux, and of Romola herself – there is an unseemly rush to denigrate each other's contributions and beneath it all the sense of an underlying, unspoken (and spurious) question: who was greater, the Showman or Petrushka?

The first and perhaps the greatest thing Diaghilev did for his friend was to provide him with an arena in which art was exalted into the noblest of pursuits. Lynn Garafola phrases it best. His 'generosity [to his protégés, Nijinsky being the first among equals] was boundless: he gave them all the accumulated wisdom of his years and all the fruits of his broad experience, in addition to a knowledge of the arts, an appreciation of aesthetics, and an introduction to anyone who was anyone in the circles of high bohemia. Money was no object: he paid for months of experiments in the studio and hundreds of rehearsal hours with dancers, for music by the greatest composers and sets by the finest artists. No Pygmalion ever served his Galatea as devotedly as Diaghilev served his lover-choreographers.'

However, the very intensity of this generosity – and what was expected in return – was untenable. The sacrifices Art and Beauty demanded were great: no home, no rest, no friends except those with whom Diaghilev surrounded himself, nothing permitted except the one overriding aim – immortality. Champagne was allowed, but Vaslav seldom drank. Diaghilev may have made his favourites into gods (as Marie Rambert put it) but none of them could 'sustain it [without him] …

Not at the height at which they were with him, because it was too high for anyone.'

Diaghilev created, in the Ballets Russes, something that was immeasurably greater than the sum of its parts. He 'was the permeating genius who was behind it, through it, around it and before it; responsible in undefinable ways (as well as those that are definably within the province of a director) for every gesture, light and shade, and measure of tempo. Of all the great artists he has trained, which one ever achieved without him that which was possible with him?' Nijinsky was not the only one of Diaghilev's spurned or disgruntled colleagues who could never replicate the creative atmosphere they had experienced alongside him.

Perhaps this is where the problem lies. Ultimately Diaghilev fell out with most of the people with whom he worked and on whom he depended, whether they were friends or lovers. He tried to bind his collaborators to him by creating an almost claustrophobic sense of family within his company and, in Vaslav's case, by relying too quickly on him to be his only choreographer, without allowing him a period of apprenticeship (Fokine by contrast had several years, between 1900 when he began composing and 1907 when Pavlova danced his Dying Swan, to hone his ideas away from the public eye) or enough time off; and, when they chafed against his dominion, he turned almost vengefully against them.

But the great achievement of this volatile group of artists, apart from their work, was their propagation of ballet, as we know it today, across the world. The diaspora of the Ballets Russes would promote or found national or municipal companies in six continents in the decades after Diaghilev's death and this is perhaps the greatest legacy of Diaghilev's genius for attracting, recognising and nurturing talent.

Many of these artists had known and worked with Nijinsky and they preserved a quite different memory of him than that disseminated by Romola or Diaghilev. Marie Rambert, for example, had danced the role of a Nymph in Nijinsky's 1913 production of *Faune*. Later she would go on to mount the ballet herself for the company that would become the Ballet Rambert, her own memorial to the man she had loved.

Diaghilev's later lovers form an interesting subsection of this group because apart from Massine none of them met Nijinsky until after his breakdown, but their collective obsession with him – I do not think that is too strong a word – would colour their subsequent careers. 'Any outstanding work of merit in my career with the Russian Ballet was inspired by a man I had never known, and then by the haunting memory of someone I had seen more as a vision than as a living person,' Anton Dolin would write.

In his books Serge Lifar claimed that Nijinsky had been merely Diaghilev's cypher as a choreographer, parroting back what a bitter Diaghilev had almost certainly told him – that he had been responsible for everything good about Nijinsky's ballets and dismissing the rest – and yet he moved heaven and earth (nearly), braving Romola's wrath, to get Nijinsky's body to Paris so that they could lie beside one another for all eternity – leaving Diaghilev, the man he had called his soulmate, alone in a Venetian cemetery.

This issue – of who was responsible for what – dogs all Diaghilev's collaborators, but Nijinsky in particular. It was Fokine to whom Diaghilev was referring when he declared he could make a choreographer out of an inkstand, but he damned them all by implication; only Balanchine, whose later career eclipsed the work he did for Diaghilev, escaped this taint. In Spain in 1916 Diaghilev blithely told Nijinsky that he had explained to Massine all the steps and gestures for *Les Femmes de bonne humeur*, which Massine then showed the other dancers – just what he would later say to Lifar about Nijinsky and *Faune*.

I find it interesting that Diaghilev (or his promoters) could in one breath claim Nijinsky's work as his own and in the next dismiss it as uncommercial, intellectually inadequate and immature. Surely if he really had created *Sacre*, for instance, as he claimed to Lifar, he would not have dropped it from the Ballet's repertoire so quickly. It is no accident that when, in the late 1920s, interest in *Sacre* had been rekindled but *Jeux* was still considered Nijinsky's weakest ballet, Diaghilev told Lifar that *Sacre* was wholly his but the part he had played in *Jeux* was 'much more limited'. Vaslav knew he did it: in his diaries he wrote, 'I know that Diaghilev likes saying they [the ballets] are his, because he likes praise'. 'Diaghilev did not like me, because I composed ballets by myself. He did not want me to do things by myself that went against his grain.'

Almost everyone involved with the Ballets Russes at one time or another sought to trumpet their own achievements at the expense of their collaborators. Lifar quotes Benois saying that, 'It was we, the painters – not the professional stage painters, but the real painters – who, profoundly attracted by the stage, took up stage design and so helped mould the art of dancing along new lines.' Massine also attempted to play down Diaghilev's role. 'We were all of us caught up in the violence of the artistic creation in Paris of the period. No escape was possible, and the ballet expressed what the poets, painters and musicians had to say ... Diaghilev followed.'

Many of them tried to do this at Nijinsky's expense; Nijinsky, who could not answer back. As Lincoln Kirstein, to whom Nijinsky owes in great part the rehabilitation of his reputation from the 1970s onwards, observed, it was 'convenient for many reasons for Cocteau (who knows perhaps more than anyone), even for Fokine, for his other colleagues, dancers and musicians, to keep either a deprecatory silence about his creative expression (apart from his dancing) or to flatly run it down'. In short, making Nijinsky look bad often made his collaborators or successors look good, and regardless of her motivations the only person who cared about this, to begin with, was Romola.

The battle between Diaghilev and Romola is another epic element of the Nijinsky myth. It is true that, as Arnold Haskell wrote, Diaghilev was uninterested in personal gain and had always lived precariously for the sake of Art: every penny he had 'went into his dreams'. His pursuit by Romola through the law courts for the salary Nijinsky had been neither paid nor, it has to be said, promised, was a body blow. It is possible that, as Nijinsky imagined when he married, he might have been able to return to Diaghilev's artistic bosom (if not his physical one), as Benois and Fokine had, if it hadn't been for Romola's refusal to compromise with the man she knew her husband would always consider his mentor.

It is also clear in her biography of Nijinsky that Romola thrilled to her duel with Diaghilev, pitting her wits and determination against this magnificent rival. With undisguised glee she recounted her first interview with Diaghilev, during which she convinced him that she was in love with Bolm and had barely noticed Nijinsky, and procured his permission to follow the Ballet by playing on his desire to impress her friend, an influential critic. On the surface, she wrote, a debonair impresario was granting a request to a young society girl; 'in reality, two powerful enemies had crossed swords for the first time ...[a] fine, covert duel ... was being fought between and behind words'. When she left the room with permission to take lessons with Cecchetti, 'I could scarcely believe I had succeeded in fooling such an inconceivably clever man'. She presented herself as having saved Nijinsky, a captive genius, from the evil Showman: a knight in a fairytale, with Vaslav cast as princess.

But Romola's depiction of her battle with the dragon is 'all the more misleading through being nearly accurate on so many points, and always highly plausible'. Diaghilev *was* an arch-manipulator; he was furious with Nijinsky for leaving him and he did undoubtedly want to diminish him in the most wounding way he knew how – as an artist – as punishment for that humiliation and heartbreak; but the thought that he was engaged with Romola in some kind of Miltonian struggle for possession of Nijinsky is laughable, and evidence only of her capacity for grandiose self-deception.

Romola's unpopularity, and the image she propagated of her husband as half-victim, half-saint, both kept his name on people's lips and turned many others in the field of dance against him. Quite deliberately, and for her own purposes, she had contravened Anna Pavlova's tenet that a great 'artist should show himself to the public only on stage, never in private life' and the fact that she insisted so vehemently on his genius made many determined to reject it.

While today the mere mention of Nijinsky's name can cause shivers of delight among his devotees, with one modern writer, the poet, Wayne Koestonbaum, riffing djinn, jinx, sky in an effort to quantify its enchantment, by the 1930s it had become 'a sign of connoisseurship not to like Nijinsky'. His role in *Schéhérazade* had become an object of parody – by none other than Balanchine. The 1949 *Dance Encyclopedia* (published the year after the film *The Red Shoes*, partly based on Diaghilev and Nijinsky's relationship, came out) even claimed that a 'Nijinsky conspiracy' was keeping his feeble flame alight. 'So few people, comparatively speaking, ever saw Nijinsky dance, that if his fame were based on his actual appearances before the public, he would now have been completely forgotten ... his role in the history of ballet and his influence on the art of ballet are extremely modest.'

The second great gift Diaghilev gave Nijinsky was making him the star of his ballets, the central figure on stage rather than an accessory to a ballerina. For the first time since the early nineteenth century, audiences came to see a male dancer – not a *porteur* but a supreme artist – and for him not just solos but entire ballets were composed around a male central figure. Diaghilev did this because he was erotically in thrall to Nijinsky. He saw him as beautiful and desirable and he presented him on stage as beautiful and desirable.

Diaghilev's private passion for Nijinsky was a defining aspect of his public success as a dancer. Whatever really happened between them, physically or emotionally, for me this is their love story, the truest expression of their partnership – why, if for no other reason, they were in some romantic sense meant to be together and why they will always be remembered as inextricably linked: Diaghilev catching his breath in a darkened theatre watching Nijinsky dance; audience and performer united by the intensity of their desire, in their different ways, to capture the same perfection.

Nijinsky came to prominence at a time of deep-seated confusion about sex and gender and at the start of a century of change that would transform how Western society viewed dissenters from the norm. Freud published his first articles on sexuality and the unconscious in the 1890s. Despite flourishing 'gay scenes' in Paris, Berlin and St Petersburg, homosexual scandals were still rocking the established order all over Europe: Oscar Wilde's case was the most notorious, but even political trials like those of Alfred Dreyfus in France and Roger Casement in Ireland had homosexual subtexts. At the same time, gay men with public profiles like Wilde and Diaghilev were increasingly unwilling to disguise or deny their preferences.

Women were also subverting traditional roles on a broader level, with the suffragettes demanding a say in government but also privately refusing to accept nineteenth-century stereotypes of how they should behave. Ida Rubinstein commissioned a ballet in which she played St Sebastian; other prominent but unfeminine women of the time, many of whom Nijinsky knew, included Virginia Woolf, Sarah Bernhardt, Edith Sitwell, Zinaida Gippius and even his sister Bronia.

Diaghilev laboured under no illusions about himself. He knew he was gay and what was more he believed being gay was better than being straight – all the proof he thought he needed was that throughout history the great creators from Socrates to Christ to Leonardo had been homosexual (evidently it never occurred to him that women have not had the same opportunities to be creative). One of the things he and Stravinsky always disagreed about was his prosyletising insistence that Stravinsky would be a greater artist if he could detach himself from women.

With regard to the ballet in general, 'although he was showman enough to emphasise the beauty of the female body' on stage, Diaghilev's preference for boyish slenderness (he used to say, 'there is nothing uglier than a woman's thighs') made him ban short classical tutus for all his dancers except those with the longest, thinnest legs and shaped the attenuated physique that prevailed for female dancers throughout the twentieth century. Nicolas Nabokov, cousin of Vladimir and a composer who worked with Diaghilev in the 1920s, believed that Diaghilev deliberately embraced the 'scandal' of his homosexuality in promoting the Ballets Russes and Nijinsky. 'The risk, and the sense of otherness, was a powerful source of Diaghilev's mystique, and he used it knowingly.'

Thus, according to Richard Buckle, did Nijinsky's entrance on stage in his pearl choker as Armida's Slave in Paris in 1909 speed 'this most homosexual of centuries on its vertiginous course'. Throughout the century an interest in dance in general and the Ballets Russes and Diaghilev and Nijinsky in particular was a signal of unmasculine interests and intentions: in *A Queer History of the Ballet* (2007), Peter Stoneley lists as examples of this the young Harold Acton dancing instead of playing football at Eton and Edmund White as a boy imitating the Favourite Slave in his mother's turban. Almost unwittingly Nijinsky became a gay icon, for want of a better phrase: a beacon for homosexual men and women charting a new course, moving away from needing to keep their true selves hidden from the world.

One of these people, strangely enough, may have been Romola Nijinsky herself. Although it was not until Buckle's biography of Nijinsky that his relationship with Diaghilev was discussed openly – coinciding with the advent of the gay liberation movement – Romola played her own part in this aspect of Nijinsky's legend. After his breakdown, her great loves were women, and the books she wrote about Nijinsky make absolutely clear both what the relationship between her husband and Diaghilev was and that she understood the nature of it. 'To make Sergey Pavlovich happy was no sacrifice to Vaslav,' she wrote. 'And Diaghilev crushed any idea of resistance, which might have come up in the young man's mind, by the familiar tales of the Greeks, of Michelangelo and Leonardo, whose creative lives depended on the same intimacy as their own. The relationship between them was so real that it was therefore universally taken for granted. Diaghilev and Nijinsky were one in private life …'

Despite all her fame being attached to her role as a devoted wife, Buckle called Romola 'predominantly homosexual'; certainly her sexuality was complex. Repeatedly in writing about her husband she marvelled at his ability to assume a woman's form, imitating the peasant dances and gypsy girls he had seen in his youth and dancing for her the women's roles in the ballets he was creating in the mid-1910s, and the way it stimulated her. 'Never, never, have I seen among all the great *prima ballerinas* anybody so tender, so maidenly, so light, so harmonious, so perfect in their attitudes, and so matchlessly equal on their toes.'

Apparently he even planned a ballet for her, based on Pierre Louÿs's *Les Chansons de Bilitis*, arranged by Debussy, the story of a young Greek girl of antiquity who, in the first act, has as her lover a shepherd and, in the second, another young girl – a fable Romola evidently saw as a mirror for her own life.

Just as much as Diaghilev, Romola was attracted by Vaslav's androgynous quality on stage and acclaimed it as an element of his genius. Sometimes, she wrote, she felt like the women of mythology must have felt when a god made love to them, because despite the intensity of his passion there was always something unattainable about Nijinsky. Her bias was echoed by Nijinsky's first biographer Buckle, who was too young to have seen him dance. He described an awkwardness for Vaslav 'in the normal man–woman relationship in ballet', implying that he needed to wear a mask to convincingly partner a woman.

But Haskell commented rightly that it was absurd to call Nijinsky effeminate just because he was beautiful on stage; indeed, in *Schéhérazade* and *Faune* it was his overwhelming virility that shocked audiences. Most observers who did see him have made clear that Nijinsky was not feminine, on stage or off. Cyril Beaumont said that rather than seeming to be either overtly masculine or overtly feminine, he appeared instead 'of a race apart, of another essence than ourselves, an impression heightened by his partiality for unusual roles, which were either animal-like, mythological or unreal. On the stage he seemed surrounded by some invisible yet susceptible halo.'

While it is impossible and irrelevant now to try to assess whether Nijinsky was a masculine presence on stage or not – by yesterday or today's standards – what is evident is that for audiences he 'made the relation between the dancer's sexuality and the dancer's art absolute', whatever vocabulary the critics used. His work expressed 'Freud's chart of man's developing psyche,' according to Lincoln Kirstein in 1970: 'in *Faune*, adolescent self-discovery and gratification; in *Jeux*, homosexual discovery of another self or selves; in *Le Sacre du printemps*, fertility and renewal of the race.' 'If the trilogy of *Faune*, *Jeux* and *Sacre* has any biographical meaning at all,' dance critic Arlene Croce wrote in 1982, 'it is a biography of the orgasm: at first self-induced, later consciously manipulated through the piquancy and perversity of intimate relations, and finally a vast and sweated communal seizure, with death and life occurring together in a shattering rhythm.'

Freud explicitly associated sex with creativity, suggesting that sublimated desires might bubble up and be rechannelled as art. Rudolf Nureyev agreed. He saw creativity as 'very much akin to sex, sexual drive or sexual appetite if you wish' and he, like Nijinsky, projected incredible sexual energy on stage. Since his breakdown, Nijinsky's creativity – Stravinsky said that his 'creative imagination [was] … almost too rich' – and his sexuality have been inextricably linked to his madness.

Dance has a long association with insanity, most famously in the 1841 ballet *Giselle* which tells the story of a girl who goes mad after having had her heart broken and who then, after dying, protects her faithless lover from the Wilis, beautiful but evil spirits from Slavonic folklore who dance young men to their deaths. The elegant, elongated redhead Jane Avril, *'sylphide étrange'* and model for many of Toulouse-Lautrec's images of *fin de siècle* Montmartre nightlife, was hospitalised as a girl with the nervous condition then known as St Vitus' Dance before taking her place on the stage of the Moulin Rouge. She was still dancing in the same decade Nijinsky arrived in Paris.

Even before his breakdown – though most of these accounts were written with the benefit of hindsight – people around him sensed something about Nijinsky that was unsettling. Cecchetti told Romola not to get close to him, Stravinsky detected worrying gaps in his personality, Charlie Chaplin found his presence unnerving, and set designer Robert Edmond Jones said he carried around with him an atmosphere almost of oppression. In old age Lydia Lopokova told author Henrietta Garnett that Nijinsky was always 'potty. His soul had holes in it, but when he danced then his holes were healed, then he became alive and he was not unhappy any more.'

I find it hard to believe that the struggles faced by Nijinsky as a child and the tragedies he saw enacted all around him throughout his life did not heighten his vulnerability, making dance his sole means of escape from a brutal world: his father leaving them and the struggles borne by his mother to raise her children alone; his brother's illness and incarceration; the excruciating intensity of the working atmosphere of the Imperial Theatres and then the Ballets Russes; the pressures of his celebrity; the strains of his relationship with Diaghilev and its devastating end; his haphazard marriage to a self-absorbed woman who worshipped but made no effort to understand him; and the waste and wreckage of the Great War and the revolution tearing his homeland apart – a place to which he knew he could never return. Illness and death were always near. Of his six classmates at the Imperial Theatre School alone, four died tragically in their twenties. He was the fifth and Anatole Bourman the sixth.

When Nijinsky was diagnosed and throughout the remainder of his life, quite different factors were thought to have contributed to his illness. Freud speculated that schizophrenia was caused by repressed homosexual urges; later psychoanalysts would suggest that overprotective mothering might stimulate it; in the 1930s Anton Boisen (founder of the clinical pastoral education movement and sufferer from mental illness, who believed some types of schizophrenia could be understood as crises of the soul, rather than the mind) thought it sprang from an intolerable loss of self-respect. Alfred Adler believed Nijinsky suffered from an inferiority complex stemming from the social disjunct between his deprived childhood and the sophisticated world in which he moved as an adult, what the sociologists Richard Sennett and Jonathan Cobb have called 'the hidden injuries of class'. Nijinsky may have been subject to all of these conditions, but probably no doctor today would say they had caused his illness. Perhaps Nureyev, who could imagine what it felt like to be Nijinsky better than most, got it right. At first, he said, he had assumed that the end of his relationship with Diaghilev had made Nijinsky go mad; later he came to believe that Nijinsky's 'mind broke because he could no longer dance'.

At times during the last thirty years of his life Nijinsky was brutally restrained and heavily drugged; at others he was cruelly neglected or thrust back into the public eye to satisfy other people's ambitions. The

contrast between Nijinsky before and after 1919 – the weightless figure glowing in the spotlights and the stodgy, blank face of the mental
patient – is the most tragic image from the story of his life.

'Balanchine always said that his ballets are like butterflies: they live for
a season.' Ballet is a notoriously hard art to communicate. Like wordless
poetry it seeks to express mysteries just out of reach. If you weren't at
a particular performance you wouldn't be able to recreate what it was
like – even if you watched the same piece being performed again the
next night. 'At the moment of its creation it is gone.'

The art of an individual artist is even more ephemeral. When Pavlova died in 1931, Lopokova observed that 'a dancer can leave nothing
behind her. Music will not help us to see her again and to feel what
she gave us, nor the best words.' But though the best words cannot
make dance come alive again, they can help us understand the power
of an artist and what he or she communicated to their audience; and
the creative memory of other artists, their training and technique, their
will to be artists and to carry on the traditions they represent, preserve
the achievements of their predecessors in indefinable but fundamental
ways. Though it may be impossible to 'know how the great Taglioni
[Marie Taglioni, 1804–1884] danced … her art is not dead. Some little
girl in London, Paris or Milan dances differently today because Taglioni
once existed. She will carry part of Taglioni with her onto the stage.'

Every great artist is the product of his training and surroundings
and Nijinsky was no exception. His parents' experience and passion,
the tuition of the Legat brothers and Cecchetti, working as part of the
Mariinsky at the end of fifty years of Marius Petipa's supremacy, Fokine
creating ballets for him and Diaghilev working to give him everything he
needed off stage and on combined to create a background and environment in which he could shine.

Beyond that it was up to Nijinsky. Technique, craft, experience
and practice will only take the artist so far; the next level is a kind
of transfiguration, a spiritual awareness, a surrender. This is what cre-
ates the sense of exaltation in the audience – the knowledge that they

are witnessing something on a higher plane, the 'spiritual activity in physical form', as Merce Cunningham and Lincoln Kirstein have defined dance. With Nijinsky, as Rambert wrote after his death, 'his technique was completely subordinate to his expression'.

All the dancers from the Imperial Theatre School had incredible elevation, but what was unique about Nijinsky, according to Karsavina, was his 'incorporeal lightness', the way he appeared to float over the stage as if he had left the ground behind. Despite his muscularity, the effortlessness of his style could make him seem almost indolent and his *port de bras*, though classical in line, according to his training, was unconventionally supple and expressive.

'Never has any other dancer been able to seize upon one's imagination and sweep one into forgetfulness of the mechanics of dancing as Vaslav Nijinsky,' wrote his schoolmate Anatole Bourman. Throughout her life Bronia was captivated by her brother's art, which for her depended not upon his virtuosity or elevation, extraordinary though those were, but on 'the nature of the Dance, living in him, body and soul'. For Massine, his work was simply 'the highest form of artistic perfection'.

Nadine Legat, wife of Vaslav's teacher Nikolai and herself a *prima ballerina* of the Imperial Theatres, told Tamara Nijinsky that for her there would always be 'two Nijinskys – Nijinsky "the dancer", whom the world enjoyed watching, loved and even idolised, and Nijinsky the "superman" – barred from us through his detachment from the material world which he had outgrown, and to which he did not wish to belong … To me Nijinsky was never mad. It was the world that was blind (if not mad) because it could not see, understand, or reach his height … therefore he lived in his own world.'

The gulf between what Nijinsky seemed to be onstage and what he really was offstage fascinated his contemporaries, both before and after his breakdown. 'Where the essential Nijinsky existed was a constant mystery,' admitted his wife. Tamara Nijinsky has offered this assessment of her father's character, after years of trying to find out what he had been like: unimpressed by status, uninterested in money, 'wrapped up in his art for which he lived and breathed; he only felt rapport for people on the same wavelength'. In manner reserved, in speech succinct, he sought 'escape from people fawning upon him; only when he danced did the incredible metamorphosis take place'. It makes me wonder whether it would have been somehow always impossible for his offstage self to match up to his ineffable onstage experiences.

Even his friends often thought the dancer was his true self. 'Nijinsky alone could use his body as a symbol of imponderable ideas while it moved in fluid physical intensity. The world of canvas scenery, costumed bodies, and painted faces, was his reality. It was Nijinsky himself who leapt out into space in red rose-petalled grace in *Spectre de la Rose*; it was an uninhabited hulk of heavily breathing man that rose from the thick mattress held outside the window by six pairs of strong hands, to cushion his fall,' wrote Muriel Draper. 'Atop the flimsy impermanence of a tottering show-booth in a country fair, the soul of Nijinsky questioned God with little useless folded hands, while unanswering crowds of spectators revolved in dead merriment below.'

'You could never believe that this little monkey, with sparse hair, dressed in a wide overcoat, a hat balanced on top of his skull, was the public idol. Yet he was the idol,' wrote Jean Cocteau. 'On stage, his over-developed muscular system appeared supple. He grew taller (his heels never touched the ground), his hands became the foliage of his gestures, and his face radiated light.'

The power of his stage presence came to be an ambiguous burden. 'Too familiar with the triumph of grace, he rejects it,' Cocteau wrote elsewhere. Nijinsky 'carries in him that fluid which stirs crowds, and he despises the public (whom he does not refuse to gratify)'. It was this feeling, surely – the impulse that made him tell newspapers that playing the Rose made him feel sea-sick – that made him so determined to create ballets over which he maintained total control rather than merely dance other people's ideas of what he did best.

Fokine had been the inheritor of and challenger to Petipa's formal traditions of virtuosity and splendour designed to reflect the pageantry and flatter the vanity of an imperial court. Wonderfully convincingly he conjured up past worlds and far-off places, using flowing movement rather than mime to create drama, and he did this by taking the dancers into his confidence to elicit from them the emotions he wanted expressed on stage. Along with Pavlova, no one embodied this style better than Nijinsky, yet when he embarked upon his own choreographic work it was an implicit denial of Fokine's work.

Although it is wrong to think of Nijinsky as having rejected the classical canon – on the contrary, until his break with Diaghilev, he remained immersed in it, sprinkling water on the floor in Cecchetti's class as humbly and enthusiastically in 1913 as in 1908 – he recognised its limitations. He was determined to speak for his own, modern world rather than to create exotic historical fantasies. 'I do not like past centuries, because I am alive.'

Having taken what he could from Fokine, he discarded his sinuous, curving lines and unbridled sensuality and violence in favour of almost Byzantine angles, austerity and rigour: no sentiment, no emotion, just ideas expressed as pure movement. 'What kind of beauty is hidden in this spare, restricted dancing?' asked Jacques Rivière, comparing Nijinsky's style to Fokine's in his review of *Sacre*. 'All one can read in it [Fokine's dancing] is a vague, entirely physical and faceless joy ... By breaking up movement, by returning to the simplicity of gesture, Nijinsky has restored expressiveness to dancing. All the angularities and awkwardness of this choreography keep the feeling in ... The body is no longer an escape-route for the soul: on the contrary, it gathers itself together to contain the soul.'

Nijinsky even came to see Diaghilev as outdated. 'I could not agree with him in his taste in art,' he would write. 'I want to prove that all Diaghilev's art is sheer nonsense. I know all his tricks and habits. I was Diaghilev. I know Diaghilev better than he does himself.' Creating was the only place where he could both be himself without being desired from the stalls and where he could rebel – against his training, against the traditions of which he knew himself to be a part and against Diaghilev's control over him. 'Now that I am a creator myself, I don't any longer need you in the way that I did,' the character of Nijinsky says to Diaghilev in Nicholas Wright's 2011 play, *Rattigan's Nijinsky*. 'I must belong to myself and no one else.'

'Absolutely everything he invented from the beginning, and everything that he invented was contrary to everything he had learned,' said Marie Rambert. 'I would not hesistate to affirm that it was he, more than anyone else, who revolutionised the classical ballet and was fifty years ahead of his time.' Ninette de Valois agreed; for her Nijinsky was an even greater choreographer than dancer.

He also transformed the way choreographers were viewed, the respect accorded to the role as distinct from the work. In the early years of the twentieth century the choreographer was still seen almost as a theatrical technician, bringing the artistic direction of the stage designer and librettist to life. But building on the ground that Fokine had seized, with Nijinsky insisting on total control over every detail of his compositions, the choreographer would become for the first time and unequivocally an artist in his own right.

What seems to me to have been modern about Nijinsky's style was his capacity to experiment, to re-examine established ways of moving and seeing and try to create from those discoveries a new aesthetic. Motivated by the same impulses as many of the visual artists and writers who were his contemporaries, he sought to pare down a tradition he saw as having become over-embellished and sentimental to return to first principles. He refused to be satisfied with prettiness or the charms of predictability, seeking instead a new distillation of reality and beauty.

One aspect of this disregard for convention was his conviction that art should not be confined by gender. His willingness to dance en pointe if Diaghilev had let him play the Firebird or in *Jeux* and his blurring of gender roles on stage demonstrates to me not a desire to take on feminine qualities, as many interpreted it at the time, but rather courage in taking risks and a passion for creating something new – a curiosity about finding out what his body and his art were capable of. 'Had Nijinsky tried to follow an approved pattern of male perfection, he would never have given the full measure of his genius,' wrote Karsavina. His willingness to challenge assumptions was an essential aspect of what he achieved on stage. The fact that his sexuality would not be an issue to audiences today is a triumphant legacy for a man who was defined by his sexuality in his lifetime.

It is hard to recreate a sense of the importance of art at the start of the twentieth century. In his 1977 autobiography, the critic and writer Arnold Haskell regretted the loss of the idea he had known in his youth that art was inspirational and important. People were schooled in it, they sought to understand it, they had faith in it as something numinous and transcendant, something that made man greater than a lump of clay or a hairless ape. He mourned that sense of urgency. No longer would a friend bang on his door to say, Come, come now; we're going to see Nijinsky. Haven't you seen *Faune* yet? – Don't worry about what you're wearing, the taxi's waiting, we must get there in time – before racing him off to the theatre.

Haskell never saw Nijinsky dance, but those audiences who did were enraptured by him; there is an appreciable difference between what they said they saw in him and what they described seeing in other dancers. The essay accompanying a book of prints of Nijinsky published by the illustrator George Barbier in 1913 raved about him in the fragrant prose of the time, translated by the young Cyril Beaumont. 'Ah! What poet could tell of the mysterious boon we accept from this foreign fairy with the oriental face, and weightless body? The spell of his subtle talent and his wondrous youth gives back to us, in desire without a pang, some magical illusion of our departed youth. It is as if this divine genius for defying the earth's attraction and for treading the unseen paths of the air belonged to us too a little.'

The critic Carl Van Vechten, one of several people who 'remembered' being at the Théâtre des Champs-Elysées for the premiere of *Sacre* (but was actually there for one of the later performances), and who saw Nijinsky both in Paris in 1912 and 1913 and in New York in 1916, declared that as a performer he had no rivals. Nijinsky was simply 'the greatest of stage artists ... he communicates more of beauty and emotion to me as a spectator than other interpretative artists do': 'his dancing has the unbroken quality of music, the balance of great painting, the meaning of fine literature, the emotion inherent in all these arts'.

Another American critic, Stark Young, agreed. 'I have never seen any other artist so varied in his compulsion, so absorbing in his variety, so glamorous in his stage presence as was Nijinsky.' The theatre designer Edward Gordon Craig, who deplored most of Diaghilev's excesses (Diaghilev teased him about wanting to get rid of actors altogether since he so loved abstraction), shouted with delight when Nijinsky as the Rose leapt into the wings, though he found his 'tiny, almost unnoticeable movements even more marvellous than his dancing and later observed that all he did was Art'.

In roles that had as their common theme a sense of myth and otherworldliness, Nijinsky communicated to his audience a sense of the 'saturated moment' described by Virginia Woolf and T. S. Eliot – a mystical combination of thought, sensation and experience that created a unified poetic whole. 'Looking at him, one is in an imaginary world, entire and very clear.' When Robert Walser saw him dancing at Bellevue, soon after he was institutionalised, he thought his dancing was like a fairy tale, with all the layers of meaning that implies.

Nijinsky had a passionate connectedness to his work, identifying himself completely with his art. He was different in every role, submerging himself into the part he was playing without any sense of the post-war irony or detachment which has characterised later twentieth-century performance. 'It was not only the face, the façade, that changed, but the mind and the personality behind it which altered. The change was not skin-deep, but soul-deep,' wrote Cyril Beaumont. Reading these words again as I type them, the nature of Nijinsky's illness comes insistently and poignantly to mind. He could 'play upon movement in the same way that a great actor clothes words now with fire, now with the most melting tenderness'.

Perhaps the closest we can get to Nijinsky today is his various publicity photographs in which the intensity of his gaze and the immediacy of his presence is so powerful that you almost forget you are looking at a piece of paper. When Lincoln Kirstein's *Nijinsky Dancing*, containing reproductions of several of these portraits, came out in 1975, Clement Crisp said that no live Petrushka had ever moved him as much as these photographs of Nijinsky in character.

The dance critic Edwin Denby noted that in these pictures Nijinsky's poses were never exhibitionistic. He was so centred in the pelvis and, because of that, had such extraordinary balance, that when he lifted a leg it was as if a table was being lifted by one leg while keeping the top horizontal; he used the whole foot, not just the ball. 'He looks as if the body remembered the whole dance, all the phases of it, as he holds the one pose; he seems to be thinking, I've just done that, and then after this I do that, and then that, and then comes that; so his body looks like a face lighting up at a single name that evokes a whole crowd of remembered names.'

'I do not see anything in these pictures that would lead one to suppose that Nijinsky's subsequent insanity cast any premonition-ary shadow on his phenomenally luminous dance intelligence,' Denby wrote. 'In their stillness Nijinsky's pictures have more vitality than the dances they remind us of as we now see them on stage.'

What endures of Nijinsky's work is of course impossible to pin down and there is an ongoing academic debate about what exactly he should be remembered for. As Joan Acocella wrote, concluding her Introduction to his diary with the thought that he was 'probably' a genius, 'never was so much artistic fame based on so little artistic evidence: one eleven-minute ballet, *Faun*, plus some photographs'. It is true that no one can judge a work of art they have not seen. But that does not stop me wishing I had had the chance.

Paris, 29 May 1913. Onstage in the noisy, overheated theatre, the Chosen One waits to begin the solo that is at the heart of her tribe's appeasement of their cruel gods. She has been selected from among her companions and prepared for the ritual by the elders of the tribe; the responsibility with which she has been entrusted weighs heavily upon her. The noise of the orchestra – and of the hissing, cat-calling audience – crashes around her like thunder.

Her head hangs down, her heels and elbows jut out, her trembling knees turn awkwardly in. The uncomfortable pose is an expression of her internal state, at once proud, scared, brave, hopeful, angry and ecstatic. Her peers encircle her, focused on her, willing her on to her end. She must dance with her whole self, or the sacrifice will not work; they have chosen her to be their victim, their most precious victim, and she represents them all. When the music begins and she starts to dance, they marvel at her courage, power and beauty even as they watch for her to fall.

Later observers have found in *Sacre* an irresistible prelude to the Great War, the portent of an entire society's self-destruction. The Maiden's obedient, almost joyful submission to the rite, the way she is honoured by her people rather than mourned, the celebration of life and youth through sacrificial death – all these were impulses that animated the generation who fought and died between 1914 and 1918. As the cultural historian Modris Eksteins has written, the Chosen Maiden in *Sacre* would become, a few years later, the Unknown Soldier, memorialised in national tombs all over Europe – an ambivalent tribute to which I imagine Nijinsky would have been acutely sensitive.

Throughout his long afterlife, the fatal, frenzied solo of the Chosen Maiden has become a vivid metaphor for the tragic figure of Nijinsky going insane, dancing himself to lunacy but perhaps only feeling truly alive as he danced. If the music and choreography of *Sacre* 'can be interpreted as a sign that the end of civilisation was at hand', then Nijinsky becomes at once the emblem and prophet of modernity and its victim.

Very few lives have clearly definable points at which everything changes, but for Nijinsky one of those points was the first night of *Le Sacre du printemps*. It sped on a series of events – events which were *en train* anyway, but which were hastened or made inevitable by *Sacre's* bold, perhaps foolhardy, refusal to cater to the traditional ballet audience and consequent commercial failure, and which would inexorably lead to the tragedy of Nijinsky, less than six years later, being committed to Bellevue as a madman.

Because of his vertiginous fall, the heights he scaled and the depths to which he plunged, and because it is almost impossible to recapture anything of what he achieved, the memory of Nijinsky survives today like a fly caught in amber. He has become for me a glorious, glowing emblem of youth and talent, cut off in its prime but preserved forever as a reminder that art and beauty will always be the highest of human ideals.

Notes and References

(The sources have been abbreviated in this section and can be found in full in the Bibliography.)

I YAPONCHIK, 1889–1905

6   'a woman … in the ballet': Z. Fitzgerald, *Save Me the Waltz* (New York, 1968), p. 113.

7   'We were born': Bronia Nijinska, *Early Memoirs* (Durham, NC, 1981), p. 1.

8   This is the date Bronia Nijinska gives (the night of 27–28 February, old time (Russian calendar before the Revolution); see Nijinska, *Early Memoirs*, p. 12); though Vaslav's birth certificate has the date 10 January 1890, it is thought that Eleonora Nijinsky tried to buy him an extra year before he was required to perform his National Service by making him appear younger than he was.

9   'fairy-tale … so many directions': Nijinska, *Early Memoirs*, p. 15.

9   'My parents considered': V. Krasovskaya, *Nijinsky* (New York, 1979), p. 5, from an interview in *Je sais tout* magazine.

9   'wild, fierce … his body': Romola Nijinsky, *Nijinsky; and, The last years of Nijinsky* (London, 1980), p. 280.

10   'With his … then again': Nijinska, *Early Memoirs*, pp. 20–21.

10   'How high he': ibid., p. 26.

10   'first appearance': ibid., p. 28; *T.P.'s Magazine*, London, May 1911.

10 'Throughout our childhood': Nijinska, *Early Memoirs*, p. 25.

13 'It was as if': ibid., p. 57.

14 'a charming little': Isadora Duncan, *My Life* (New York, 1995), p. 119.

14 'Before leaving ... to go': Nijinska, *Early Memoirs*, p. 77.

15 'praised me very': ibid., p. 78.

17 'The little devil': T. Karsavina, *Theatre Street* (London, 1948), p. 151.

17 'Are you a': Nijinska, *Early Memoirs*, p. 85.

17 'made to feel': A. Bourman, *The Tragedy of Nijinsky* (London, 1937), p. 6. Though he is wildly unreliable about later parts of Nijinsky's life, to the point of inserting himself into scenes where he is known not to have been present, Bourman was one of six boys in Nijinsky's year at the Imperial Theatre School and therefore his account of their school-life must be worth something.

18 'anger and jealousy': ibid., p. 20. Bourman accuses Georgy Rozai in particular of this jealousy (and this crime), but Nijinska's account of the accident has Bourman and another boy, Grigory Babich, equally culpable.

18 'I played a': V. Nijinsky, *Nijinsky's Diary* (New York, 1999), p. 116.

18 'unneccessary torment': M. Fokine, *Memoirs of a Ballet Master* (London, 1961), p. 16.

19 'That to me': J. Kavanagh, *Rudolf Nureyev: The Life* (London, 2008), p. 21.

20 'The theatre in': Karsavina, *Theatre Street*, p. 190.

21 'felt a great': Nijinsky, *Nijinsky's Diary*, p. 115.

21 'You have ... your brother': Nijinska, *Early Memoirs*, p. 127. Later in his career Fokine saw Nijinsky as a rival, and as a consequence his memoirs offer Nijinsky only the barest minimum of praise through evidently gritted teeth; it is interesting therefore to read Bronia's account of his early response to her brother, whom Fokine's choreography made a star and who in turn took Fokine's ballets to new heights.

22 'exalted, vibrant, free': Karsavina, *Theatre Street*, p. 378, quoting Nadine (Nadia) Legat, Nikolay's wife.

22 'to a plane': ibid., p. 378, quoting Nikolay Legat.

22 'above all ... and earth': J. Homans, *Apollo's Angels: A History of Ballet* (London, 2010), p. xxii.

22 'convent-like': Karsavina, *Theatre Street*, p. 58.

29 'torture chamber': Duncan, *My Life*, p. 121.

23 'tunic of cobweb': ibid., p. 119.

23 'Like eager … and vividness': Duchesse de Gramont, *Years of Plenty* (London, 1932), p. 339. She continues, 'After that, she became Isadora Duncan.'

23 'reminded us … art form': Fokine, *Memoirs of a Ballet Master*, p. 256.

23 'soul wept with': Duncan, *My Life*, p. 119.

24 'by talent'. S. Scheijen, *Diaghilev* (London, 2009), p. 143.

26 This ethnographic: L. Garafola, *Diaghilev's Ballets Russes* (New York, 1989), p. 6 et seq.

26 'complete unity of': Homans, *Apollo's Angels: A History of Ballet*, p. 293.

26 'to participate': M. Rambert, *Quicksilver: The Autobiography of Marie Rambert* (London, 1991), p. 61.

27 'for the audience's … the dance': Fokine, *Memoirs of a Ballet Master*, p. 132.

27 'an articulate … slightest detail': ibid., p. 132.

28 'As he extends': Nijinska, *Early Memoirs*, p. 517.

28 'like a bashful': Bourman, *The Tragedy of Nijinsky*, p. 77. Bourman doesn't refer specifically to this performance, but more generally to Nijinsky's early performances.

2 THE FAVOURITE SLAVE, 1906–1909

29 'not merely to be': Nijinska, *Early Memoirs*, p. 157.

29 'Bronia, tell … doushka': ibid., p. 159.

30 Ibid., pp. 190–2: I have disregarded the secondary account of Romola Nijinsky, who described this last meeting between Vaslav and Foma as a sentimental reunion.

31 'amongst the chosen': Karsavina, *Theatre Street*, p. 123.

31 'a charming boy': M. Kshesinskaya, *Dancing in St. Petersburg* (Alton, Hants, 2005), p. 110.

31 'what secrets Nijinsky': Nijinska, *Early Memoirs*, p. 248.

31 'like some exotic': A. Oliveroff, *Flight of the Swan: A Memory of Anna Pavlova* (New York, 1935), p. 23.

32 'unworthy of her genius': S. Lifar, *Serge Diaghilev: His Life, His Work, His Legend* (London, 1940), p. 139.

32 'sought more success': A. L. Haskell, *Balletomania: The story of an Obsession* (London, 1977), p. 56.

32 'If a dancer': A. Pavlova, *Pages of My Life* (New York, 1947), p. 10.

32 'the quiet joys': Oliveroff, *Flight of the Swan: A Memory of Anna Pavlova*, p. 61.

32 'shows onstage. You watch': Kavanagh, *Rudolf Nureyev: The Life*, p. 645.

33 'I had my arms': Nijinska, *Early Memoirs*, p. 196.

33 'I started to dance … about me': Nijinsky, *Nijinsky's Diary*, p. 118.

33 Nijinska says Vaslav was recovering in the spring of 1908, nursed by Prince Lvov's (see below) valet. She speculates that Bourman's taunts about his relationship with Lvov prompted Vaslav to go with him to the prostitute where he could prove that he was a man.

34 Prince Nikolay Yusupov: Homans, *Apollo's Angels: A History of Ballet*, p. 53.

34 'Ballet is': Fokine, *Memoirs of a Ballet Master*, p. 52.

34 1,000 roubles: Romola Nijinsky, *Nijinsky; and, The last years of Nijinsky*, p. 426. She says this sum was given at his introduction to Diaghilev, but since Lvov wouldn't have wanted money and Diaghilev wouldn't have paid it, I think it more likely that she got her facts slightly wrong (not uncommon) and it was paid by Lvov for his initial introduction to Nijinsky. See also Bourman, *The Tragedy of Nijinsky*, p. 122. R. Buckle names the pander as Boris Alexandrov.

34 'He loved me': Nijinsky, *Nijinsky's Diary*, p. 163.

35 'marvellously … stupefied': Nijinska, *Early Memoirs*, p. 217.

36 'it was a bad sign': M. Keynes (ed.), *Lydia Lopokova* (London, 1983), p. 46.

36 'perfection in the': Nijinska, *Early Memoirs*, p. 248.

37 I have paraphrased Nijinska, *Early Memoirs*, p. 231.

37 'for the rest of my life': ibid., p. 218.

38 'Before, he had only known school … innocence': Romola Nijinsky, *Nijinsky; and, The last years of Nijinsky*, p. 60. To be taken with the usual pinch of salt required for Romola's stories.

38 'that very rare feeling … hero': A. S. Benois, *Reminiscences of the Russian Ballet in London* (London, 1941), p. 251 (phrases cited in different order from original source).

39 'dying of curiosity': ibid., p. 256.

39 'a magnificent bear': Serge Lifar in J. Drummond (ed.), *Speaking of Diaghilev* (London, 1997), p. 292.

39 'one tooth on the edge': J. Cocteau, *Journals* (London, 1957), p. 55.

39 'looked one through': A. Dolin, *Autobiography* (London, 1960), p. 28.

39 I know he smoked, but I am only guessing that he smoked Sobranie; it is such a peculiarly Russian smelling cigarette. The company was founded in 1879.

40 'his bluelit nights': quoted in Lifar, *Serge Diaghilev*, p. 19.

40 'peculiar lazy grace': Karsavina, *Theatre Street*, p. 352.

40 'looked up to him': C. W. Beaumont, *The Diaghilev Ballet in London* (London, 1940), p. 8.

40 'It is the Seryozhas': quoted in Scheijen, *Diaghilev*, p. 82.

40 'the only one': quoted in Scheijen, ibid., p. 78.

41 'The dream and': to Leo Tolstoy, quoted in J. Pritchard (ed.), *Diaghilev and the Golden Age of the Ballets Russes, 1909–1929* (London, 2009), p. 40.

41 'Everything is here': quoted in Scheijen, *Diaghilev*, p. 58.

41 'part of history': Nijinsky, *Nijinsky's Diary*, p. 109.

41 'We are a generation': quoted in L. Garafola and N. V. N Baer (eds), *The Ballets Russes and its World* (New Haven, CT, 1999), p. 92.

41 'sly dandified primness': Karsavina, *Theatre Street*, p. 201.

41 'one think of champagne': J. Melville, *Diaghilev and Friends* (London, 2009), p. 11, quoting (I assume) Diaghilev.

42 'an individual gift': quoted in Scheijen, *Diaghilev*, p. 101.

42 'there could be': ibid., p. 6.

42 'for all his': Mstislav Dobuzhinsky quoted in Scheijen, *Diaghilev*, p. 132.

42 'The end ... the Resurrection!': quoted in Scheijen, *Diaghilev*, p. 134.

43 'my greatest': P. Stoneley, *A Queer History of the Ballet* (London, 2007), p. 58.

43 'elegant but unremarkable': L. Massine, *My Life in Ballet* (London, 1928), p. 47.

43 'wicked': Stoneley, *A Queer History of the Ballet*, pp. 68–9.

44 'made me see': Karsavina, *Theatre Street*, p. 283.

44 'the clamorous demands ... sensual demands': quoted in Scheijen, *Diaghilev*, pp. 114–15 (phrases cited in different order from original source).

46 'uninteresting': Benois, *Reminiscences of the Russian Ballet in London*, p. 289.

46 'to lose its human': Nijinska, *Early Memoirs*, p. 210.

46 'greatly impressed': ibid., p. 253.

46 'to their conversations': ibid., p. 258.

47 'to please Diaghilev': quoted in Scheijen, *Diaghilev*, p. 162.

47 'help cultivate': quoted in Scheijen, ibid., p. 162.

47 'his most fervent': quoted in Scheijen, ibid., p. 169.

47 It was first on the list he and Astruc wrote in June 1908 of what they hoped would form their 1909 season. See R. Buckle, *Nijinsky* (London, 1971), p. 63.

48 'a child who': Karsavina, *Theatre Street*, p. 170.

48 'barefoot childish hoppings': Nijinska, *Early Memoirs*, p. 224.

48 'the green box trees': quoted in R. Burt, *The Male Dancer: Bodies, Spectacle, Sexualities* (London, 1995), p. 13. Burt adds that at this time the male nude as a subject for painting and sculpture also disappeared, and plain, dark suits became a bland and sexless uniform for men of all classes.

49 five times: N. Macdonald, *Diaghilev Observed by Critics in England and the United States, 1911–1929* (London, 1975), p. 6.

49 'I hated him': Nijinsky, *Nijinsky' Diary*, p. 103.

50 'many beautiful women': ibid., p. 205.

50 'I knew perfectly': Dolin, *Autobiography*, p. 44.

51 'I came … long time': Nijinska, *Early Memoirs*, p. 262. Some observers speculated that Lvov's motive in trying to set him up with Diaghilev was to get rid of a lover of whom he had become bored, but I think Bronia and Nouvel's accounts tally together better in this interpretation of events.

3 DIEU DE LA DANSE, 1909–1910

52 'the lovely sight': Karsavina, *Theatre Street*, p. 219.

52 'the tangled mass': D. Milhaud, *Notes without Music* (London, 1952), p. 19.

53 'little ladies … canary-bird': de Gramont, *Years of Plenty*, pp. 24–5.

54 'a fairy godmother': Valentine Gross quoted in F. Steegmuller, *Cocteau: A Biography* (London, 1970), p. 69.

54 '*tournée des mécènes*': A. L. Haskell, *Ballet Russe: The Age of Diaghilev* (London, 1968), p. 11.

55 'benevolent giant': Drummond (ed.), *Speaking of Diaghilev*, quoting Marie Rambert, p. 110.

55 'A conference was': A. Khan, *The Memoirs of the Aga Khan* (London, 1953), p. 109.

55 'It was impossible': Romola Nijinsky, *Nijinsky; and, The last years of Nijinsky*, p. 120.

55 'bare of adornment': Karsavina, *Theatre Street*, p. 215.

55 'did not want': M. Calvocoressi, *Music and Ballet: Recollections of M. D. Calvocoressi* (New York, 1978), p. 226.

56 'that would amaze': Benois, *Reminiscences of the Russian Ballet in London*, p. 282.

56 'shouted himself hoarse': Karsavina, *Theatre Street*, p. 201.

56 'had seen a Japanese': ibid., p. 214.

57 'His whole body': Nijinska, *Early Memoirs*, p. 270.

57 'a storm of applause': Karsavina, *Theatre Street*, p. 197.

57 'The familiar barriers ... up there': ibid., pp. 198–9.

58 'every movement ... his arm': C. W. Beaumont, *The Diaghilev Ballet in London*, pp. 16–17.

59 'wonder of wonders': *Commedia*, 20 May 1909.

59 'seen anything like': A. Rubinstein, *My Young Years* (London, 1973), p. 219.

60 'vacant eyes': M. de Cossart, *Ida Rubinstein* (Liverpool, 1987), p. 17.

60 'so thin you thought': Cocteau, *Journals* , p. 55.

61 'the cunning with': Keynes, *Lydia Lopokova*, p. 215.

61 'He couldn't stand': in Drummond (ed.), *Speaking of Diaghilev*, p. 244.

61 'not this, that': J. Bowlt, Z. Tregulova and N. R. Giordano (eds), *Feast of Wonders: Sergei Diaghilev and the Ballets Russes* (Milan, 2009), p. 21.

61 'We really did': Benois, *Reminiscences of the Russian Ballet in London*, p. 284.

61 'we all lived': S. Grigoriev, *The Diaghilev Ballet, 1909–1929*. (Harmondsworth, 1953), p. 25.

61 And as Diaghilev's most recent biographer Sjeng Scheijen observes, we must take the rapture shown by the ballet's first audiences at face value.

61 'Right away I': S. Kahan, *Music's Modern Muse* (Rochester, NY, 2003), p. 159 and Lifar, *Serge Diaghilev*, p. 161.

61 'drably provincial': ibid., p. 155.

61 'When one has': Tamara Nijinsky, *Nijinsky and Romola* (London, 1991), p. 376.

62 walk upright: Oliveroff, *Flight of the Swan: A Memory of Anna Pavlova*, p. 163.

62 'applied maximum ... so that': Nijinska, *Early Memoirs*,p. 401.

62 'In no other art': French *Vogue*, December 1986. R. Gottlieb (ed.), *Reading Dance* (New York, 2008), pp. 336–7.

62 'how perfection lay': Tamara Nijinsky, *Nijinsky and Romola*, p. 258.

62   'should be as simple': Romola Nijinsky, *Nijinsky; and, The last years of Nijinsky*, p. p. 93.

62   'he could never watch': ibid., p. 115.

63   'like an old Marquise': ibid., p. 89.

63   'With Grigoriev following': L. Sokolova, *Dancing for Diaghilev* (London, 1960), p. 39.

63   'incapable of loving': ibid., p. 37.

63   'a capacity': Benois, *Reminiscences of the Russian Ballet in London*, p. 190.

63   'pride and joy': Lifar, *Serge Diaghilev*, p. 143.

64   'new existence': Benois, *Reminiscences of the Russian Ballet in London*, p. 289.

64   'uncanny swiftness ... of Jesus': Oliveroff, *Flight of the Swan: A Memory of Anna Pavlova*, p. 23.

64   'tight, nervous ... small space': D. Bull, *The Everyday Dancer* (London, 2011), p. 159.

64   'standing in the wings': Nijinska, *Early Memoirs* , pp. 517–18.

64   'very small pair': Cocteau, *Journals*, p. 50.

64   'that murmuring': J. Cocteau, *Paris Album 1900–1914*, p. 32.

64   'We always knew': L. Sokolova in Drummond (ed.), *Speaking of Diaghilev*, p. 144.

65   'a glass ... his shoulders': Nijinska, *Early Memoirs*, p. 369.

65   'His bearing was modest': Beaumont, *The Diaghilev Ballet in London*, p. 28.

65   'just as a horse': Romola Nijinsky, *Nijinsky; and, The last years of Nijinsky*, p. 94.

65   'all the ballerinas': Nijinsky, *Nijinsky's Diary*, p. 161.

66   'great friends': Nijinska, *Early Memoirs*, p. 273.

66   'the peculiar specialities': Romola Nijinsky, *Nijinsky; and, The last years of Nijinsky*, p. 95.

66   'Bakst thought the women': Steegmuller, *Cocteau: A Biography*, p. 78, quoting Paul Morand's diary.

66   'We are all living': Karsavina, *Theatre Street*, p. 200.

67   'that she was the only woman': quoted in Scheijen, *Diaghilev*, p. 186.

68   'Look at that strength!': Buckle, *Nijinsky*, p. 95 and note.

69   'the mere fact': quoted in R. Davenport-Hine, *A Night at the Majestic* (London, 2006), p. 167.

69   'I did not want ... afraid of life': Nijinsky, *Nijinsky's Diary*, p. 198.

69   'loved Diaghilev': Nijinsky, *Nijinsky's Diary*, p. 111.

69   'this world of art': Nijinska, *Early Memoirs* , p. 306.

69   'but exhilarated at the prospect': Massine, *My Life in Ballet* , p. 47.

70   'like going to bed': J. Richardson, *Picasso*, vol. 3, *The Triumphant Years 1917–1932* (New York, 2007), p. 7.

70   Figures from Garafola, *Diaghilev's Ballets Russes*, p. 178 and Buckle, *Nijinsky*, p. 106.

71   Speculation on the genesis of *Faune*: Buckle, *Nijinsky*, p. 108 and note.

71   'an eyeglass': S. Lifar, *Ma Vie: From Kiev to Kiev* (trans. J. H. Morgan; London, 1970), p. 41.

71   'like a street urchin': quoted in Stoneley, *A Queer History of the Ballet*, p. 68.

71   'as if ... stage costume': Calvocoressi, *Music and Ballet: Recollections of M. D. Calvocoressi*, p. 209.

72   'to society what Ida': H. Acton, *Memoirs of an Aesthete* (London, 1948), p. 37.

72   'it was more wonderful': F. Rose, *Saying Life* (London, 1961), p. 70.

72   'Diaghilev's attitude': Benois, *Reminiscences of the Russian Ballet in London*, p. 303.

73   Firebird: R. Buckle, *Diaghilev* (London, 1979), p. 162, citing Boris Kochno.

73   'in those days': Benois, *Reminiscences of the Russian Ballet in London*, p. 302.

73   'impossible to describe': I. Stravinsky, *Stravinsky in Conversation with Robert Craft* (London, 1960), p. 174.

73   'extraordinary ... personality': I. Stravinsky and R. Craft, *Memories and Commentaries* (Harmondsworth, 1960), p. 35 (phrases cited in different order from original source).

73   'the elite ... own art': Nijinska, *Early Memoirs*, p. 306.

74   'because I was': Nijinsky, *Nijinsky's Diary*, p. 89.

74   'at ease ... social blunder': Nijinska, *Early Memoirs*, pp. 306–7.

74   'essay in choreography': Buckle, *Nijinsky*, p. 130.

74   'supremely right ... heartache': Nijinska, *Early Memoirs* p. 282.

74   'I do not wish to share': ibid., , p. 283.

75   'He was almost always alone': ibid., p. 293.

75   'that it ... to speak': Nijinsky, *Nijinsky's Diary*, p. 52.

75   'magic lantern': quoted in Haskell, *Ballet Russe: The Age of Diaghilev*, p. 75.

76 *'Que veux-tu?'*: Benois, *Reminiscences of the Russian Ballet in London*, pp. 310–11.

77 'not unlike the bloom': Beaumont, *The Diaghilev Ballet in London*, p. 33.

77 'inexpressibly wild': C. W. Beaumont, *Michael Fokine and his Ballets* (London, 1935), p. 42.

77 'Nobody will believe me': C. M. Joseph in L. Garafola and N. V. N. Baer (eds), *The Ballets Russes and its World* (New Haven, 1999), p. 201.

77 'conscious of his performances': Stravinsky and Craft, *Memories and Commentaries*, p. 36.

77 'the grief of the repentant seducer': Benois quoted in L. Kirstein, *Nijinsky Dancing* (London, 1975), p. 83.

77 'his dancing was': Beaumont, *The Diaghilev Ballet in London*, p. 24.

77 'an acrobatic cat': D. Parker, *Nijinsky* (London, 1988), p. 104.

4 PETRUSHKA, 1910–1911

78 'his usual brilliance': Nijinska, *Early Memoirs*, p. 310.

79 'I spit ... at us': ibid., p. 311.

79 'But there was': ibid., p. 314.

79 the music of Debussy: Bronia's *Memoirs* indicate that even at this early stage he knew the music would be Debussy's, but other sources suggest that the music was the last thing to fall into place, after Nijinsky had got quite far with his choreographic ideas. The fact that the music and his movements seem far apart in the piece might corroborate this.

79 'I want to move away': Nijinska, *Early Memoirs*, p. 315.

80 'as if to encourage': M. Chagall, *My Life* (London, 1965), p. 92.

80 'an indecent ... will be': Nijinska, *Early Memoirs*, pp. 319–20.

81 'Paris is tolerant': quoted in Scheijen, *Diaghilev*, p. 218.

81 'conceited artist': Benois, *Reminiscences of the Russian Ballet in London*, p. 318.

82 'Vaslav was now': ibid., p. 318.

82 'Appalling scandal': quoted in Scheijen, *Diaghilev*, p. 217.

82 'where ballets': Nijinska, *Early Memoirs*, p. 325.

82 'A completely new path': ibid.,p. 324.

84 'You don't understand': Karsavina, *Theatre Street*, p. 240.

84 'looking very pompous': Benois, *Reminiscences of the Russian Ballet in London*, p. 340.

84 'a celestial insect': Romola Nijinsky, *Nijinsky; and, The last years of Nijinsky*, p. 137.

84 'suggested a cluster of leaves': Beaumont, *The Diaghilev Ballet in London*, p. 28.

84 'When he danced': Rambert quoted in Drummond (ed.), *Speaking of Diaghilev*, p. 115.

84 'the most perfect': Beaumont, *The Diaghilev Ballet in London*, p. 26.

84 'grace, freshness … the Rose': E. Cecchetti and O. Racster, *The Master of the Russian Ballet* (London, 1922), p. 217.

85 'The fact that': Fokine, *Memoirs of a Ballet Master*, p. 182.

85 'the artistry by which': V. Gross, *Nijinsky on Stage*, p. 67.

85 'played the chord': D. Monteux, *It's All in the Music: The Life and Work of Pierre Monteux* (London, 1966), p. 77.

86 'all solicitude as': Rambert, *Quicksilver: The Autobiography of Marie Rambert*, p. 57.

86 'What grace coupled': K. Kopelson, *The Queer Afterlife of Vaslav Nijinsky* (San Francisco, CA, 1997), p. 113; see also Steegmuller, *Cocteau*, p. 84 and J. Cocteau, *The Cock and the Harlequin* (*Le Coq et l'Arlequin*), translated by R. H. Myers (London, 1921), p. 42.

87 'the "lowest sort"': V. Stravinsky and R. Craft, *Stravinsky in Pictures and Documents* (London, 1960), p. 26.

87 'that sets itself' quotation continued, but in a better translation, in Homans, *Apollo's Angels: A History of Ballet*, p. 290.

87 'in perfect … of execution': Fokine, *Memoirs of a Ballet Master*, p. 194.

88 'The costumier … and glamorous': M. Sert, *Two or Three Muses* (London, 1953), p. 129.

88 'Only Monteux': Monteux, *It's All in the Music: The Life and Work of Pierre Monteux* , p. 76.

89 'enchanted': Benois, *Reminiscences of the Russian Ballet in London*, p. 337.

90 'Only the swinging': Nijinska, *Early Memoirs*, p. 373.

90 'Of the once bright-red cheeks': Nijinska, *Early Memoirs*, p. 373.

90 'A friend … very clear': E. Denby quoted in Paul Magriel, *Nijinsky, Pavlova, Duncan: Three Lives in Dance* (New York, 1977), pp. 19–20.

90 'an entire poem': Stravinsky and Craft, *Stravinsky in Pictures and Documents*, p. 67.

90 'amplified the crazy doll': Romola Nijinsky, *Nijinsky; and, The last years of Nijinsky*, p. 128.

91 'seemed to have': Beaumont, *The Diaghilev Ballet in London*, p. 45.

91 distilling something ... its loss: see Garafola, *Diaghilev's Ballets Russes*, pp. 29, 32, 48.

91 'personality, the imprisoned genius': Keynes, *Lydia Lopokova*, p. 211.

91 'a Hamlet': Buckle, *Nijinsky*, p. 159.

91 'to help the actor': Valery Bryusov essay quoted in Garafola, *Diaghilev's Ballets Russes*, p. 27.

91 'seen the finest actor': Romola Nijinsky, *Nijinsky; and, The last years of Nijinsky*, p. 129.

91 'the most ... ever seen': Stravinsky and Craft, *Memories and Commentaries*, p. 37.

92 'the mythical outcast': R. Gathorne-Hardy (ed.), *Ottoline: the Early Memoirs of Lady Ottoline Morrell* (London, 1964), p. 227.

92 'in the midst': S. Grigoriev, *The Diaghilev Ballet, 1909–1929* (Harmondsworth, 1953), p. 55.

92 'People thought and talked': T. Beecham, *A Mingled Chime* (London, 1973), p. 149.

92 'with their diamond tiaras': Charles Ricketts quoted in Buckle, *Diaghilev*, p. 232.

92 society girls: Lady Diana Cooper actually did; see Melville, *Diaghilev and Friends*, p. 122.

92 'Now I knew': M. Green, *Children of the Sun: A Narrative of 'Decadence' in England After 1918* (New York, 1977), p. 30.

93 '*Je ne sais pas*': M. Draper, *Music at Midnight* (Kingswood, Surrey, 1929), p. 143.

93 'he ate and drank': ibid., p. 188.

93 'Always he demanded': Lifar, *Diaghilev*, p. 299.

94 'the most rigorous seclusion': Romola Nijinsky, *Nijinsky; and, The last years of Nijinsky*, p. 113.

94 'to go ... Certainly not': Steegmuller, *Cocteau: A Biography*, p. 80.

94 'childishly spoiled': Stravinsky and Craft, *Memories and Commentaries*, p. 35.

94 'on the pretext': Nijinska, *Early Memoirs*, p. 339.

94 '*mon petit*'... restless: Count Harry Kessler and Kuzmin quoted in Scheijen, *Diaghilev*, p. 238.

94 'thought I went out ... horrible': Nijinsky, *Nijinsky's Diary*, p. 18.

94 'I received a moral blow ... a beast': ibid., p. 20.

95 'You have slapped ... of China': Karsavina, *Theatre Street*, p. 285 and Buckle, *Nijinsky*, p. 156. This took place in 1910. I am assuming that

Diaghilev used the feminine pronoun because it simply wouldn't have been acceptable to use the male. Whatever he may have thought Karsavina understood about his personal life, I don't think he would ever have referred to it directly with her. In the unlikely case he had said 'he', she would almost certainly have changed it herself for publication.

5 FAUNE AND JEUX, 1911–1913

96 'That's not so great … the ballet': Benois, *Reminiscences of the Russian Ballet in London*, p. 318.

97 'carry out my artistic ideas': Lifar, *Diaghilev*, p. 142.

97 'Oh, he was like the rest of them': C. Spencer, *Léon Bakst* (London, 1978), p. 98.

97 lacked taste: from Haskell, *Ballet Russe*, p. 74. Since Haskell relied heavily on Walter Nouvel's interpretation of events, we can assume that Diaghilev's 'close collaborator' to whom Haskell credits this assertion was Nouvel.

97 'sweetly sentimental': Nijinska, *Early Memoirs*, p. 315.

97 'Leaping to his feet': Lifar, *Diaghilev*, p. 146.

97 Meyerhold: *Faune* transposed to the dance stage Meyerhold's 'static Theatre' with its 'two-dimensionality, stylised posture, foreshortened stage, depersonalised performing style, totalising design, and slow "signifying" movement'. Garafola, *Diaghilev's Ballets Russes*, p. 54.

97 'moving bas-relief': Haskell quoted in Garafola, *Diaghilev's Ballets Russes*, p. 52.

98 'the source … own way': Nijinska, *Early Memoirs*, p. 315.

98 'laboratory experiments in': Haskell, *Balletomania*, p. 82.

98 'Explaining is the wrong word': Rambert, *Quicksilver: The Autobiography of Marie Rambert*, p. 59.

98 'without any preparation … the movement': Nijinska, *Early Memoirs*, p. 316 (phrases cited in different order from original source).

99 'unexpected and unusual severity': ibid., p. 328.

99 'remoteness of music': Buckle, *Nijinsky*, p. 164.

100 'compensate for': Scheijen, *Diaghilev*, p. 241.

100 perfectly musically literate: see also S. C. Berg, *Le Sacre du printemps: Seven Productions from Nijinsky to Martha Graham* (Ann Arbor, MI, 1988), p. 26.

100 'music made visible': C. W. Beaumont, *Bookseller at the Ballet: Memoirs 1891 to 1929* (London, 1975), p. 100.

100 'the courage to stand still': Buckle, *Diaghilev*, p. 251.

100 'horribly decadent': Stravinsky, *Stravinsky in Conversation with Robert Craft*, p. 165.

101 'she never makes one forget': Buckle, *Nijinsky*, p. 214.

101 'Oh, Mathildoshka … two feet': Romola Nijinsky, *Nijinsky; and, The last years of Nijinsky*, p. 160.

102 'almost as a priest … uncanny feeling of apprehension': Romola Nijinsky, *Nijinsky; and, The last years of Nijinsky*, p. 16.

102 'When she unfolded': Karsavina in Drummond (ed.), *Speaking of Diaghilev*, p. 18.

103 'dancers dreaded': Grigoriev, *The Diaghilev Ballet, 1909–1929*, p. 66.

103 'Up to then … choreographic plan': Nijinska, *Early Memoirs*, p. 427.

103 'the movement he gave': Rambert, *Quicksilver: The Autobiography of Marie Rambert*, p. 62.

103 'merely an extension … that speaks': Jacques Rivière quoted in Burt, *The Male Dancer: Bodies, Spectacle, Sexualities*, p. 90.

103 'never seen him': Macdonald, *Diaghilev Observed by Critics in England and the United States, 1911–1929*, p. 88, telegram of 18 April 1912.

104 'You will see … understood it': Nijinska, *Early Memoirs*, p. 431.

104 '"creating" a choreographer': Fokine, *Memoirs of a Ballet Master*, p. 202.

104 'This was a very unhappy': Monteux, *It's All in the Music: The Life and Work of Pierre Monteux*, p. 93.

104 'shabby, jealous little group': A. Gold and R. Fizdale, *Misia: The Life of Misia Sert* (New York, 1980), p. 156.

105 'with the weight … and sulky': Cocteau, *Journals*, p. 54.

105 300,000 francs: Garafola, *Diaghilev's Ballets Russes*, p. 187.

105 'doubts in the wings': Nijinska, *Early Memoirs*, p. 434.

105 *'plus nu que nu'*: Steegmuller, *Cocteau: A Biography*, p. 77.

105 'In the costume … be human': Romola Nijinsky, *Nijinsky; and, The last years of Nijinsky*, p. 170.

106 'introversion, self-absorbtion': Homans, *Apollo's Angels: A History of Ballet*, p. 309.

106 'thrilling. Although his movements': Sokolova, *Dancing for Diaghilev*, p. 40.

106 'Nobody was certain': Romola Nijinsky, *Nijinsky; and, The last years of Nijinsky*, p. 172.

107 'I wish that': quoted in Nijinska, *Early Memoirs*, p. 437.

107 'this wonderful evocation': quoted in Buckle, *Diaghilev*, p. 226. For a fuller understanding of this scandal, see Scheijen, *Diaghilev*, pp. 249–51 and Count Harry Kessler's diaries (published in German in 2005).

107 'WICKED PARIS': Macdonald, *Diaghilev Observed by Critics in England and the United States, 1911–1929*, p. 78.

107 'safe haven of': Garafola, *Diaghilev's Ballets Russes*, p. 57.

107 'the seesaw … against instinct': ibid., p. 58.

107 'Of course Nijinsky': Steegmuller, *Cocteau: A Biography*, p. 73.

107 'adored the … by it': Stravinsky and Craft, *Memories and Commentaries*, p. 36.

108 'I did not think': Nijinsky, *Nijinsky's Diary*, p. 203.

108 'Once you mastered': L. Sokolova in Drummond (ed.), *Speaking of Diaghilev*, p. 146.

108 'The sensation': Sokolova, *Dancing for Diaghilev*, p. 40.

108 'a refutation … without parallel': Oliveroff, *Flight of the Swan: A Memory of Anna Pavlova*, p. 163.

108 'to his own purpose': Rambert, *Quicksilver: The Autobiography of Marie Rambert*, p. 63.

108 '*Je ne suis pas*': Romola Nijinsky, *Nijinsky; and, The last years of Nijinsky*, p. 136.

108 'in spite of Diaghilev's': Benois, *Reminiscences of the Russian Ballet in London*, p. 290.

109 'evolved a sculptural line': Massine, *My Life in Ballet*, p. 84.

109 'revealed not one': Lifar, *Diaghilev* , p. 143.

109 'ill-concealed impatience': Buckle, *Diaghilev*, p. 235.

109 'very nervous … and jailer': Gathorne-Hardy (ed.), *Ottoline: the Early Memoirs of Lady Ottoline Morrell* , p. 227.

109 'sat in the garden': Lady Juliet Duff quoted in Buckle, *Nijinsky*, p. 261.

109 'I do not know': Nijinsky, *Nijinsky's Diary*, p. 41.

109 'naively … all evening': Stravinsky and Craft, *Memories and Commentaries*, p. 36. In Lady Juliet Duff's version of the event, he called her 'perroquet', a reference to her aquiline nose. See Buckle, *Nijinsky*, p. 261.

110 comparing her to a giraffe: It was a compliment. 'Lady Morrell is so tall, so beautiful, like giraffe'; Romola Nijinsky, *Nijinsky; and, The last years of Nijinsky*, p. 187.

110 'He was so different': Gathorne-Hardy (ed.), *Ottoline: the Early Memoirs of Lady Ottoline Morrell* , p. 239.

110 'from another world': ibid., p. 227.

110 'There were … his art': M. Seymour, *Ottoline Morrell: Life on a Grand Scale* (London, 1998), p. 231.

110 Bedford Square: see William Plomer's poem, 'The Planes of Bedford Square', which describes Nijinsky watching a game of tennis and crying out, *'Quel décor!'*

110 'no *corps de ballet*': Buckle, *Diaghilev*, p. 234, citing Jacques-Emile Blanche's description of the dinner.

111 'A woman and a man': Nijinsky, *Nijinsky's Diary*, p. 46.

111 'The man that I see': *Le Figaro*, 14 May 1913, cited in Nijinska, *Early Memoirs*, p. 467.

111 'When today one sees a man stroll': same interview cited in Garafola, *Diaghilev's Ballets Russes*, p. 59. See also Parker, *Nijinsky*, p. 111.

111 'waltz with changing partners': M. Hodson, *Nijinsky's Bloomsbury Ballet* (Hillsdale, NY), p. 263.

111 'The Faun is me': Nijinsky, *Nijinsky's Diary*, p. 207.

112 'Sin': Scheijen, *Diaghilev*, p. 268.

112 'perverted degeneracy': Fokine quoted in Buckle, *Nijinsky*, p. 249.

112 'If we don't lay down the law': Scheijen, *Diaghilev*, p. 252, quoting Kessler's diary.

113 *'Il ne supporte plus les désordes sexuels'*: E. Aschengreen, *Jean Cocteau and the Dance* (Gyldendal, 1986), p. 229 n. from a 1953 entry in Cocteau's journal.

113 'happy and proud': Romola Nijinsky, *Nijinsky; and, The last years of Nijinsky*, p. 182.

114 'from hotel to hotel': Cocteau, *Journals*, p. 54.

114 'I gave my whole heart to it': Nijinsky, *Nijinsky's Diary*, p. 164.

114 'I soon discovered': Romola Nijinsky, *Nijinsky; and, The last years of Nijinsky*, p. 17.

114 'with an aloof, distant air … never warmth': ibid., pp. 21–2.

115 'a rather risqué situation': C. Debussy, *Letters*, trans. R. Nichols (London, 1987), p. 260, 12 September 1912.

115 'He replied that': Calvocoressi, *Music and Ballet: Recollections of M. D. Calvocoressi*, p. 208.

115 'the best … tell you': Karsavina quoted in Nijinska, *Early Memoirs*, pp. 465–6.

116 'ballerina mentality ... forgive you': Rambert, *Quicksilver: The Autobiography of Marie Rambert*, p. 68.

116 'felt that ... a woman': Nijinsky, *Nijinsky's Diary*, p. 201.

117 'could not compose it ... never finished': ibid., p. 206.

117 'blank ... Debussy's score': Grigoriev, *The Diaghilev Ballet, 1909–1929*, pp. 91–2.

117 'What beauty ... in this?': Rambert, *Quicksilver: The Autobiography of Marie Rambert*, p. 56.

117 'second installment': Garafola, *Diaghilev's Ballets Russes*, p. 63.

118 'Monsieur Dalcroze ... young savage': Debussy, *Letters*, p. 272, 9 June 1913.

118 'had some ... and immature': Grigoriev, *The Diaghilev Ballet, 1909–1929*, p. 91.

118 'Everything in the choreography': Nijinska, *Early Memoirs*, p. 445.

118 'He was like a crumpled rose': Buckle, *Diaghilev*, p. 256.

118 'Japanese food': ibid., p. 250.

119 'Rose is a rose': Hodson, *Nijinsky's Bloomsbury Ballet*, p. 5.

119 'I must make': Buckle, *Diaghilev*, p. 238.

6 LE SACRE DU PRINTEMPS, 1910–1913

120 'entranced ... and Nijinsky': L. M. Easton, *The Red Count* (Berkeley, CA, 2002), p. 202.

120 'Bowls of monstrous strawberries': ibid., p. 203.

120 originator of the initial concept: Rambert, *Quicksilver: The Autobiography of Marie Rambert*, p. 63; P. Hill, *Stravinsky and the Rite of Spring* (Cambridge, 2000), pp. 4–6; Scheijen, *Diaghilev*, p. 212.

122 'to present the power': N. Misler in Bowlt, Z. Tregulova and N. R. Giordano (eds), *Feast of Wonders*, p. 77.

122 'some unconscious folk memory': P. C. van den Toorn, *Stravinsky and The Rite of Spring* (Oxford, 1987), p. 12.

123 'the foot ... to honour': Lifar, *Serge Diaghilev*, p. 200; letter from NR to SD.

123 'the picture of': van den Toorn, *Stravinsky and The Rite of Spring*, p. 3.

123 'they were wild about it': Hill, *Stravinsky and the Rite of Spring*, p. 26.

123 'dull, rumbling explosions': Lifar, *Ma Vie*, p. 5.

123 'the violent Russian spring': Stravinsky, *Stravinsky in Conversation with Robert Craft*, p. 164.

123 'extraordinary new ... conduct it.'": Monteux, *It's All in the Music: The Life and Work of Pierre Monteux*, pp. 88–9.

124 'When they finished ... the roots': Hill, *Stravinsky and the Rite of Spring*, p. 27.

124 'by a beautiful nightmare ... some jam': Debussy, *Letters*, p. 265; 5 November 1912.

124 'new forms must be created': Stravinsky and Craft, *Stravinsky in Pictures and Documents*, p. 30.

125 'was as helpless as a child': Grigoriev, *The Diaghilev Ballet, 1909–1929*, p. 76.

125 'something he brought': Sokolova in Drummond (ed.), *Speaking of Diaghilev*, p. 145.

125 'twice as fast': Rambert, *Quicksilver: The Autobiography of Marie Rambert*, p. 58.

126 'idea of the ballet': L. Kirstein, *Dance: A Short History of Classic Theatrical Dancing* (New York, 1969), p. 114.

126 'incessantly thinking out new ballets': Gathorne-Hardy (ed.), *Ottoline: the Early Memoirs of Lady Ottoline Morrell*, p. 227.

127 'As I danced': Nijinska, *Early Memoirs*, p. 450.

127 'Nijinsky works with passionate zeal': Stravinsky and Craft, *Stravinsky in Pictures and Documents*, p. 92.

127 'Gentlemen, you do not have to laugh': T. F. Kelly, *First Nights* (New Haven, CT, 2000), p. 281.

128 'with little bits of paper': Sokolova, *Dancing for Diaghilev*, p. 42.

128 'is the life of the stones': Macdonald, *Diaghilev Observed by Critics in England and the United States, 1911–1929*, p. 90; Nijinsky interviewed by the *Pall Mall Gazette*, 2 February 1913.

128 'declared his feud': Karsavina, *Theatre Street*, p. 236.

129 'the artist who loves all shapes': Nijinsky, *Nijinsky's Diary*, p. 56.

129 'La grace, le charme': Magriel, *Nijinsky, Pavlova, Duncan: Three Lives in Dance*, p. 20.

129 'Another vision than': E. Burns (ed.), *Gertrude Stein on Picasso* (New York, 1970), p. 65.

129 'unable to reach them': Nijinska, *Early Memoirs*, p. 461.

129 'that it was an excellent sign': Grigoriev, *The Diaghilev Ballet, 1909–1929*, p. 90.

129 'pagan worship, the religious instinct': Gathorne-Hardy (ed.), *Ottoline: the Early Memoirs of Lady Ottoline Morrell* , p. 239.

130 'as if he felt': Nijinska, *Early Memoirs*, p. 475.

130 'a wild creature ... him before': Sokolova, *Dancing for Diaghilev*, p. 38.

131 'If the work continues like this': Stravinsky and Craft, *Stravinsky in Pictures and Documents*, p. 94; 25 January 1913.

131 'You are the only one ... *muzhik*': Nijinska, *Early Memoirs*, p. 462.

131 'a blackguard, a brigand': Rambert, *Quicksilver: The Autobiography of Marie Rambert*, p. 58.

132 'how exhausting and fatiguing': Nijinska, *Early Memoirs*, p. 462.

132 'himself away with a wild leap': Nijinska, *Early Memoirs*, p. 464.

132 'more than human': Bourdelle quoted in Magriel, *Nijinsky, Pavlova, Duncan: Three Lives in* Dance, p. 56.

133 'in that sad delightful ... very quickly': Lifar, *Diaghilev*, p. 202; G. Astruc, *Le Pavillon des fantômes* (Paris, 1929), p. 286.

133 'I realised that Diaghilev': Nijinsky, *Nijinsky's Diary*, p. 110.

133 'going through a dreadful period': Gold and Fizdale, *Misia: The Life of Misia Sert*, p. 153.

133 'a little in love with him': Nijinska, *Early Memoirs*, p. 462.

134 'Get out ... and parrots': Krasovskaya, *Nijinsky*, p. 267.

134 'Nijinsky didn't take': Rambert, *Quicksilver: The Autobiography of Marie Rambert*, p. 58.

134 'no danger': Nijinska in conversation with Buckle; Buckle, *Diaghilev*, p. 247.

134 'the greatest tragic dance': Rambert, *Quicksilver: The Autobiography of Marie Rambert*, p. 63.

134 'His movements were epic': Marie Rambert to Clement Crisp, 1962; draft of an article for *Dance Research* magazine found in the Rambert Ballet's archive.

134 'picture-postcard': Kirstein, *Nijinsky Dancing*, p. 145.

134 'I think the whole thing': Cecchetti and Racster, *The Master of the Russian Ballet*, p. 226.

135 'the thousand varieties of snobbism': Cocteau, *The Cock and the Harlequin*, p. 48.

135 'I am happy to have found': 'Montjoie' in *Dossiers de Presse*, 29 May 1913, reproduced in Hill, *Stravinsky and the Rite of Spring*, p. 95.

135 'Whatever happens': Grigoriev, *The Diaghilev Ballet, 1909–1929*, p. 92.

136 'impervious and nerveless': Stravinsky, *Stravinsky in Conversation with Robert Craft*, p. 46.

136 'You may think': Monteux, *It's All in the Music: The Life and Work of Pierre Monteux*, p. 90.

136 'Exceptionally long-sleeved': Sotheby's Ballets Russes Catalogue 1972, lot 68 iv.

136 'as irritating to': Beaumont, *The Diaghilev Ballet in London*, p. 75.

137 'If that's a bassoon': P. Blom, *The Vertigo Years* (London, 2008), p. 288.

137 'with a … don't understand it': Gold and Fizdale, *Misia: The Life of Misia Sert*, p. 151.

137 'First listen!': Astruc, *Le Pavillon des fantômes*, p. 286.

137 'to exclude the audience': T. Scholl, *From Petipa to Balanchine: Classical Revival and the Modernisation of Ballet* (London, 1993), p. 74.

137 'I am sixty years old': Romola Nijinsky, *Nijinsky; and, The last years of Nijinsky*, pp. 199–200 and Cocteau, *The Cock and the Harlequin*, p. 49.

137 'an utterly new vision': Scheijen, *Diaghilev*, p. 271.

138 'Down with the whores': Kelly, *First Nights*, p. 293.

138 'the refined primitivism': Roerich p. 89.

138 'What an idiot … *dura publika*': Drummond (ed.), *Speaking of Diaghilev*, p. 113.

138 'She seemed to dream': André Levinson quoted in Kirstein, *Dance: A Short History of Classic Theatrical Dancing*, p. 288.

138 'no cathartic outpouring': Homans, *Apollo's Angels: A History of Ballet*, p. 311.

139 'Nothing could be': Scholl, *From Petipa to Balanchine: Classical Revival and the Modernisation of Ballet*, p. 75.

139 'This is not': Jacques Rivière quoted in Buckle, *Nijinsky*, p. 299.

139 'a bleak and intense celebration': Homans, *Apollo's Angels: A History of Ballet*, p. 311.

139 'excited, angry … what I wanted': Aschengreen, *Jean Cocteau and the Dance*, pp. 8–9.

140 'dress coat and top hat': Scheijen, *Diaghilev*, p. 272.

140 'You cannot imagine': Cocteau, *The Cock and Harlequin*, pp. 49–50. Aschengreen cites Stravinsky, who denied Cocteau was there that night ('Cocteau's story was only intended to make himself important'; they weren't intimate enough with him then to take him to dinner 'after such an event'); Aschengreen, *Jean Cocteau and the Dance*, p. 9. But in his diary, written at the time, Kessler remembered Cocteau being there, lending Cocteau's account more credence; Scheijen, *Diaghilev*, p. 273.

140 'as if she': Romola Njinsky, *Nijinsky; and, The last years of Nijinsky*, p. 194.

140 'and watched them': ibid., p. 195.

141 'seemed now almost': ibid., p. 208.

142 'a sound ... My God!': M. Draper, *Music at Midnight* (Kingswood, Surrey, 1929), p. 145.

142 'defeated and ... this work': A. Rubinstein, *My Young Years* (London, 1973), p. 412.

142 'really *terrible* and intense': Gathorne-Hardy (ed.), *Ottoline: the Early Memoirs of Lady Ottoline* Morrell, p. 227.

142 'much more attractive': M. Holroyd, *Lytton Strachey: a Critical Biography*, Vol. 2, *1910*–1932 (London, 1968), p. 94.

142 'that boredom and sheer anguish': ibid., p. 95.

143 'in a few years': quoted in Romola Nijinsky, *Nijinsky; and, The last years of Nijinsky*, p. 208.

143 'The fact is ... in dancing': Macdonald, *Diaghilev Observed by Critics in England and the United States, 1911–1929*, p. 100.

143 'primitive music with': Debussy *Letters*, p. 270; 29 May 1913.

143 'An artist sacrifices': Nijinsky, *Nijinsky's Diary*, p. 203.

143 'uprooted ... be reborn': quoted in Blom, *The Vertigo* Years, p. 289.

143 'one of the great': Stravinsky and Craft, *Stravinsky in Pictures and Documents*, p. 102.

144 'death warrant ... my madness': Lifar, *Diaghilev*, p. 202.

144 'Where would he be': Gold and Fizdale, *Misia: The Life of Misia Sert*, p. 133.

144 'intolerable and *mal elevé*': ibid., p. 156 and Buckle, *Diaghilev*, p. 258.

144 Friends of St Stephen's: Macdonald, *Diaghilev Observed by Critics in England and the United States, 1911–1929*, p. 84.

144 'capable of giving life': Burt, *The Male Dancer: Bodies, Spectacle, Sexualities*, p. 88.

145 'I am confident': Krasovskaya, *Nijinsky*, p. 249.

145 'Nijinsky's choreography is': Stravinsky and Craft, *Stravinsky in Pictures and Documents*, p. 102, 3 July 1913.

145 'I had to tell Nijinsky': Nijinska, *Early Memoirs*, p. 473.

145 'Let Diaghilev give it': ibid., p. 474.

146 'It's a possibility': ibid., p. 475.

146 'I shall have to part': ibid., p. 475.

7 ROSES, 1913–1914

148 'Twenty-one days': Romola Nijinsky, *Nijinsky; and, The last years of Nijinsky*, p. 218.

148 'the agreeable routine': ibid., p. 217.

149 'our art': Tamara Nijinsky, *Nijinsky and Romola*, p. 87.

149 'She is also alone': Nijinska, *Early Memoirs*, p. 478.

149 'endless talks about Nijinsky': Rambert, *Quicksilver: The Autobiography of Marie Rambert*, p. 72.

149 'he was only absorbed': Romola Nijinsky, *Nijinsky; and, The last years of Nijinsky*, p. 214

150 'harboured a burning': Tamara Nijinsky, *Nijinsky and Romola*, p. 58.

151 eating his glass: Massine, *My Life in Ballet* , p. 62.

151 'courteous … *Pas casser!*': Rambert, *Quicksilver: The Autobiography of Marie Rambert*, p. 74.

151 'Oh, she … Diaghilev's lover': ibid., p. 74.

152 'Nijinsky gave me … a lift': Romola Nijinsky, *Nijinsky; and, The last years of Nijinsky*, p. 230.

152 'Romola Carlovna … *oui, oui*': ibid., pp. 231–2.

152 'her affection was not': Tamara Nijinsky, *Nijinsky and Romola*, p. 87.

153 'This is indeed': Romola Nijinsky, *Nijinsky; and, The last years of Nijinsky*, p. 232.

153 'utterly heartless … without him': ibid., pp. 235–6.

153 'not quite sure': ibid., p. 237.

153 'I am not stupid': Nijinska, *Early Memoirs*, p. 480.

154 'saying that of all': Rambert, *Quicksilver: The Autobiography of Marie Rambert*, p. 75.

154 'rather dreary … so worried': Sokolova interviewed in Drummond (ed.), *Speaking of* Diaghilev, p. 147.

155 'strong undercurrent': Tamara Nijinsky, *Nijinsky and Romola*, p. 94.

155 'they all seemed happy': Romola Nijinsky, *Nijinsky; and, The last years of Nijinsky*, p. 241.

155 'handed to Anna': ibid., p. 245.

155 'made me notice … of happiness': ibid., pp. 245–6.

157 'madly superstitious … beloved child': Sert, *Two or Three Muses*, p. 120.

157 'Diaghilev burst out again': ibid., p. 120.

157 'As high as Nijinsky': Romola Nijinsky, *Nijinsky; and, The last years of Nijinsky*, p. 257.

157 'an escape … the friendship': Haskell, *Balletomania*, p. 67.

158 'for I believe': Tamara Nijinsky, *Nijinsky and Romola*, p. 116.

158 'a being never': A. L. Haskell, *Diaghileff: His Artistic and Private* Life (London, 1935), p. 255. Through Arnold Haskell and as Stravinsky's first ghost-writer, Walter Nouvel was one of Diaghilev's staunchest defenders against the memory of his former lover. According to him, it was the already 'debauched' (Haskell and Nouvel, *Diaghileff*, p. 252) Nijinsky who pursued Diaghilev sexually, rather than the other way round; without Diaghilev, he would have been no more than 'another brilliant dancer among brilliant dancers' (Haskell, *Balletomania*, p. 66); when Nijinsky is choreographing, 'Diaghilev can truly be said to be in sole command' (Haskell and Nouvel, *Diaghileff*, p. 71); Nijinsky did not understand music; by the time of their break Nijinsky was a 'spent force' (Haskell and Nouvel, *Diaghileff*, p. 254).

158 'had to ejaculate': Nijinsky, *Nijinsky's Diary*, p. 53.

158 'experiencing a feeling': ibid., p. 155.

159 'was not mature': ibid., p. 165.

159 'the background … flaccid will': Gold and Fizdale, *Misia: The Life of Misia Sert*, p. 124.

159 'a wild orgy': ibid., p. 160.

159 'He was sitting alone': Nijinska, *Early Memoirs*, p. 489.

160 'for treating Nijinsky': Grigoriev, *The Diaghilev Ballet, 1909–1929*, p. 101.

160 'Be kind and': Buckle, *Diaghilev*, p. 264 and Stravinsky and Craft, *Memories and Commentaries*, p. 135.

160 'Of course … moral sense': Scheijen, *Diaghilev*, p. 280 and Stravinsky and Craft, *Stravinsky in Pictures and Documents*, p. 106.

161 'There was a heavenly moment': Rambert, *Quicksilver: The Autobiography of Marie Rambert*, p. 78.

162 'I asked her': Nijinsky, *Nijinsky's Diary*, p. 143.

163 'for material things': Tamara Nijinsky, *Nijinsky and Romola*, p. 43.

163 'I am only an artist': Romola Nijinsky, *Nijinsky; and, The last years of Nijinsky*, pp. 252–3.

163 'she loved me': Nijinsky, *Nijinsky's Diary*, p. 143.

163 'a young, good-looking': ibid., p. 59.

163 'the intelligent Romola': ibid., p. 56.

163 'prevent her from': ibid., p. 12.

163 'I was petrified … be helpful': Romola Nijinsky, *Nijinsky; and, The last years of Nijinsky*, p. 255.

163 'whole world had collapsed': Sokolova, *Dancing for Diaghilev*, p. 50.

165 'engagements on golden trays': Garafola, *Diaghilev's Ballets Russes*, p. 190.

165 'something like a million francs': Scheijen, *Diaghilev*, p. 284.

165 'I can't believe': Scheijen, *Diaghilev*, p. 283 and Stravinsky and Craft, *Memories and Commentaries*, p. 38.

165 'It seems incredible': Buckle, *Nijinsky*, p. 333.

165 'his legendary irresistible charm': Nijinska, *Early Memoirs*, p. 490.

166 'When we parted': ibid., p. 491.

167 'sandwiched between': Macdonald, *Diaghilev Observed by Critics in England and the United States, 1911–1929* , p. 108. Nijinsky interviewed by *T. P.'s Magazine*, 1911.

167 'to perfect himself': Nijinska, *Early Memoirs*, p. 390.

167 'He also felt': Romola Nijinska, *Nijinsky; and, The last years of Nijinsky*, p. 257.

167 'I was the intruder': ibid., p. 258.

168 'to shrink … the end': Nijinska, *Early Memoirs*, p. 501.

168 Romola says her eyes filled with tears to see Vaslav perform after a clown and before a popular singer, but here and below I have followed the Palace's programme as reproduced in Macdonald, *Diaghilev Observed by Critics in England and the United States, 1911–1929*, p. 109.

168 'with a pang … had vanished': Beaumont, *The Diaghilev Ballet in London*, p. 79.

169 'the responsibility and': Beaumont, *Bookseller at the Ballet: Memoirs 1891 to 1929*, p. 151.

169 'It was as if': Nijinska, *Early Memoirs*, p. 503.

169 'Is this what': Nijinska, *Early Memoirs*, p. 506.

169 'a wretched choice': ibid., p. 506.

170 'Mais, il est fou': Monteux, *It's All in the Music: The Life and Work of Pierre Monteux*, p. 90.

170 'busily revising his past': R. Tarushkin quoted in van den Toorn, *Stravinsky and The Rite of Spring*, p. 17.

171 'his ignorance of': I. Stravinsky, *An Autobiography* (New York), p. 40.

171 many believed his work: like the composer François Poulenc, who saw it in his teens. See Krasovskaya, *Nijinsky*, p. 272.

171 'had attempted to do': Massine, *My Life in Ballet* , p. 152.

171 'very sensitive to': Nijinska, *Early Memoirs*, p. 456.

171 'unjust': Berg, *Le Sacre du printemps*, p. 41.

171 'by far the best': Rambert, *Quicksilver: The Autobiography of Marie Rambert*, p. 59; Nijinska, *Early Memoirs*, p. 471.

171 'This year ... always admired': Romola Nijinsky, *Nijinsky; and, The last years of Nijinsky*, p. 265.

172 'Massine's aim is': Nijinsky, *Nijinsky's Diary*, p. 37.

172 'Massine a taste for fame': ibid., p. 102.

172 'terrible beauty ... in *everything*': Easton, *The Red Count*, p. 208.

172 'all the ... whole company': Buckle, *Nijinsky*, p. 342.

172 'one single excruciating': Tamara Nijinsky, *Nijinsky and Romola*, p. 111.

172 'Now I am beginning': Gold and Fizdale, *Misia: The Life of Misia Sert*, p. 123.

173 'avaricious [and] ... nobody did': Melville, *Diaghilev and Friends*, p. 127.

173 'that cretinous lackey': Holroyd, *Lytton Strachey: a Critical Biography*, Vol. II, p. 109.

8 MEPHISTO VALSE, 1914–1918

174 'All these young men': Romola Nijinsky, *Nijinsky; and, The last years of Nijinsky*, p. 272.

175 'quarrelled for eighteen months': Nijinsky, *Nijinsky's Diary*, p. 211.

175 'I loved her': ibid., p. 142.

175 'small silk panties': ibid., p. 48.

175 'an enchanted habitation': Romola Nijinsky, *Nijinsky; and, The last years of Nijinsky*, p. 279.

176 'invent signs which': M. Sandoz, *The Crystal Salt Cellar* (Guildford, 1954), p. 66.

176 'But we loved it': Romola Nijinsky, *Nijinsky; and, The last years of Nijinsky*, p. 280.

177 'I now have a family ... such conditions?': ibid., p. 317.

178 'Everyone but Kahn': Sokolova, *Dancing for Diaghilev*, p. 80.

178 'harmed rather than abetted': Tamara Nijinsky, *Nijinsky and Romola*, p. 132.

178 'extremely pretty ... creative urge': Magriel, *Nijinsky, Pavlova, Duncan: Three Lives in Dance*, pp. 46–7.

179 'I am quartered': ibid., p. 47.

179 'energy, his ardour': ibid., p. 51.

180 'suspicious of everyone': Grigoriev, *The Diaghilev Ballet, 1909–1929*, p. 111.

180 'universally loved despite': Bourman, *The Tragedy of Nijinsky*, p. 235.

180 'pompous [and] … totally': ibid., p. 253.

180 'when he came on stage': Keynes, *Lydia Lopokova*, p. 2.

180 'I had never imagined': Garafola, *Diaghilev's Ballets* Russes, p. 203.

181 'She puts into his mouth': Sokolova, *Dancing for Diaghilev*, p. 91.

181 'not high enough': Magriel, *Nijinsky, Pavlova, Duncan: Three Lives in Dance* p. 58.

181 'Your scenery is so bad': ibid., p. 56.

181 'drenched in pathos': ibid., p. 58.

182 'taken out of': Nijinsky, *Nijinsky's Diary*, p. 159.

182 'from the front lines': Garafola, *Diaghilev's Ballets Russes*, p. 73.

182 'the most magnificent': O. Sitwell, *Great Morning* (London, 1948), p. 242.

182 $250,000: Garafola, *Diaghilev's Ballets* Russes, p. 206.

182 'negro who makes love': Buckle, *Nijinsky*, p. 360.

182 ' a serious man': C. Chaplin, *My Autobiography* (London, 1964), p. 206.

182 'The mystic world': ibid., p. 205.

183 '*un très grand artiste*': Romola Nijinsky, *Nijinsky; and, The last years of Nijinsky*, p. 142.

183 'intense poignancy': Seymour, *Ottoline Morrell: Life on a Grand Scale*, p. 232.

183 'far more … they express': Gathorne-Hardy (ed.), *Ottoline: the Early Memoirs of Lady Ottoline Morrell*, p. 239.

184 'I see a divorce … worse … worse': Romola Nijinsky, *Nijinsky; and, The last years of Nijinsky*, p. 349.

185 'felt as if': ibid., p. 353.

185 'hot blooded heterosexual': Richardson, *Picasso*, vol. 3, *The Triumphant Years*, p. 7.

186 'lots of cherries': Sandoz, *The Crystal Salt Cellar*, p. 53.

186 'fatter and fatter': Gold and Fizdale, *Misia: The Life of Misia Sert*, p. 171. Letter dated 1915.

186 'burst into the lobby … prove it': Romola Nijinsky, *Nijinsky; and, The last years of Nijinsky*, pp. 357–8.

186 'the music … but, instead': Stravinsky and Craft, *Stravinsky in Pictures and Documents*, p. 512.

186 'where the violent … stand that': A. Rubinstein, *My Many Years* (London, 1980), p. 11.

187 'He had an instinctive': Massine, *My Life in Ballet*, pp. 86–7.

187 'but like two accomplices': Romola Nijinsky, *Nijinsky; and, The last years of Nijinsky*, p. 361.

187 'I sensed now': ibid., p. 362.

188 '*Femmka*, I am sorry': ibid., p. 366.

188 'I wanted to': ibid., p. 369.

189 'how beautiful he was': F. Reiss, *Nijinsky: A Biography* (London, 1960), p. 168.

189 'One of the most endearing': ibid., p. 168.

189 'as so many vermin … him bitterly': Oliveroff, *Flight of the Swan: A Memory of Anna Pavlova*, p. 168.

189 'feverishly concerned': ibid., p. 161.

190 'utterly foreign world': ibid., p. 164.

190 'better than ever': Rubinstein, *My Many Years*, p. 12.

190 'She was cunning': Nijinsky, *Nijinsky's Diary*, p. 142.

191 'Nijinsky gave a few … endless ovation': Rubinstein, *My Many Years*, p. 16.

9 SPECTRE, 1918–1950

192 'our house … happy one': Romola Nijinsky , *Nijinsky; and, The last years of Nijinsky*, pp. 386–7.

193 'I like family life': Nijinsky, *Nijinsky's Diary*, p. 225.

193 'a very happy': Tamara Nijinsky, *Nijinsky and Romola*, p. 179, quoting a letter from Marta Grant in the *Daily Telegraph*, September 1979.

193 'Romola was the most ': Marta Grant in Tamara Nijinsky, *Nijinsky and Romola*, p. 182.

193 'looked like … it already': ibid., pp. 179–80.

193 'We decided to': Romola Nijinsky, *Nijinsky; and, The last years of Nijinsky*, p. 393.

194 'God said to me': Nijinsky, *Nijinsky's Diary*, p. 14.

194 'did not slip': P. Ostwald, *Vaslav Nijinsky: A Leap into Madness* (London, 1991), p. 226.

195 'an exquisite little girl … to grow': Sandoz, *The Crystal Salt Cellar*, p. 66.

196 'Oh no! Her grandfather': ibid., p. 68.

196 'show how dances': Romola Nijinsky, *Nijinsky; and, The last years of Nijinsky*, p. 406.

196 'I will tell her': ibid., p. 406.

196 'How dare you disturb me!': ibid., p. 407.

196 'We're at war': Sandoz, *The Crystal Salt Cellar*, p. 72.

197 'Now I will dance': Romola Nijinsky, *Nijinsky; and, The last years of Nijinsky*, p. 407.

197 'And we saw': Sandoz, *The Crystal Salt Cellar*, p. 73.

198 'it was the dance': Romola Nijinsky, *Nijinsky; and, The last years of Nijinsky*, p. 408.

198 'A shiver of fear … delicious grace': Sandoz, *The Crystal Salt Cellar*, p. 75.

198 'It must be very, very difficult': Romola Nijinsky, *Nijinsky; and, The last years of Nijinsky*, p. 408.

198 'The audience came': Nijinsky, *Nijinsky's Diary*, pp. 6–7.

198 'the sentences repeated': Romola Nijinsky, *Nijinsky; and, The last years of Nijinsky*, p. 409.

199 'To my knowledge': Nijinsky (ed.), *Diary of Vaslav Nijinsky*, p. vii.

199 'means intuitive perception': ibid., p. xlix.

199 'I am afraid': ibid., p. 10.

199 'I am God in man': Nijinsky, *Nijinsky's Diary*, p. 32.

199 'Reading it is like': M. B. Siegel, *Mirrors and Scrims: The Life and Afterlife of* Ballet (Middletown, CT, 2010), p. 19.

200 'to find out': J. D. Salinger, *Franny and Zooey* (Boston, MA, 1961), p. 33.

200 'I am not a magician': Nijinsky, *Nijinsky's Diary*, p. 73.

200 'I will eat everyone': Nijinsky, *Nijinsky's Diary*, p. 154.

200 'who prevent small birds': ibid., p. 37.

201 'To understand … well developed': ibid., p. 30.

201 'I am an Egyptian': ibid., p. 44.

201 'I am a peasant': ibid., p. 184.

201 'terrible things … terrible thing': ibid., pp. 155–6.

201 'not want people to think': ibid., p. 104.

202 'You do not want to live with me': ibid., pp. 256 and 261.

202 'had enough of this': ibid., p. 10.

202 'You think I am stupid': ibid., p. 128.

202 'more than anyone else': ibid., p. 21.

203 'I do not like': ibid., p. 56.

203 'splinters and mosaics': quoted in J. Lehrer, *Proust was a Neuroscientist* (Edinburgh, 2012), p. 177.

203 'loves me in his heart': Nijinsky, *Nijinsky's Diary*, p. 89.

203 'He is a tidy man': ibid., p. 163.

203 'She thinks that love': ibid., p. 29.

203 'wants money because': ibid., p. 174.

203 'I am an unthinking': ibid., p. 52.

203 'whirring of wings': Virginia Woolf in Lehrer, *Proust was a Neuroscientist*, p. 171.

203 'The quality of abstraction … seldom understood': Nijinsky, *Nijinsky's Diary*, p. xli.

204 'Later, too, I came to understand': Stravinsky and Craft, *Memories and Commentaries*, p. 35.

204 'he had no reason': C. Wilson, *The Outsider* (London, 1990), p. 103.

204 'a verbal expression': Nijinsky, *Nijinsky's Diary*, p. 1 (FitzLyon's note).

204 'I am standing … abandoned by God': ibid., p. xxv.

204 'I feel so much pain': ibid., pp. 144–5.

204 'I have been told': ibid., pp. 151–2.

205 'something *total* … and nowhere': Kavanagh, *Rudolf Nureyev: The Life*, p. 187.

205 'more abundant life': Wilson, *The Outsider*, p. 101.

205 'the working life … entirely destructive': John Russell quoted in John Heilpern article in *The Times*, 2 January 1982.

205 'I want to dance': Nijinsky, *Nijinsky's Diary*, p. 4.

205 'with tears in her voice': ibid., p. 141.

206 'Before us we have': Accocella in ibid., p. xxvi.

206 'I am afraid of people': ibid., p. 8.

206 'I do not know': ibid., p. 60.

206 'Come on out!': ibid., p. 16.

207 '*Femmka*, you are bringing': Romola Nijinsky, *Nijinsky; and, The last years of Nijinsky*, p. 411.

207 'a trail of madness': Gathorne-Hardy (ed.), *Ottoline: the Early Memoirs of Lady Ottoline Morrell*, p. 228.

207 'a shade worn … great art': Draper, *Music at Midnight*, p. 142.

208 'living in a dream world': Scheijen, *Diaghilev*, p. 349.

209 'If that's what': Gold and Fizdale, *Misia: The Life of Misia Sert*, p. 235.

209 'Take off … clothes on': ibid., p. 235.

212 'his dancing is': Ostwald, *Vaslav Nijinsky: A Leap into Madness*, p. 224.

212 'Why am I locked up?': ibid., p. 238.

212 'Would you believe … be created': Nijinska, *Early Memoirs*, p. 514.

213 'as though an unspoken conspiracy': Tamara Nijinsky, *Nijinsky and Romola*, p. 220.

213 'I can still taste': ibid., p. 221.

213 'Vatsa, you are being lazy … am mad': Ostwald, *Vaslav Nijinsky: A Leap into Madness*, p. 266.

214 'I can't take it': Parker, *Nijinsky*, p. 10.

214 'but he did not know me': Keynes, *Lydia Lopokova*, p. 141.

214 'almost suburban … never still': Dolin, *Autobiography*, p. 33.

214 'I had the impression … not sure': Gathorne-Hardy (ed.), *Ottoline: the Early Memoirs of Lady Ottoline* Morrell, p. 228.

214 'Nijinsky is not mad': Aschengreen, *Jean Cocteau and the Dance*, p. 229 note.

215 'captive in his own mind': Stravinsky and Craft, *Memories and Commentaries*, p. 35.

215 'was to some degree': Roy Porter, *Sunday Times* article, January 1991.

215 'biologically based … to develop': Nijinsky, *Nijinsky's Diary*, p. xv.

216 Baedeker: Drummond (ed.), *Speaking of Diaghilev*, p. 62.

216 'spiritual father': Lifar, *Diaghilev*, p. 356.

216 'our two souls': Lifar, *Ma Vie*, p. 44.

216 'I was enraptured': Lifar, *Diaghilev*, p. 302.

216 'everything and everyone': Lifar, *Ma Vie*, p. 49.

217 'Loves me? … adorable!': Lifar, *Diaghilev*, p. 345 (see also Lifar, *Ma Vie*, pp. 61–2).

217 'all the tragedy': C. W. Beaumont, *Vaslav Nijinsky* (London, 1932), p. 24.

217 'he again turned his head': Karsavina, *Theatre Street*, p. 243.

218 'With his big eyes': Scheijen, *Diaghilev*, p. 431.

218 'Who is that? … Can he jump?': Karsavina, *Theatre Street*, p. 244.

218 'Then I saw': Rambert, *Quicksilver: The Autobiography of Marie Rambert*, p. 79.

218 'she could have done more': Sokolova, *Dancing for Diaghilev*, p. 47.

218 '*Je ne veux pas!*': Lifar, *Diaghilev*, p. 348.

218 'modest, self-effacing': Stravinsky and Craft, *Memories and Commentaries*, p. 45.

218 'The longer the earth turns': Lifar, *Diaghilev*, p. 237.

219 'like two mad dogs': Sert, *Two or Three Muses*, p. 163.

219 'now, suddenly, it seems as if': Scheijen, *Diaghilev*, p. 442.

219 'Many things united us': Scheijen, *Diaghilev*, p. 443; see also Stravinsky and Craft, *Memories and Commentaries*, p. 47.

220 'the burden of taking care': Tamara Nijinsky, *Nijinsky and Romola*, p. 246.

220 'tries to act': Margaret Severn in Gottlieb (ed.), *Reading Dance* , p. 692.

221 'the only man in this world': Ostwald, *Vaslav Nijinsky: A Leap into Madness*, p. 285.

222 'Long talk later': L. Kirstein, *By With To & From. A Lincoln Kirstein Reader* (New York, 1991), p. 150.

222 'By then his masterpiece': See Richard Tarushkin's article in the *New York Times*, 14 September 2012, 'Shocker Cools into a "Rite" of Passage'.

222 'sometimes one can snatch': Kirstein, *Nijinsky Dancing*, p. 35.

222 'My wife is an untwinkling star': Nijinsky), *Nijinsky's Diary*, p. 153.

223 'punishment at school … his dependency': *The Times*, 2 January 1982.

223 'this exceptional, gentle': Ostwald, *Vaslav Nijinsky: A Leap into Madness*, p. 127.

223 'complained about everything': a doctor at Bellevue quoted in ibid., p. 306.

224 'incapable of showing': Tamara Nijinsky, *Nijinsky and Romola*, p. 209.

224 'Silently, he gazed …his heart': ibid., p. 266.

224 'How good! … the air': Lifar, *Diaghilev*, p. 376.

225 'simply relished being in his presence': Tamara Nijinsky, *Nijinsky and Romola*, p. 279.

226 'I fell in love': Buckle, *Nijinsky*, p. 435.

227 'sensation mongering … very cruel': *News Review*, 11 October 1945.

227 'Sometimes he would kiss my cheek': Buckle, *Nijinsky*, p. 436.

227 'a plump and well-contented': A. L. Haskell, *Balletomane at Large: an autobiography* (London, 1972), p. 86.

228 'like a docile child': *Sunday Chronicle*, 9 April 1950.

228 'Like gypsies': Romola Nijinsky, *Nijinsky; and, The last years of Nijinsky*, p. 565.

228 'in his glory': Buckle, *Nijinsky*, p. 442.

228 'saintly … our hearts': Tamara Nijinsky, *Nijinsky and Romola*, p. 373.

10 THE CHOSEN ONE

233 'refused to accept': Tamara Nijinsky, *Nijinsky and Romola*, p. 236.

233 'And who could blame her?': Buckle, *Nijinsky* (1980 edition), p. xxxi.

233 'both her strength': Tamara Nijinsky, *Nijinsky and Romola*, p. 33.

234 'truly awful … talentless': Roy Porter article in *Sunday Times*, January 1991.

234 'You know, they got it': Drummond (ed.), *Speaking of Diaghilev*, p. 32.

235 'Very strange. There was a Russian': ibid., p. 60.

235 'generosity was boundless': L. Garafola and N. V. N. Baer (eds), *The Ballets Russes and its World*, p. 261.

236 'sustain it ...for anyone': Drummond (ed.), *Speaking of Diaghilev*, p. 114.

236 'was the permeating genius': Draper, *Music at Midnight*, p. 141.

237 'Any outstanding work': Dolin, *Autobiography*, p. 32.

237 'much more limited': Lifar, *Diaghilev*, p. 201.

238 'I know that Diaghilev': Nijinsky, *Nijinsky's Diary*, p. 206.

238 'Diaghilev did not like me': ibid., p. 103.

238 'It was we, the painters': Lifar, *Diaghilev*, p. 141.

238 'We were all of us': Haskell, *Balletomania*, p. 95.

238 'convenient for many reasons': Kirstein, *Dance: A Short History of Classic Theatrical Dancing*, p. 283.

238 'went into his dreams': Haskell, *Balletomania*, p. 67.

239 'in reality ... clever man': Romola Nijinsky, *Nijinsky; and The last years of Nijinsky*, pp. 25–6.

239 'all the more misleading': Haskell, *Balletomania*, p. 65.

239 'artist should show himself': Beaumont, *The Diaghilev Ballet in London*, p. 40.

239 The poet Wayne Koestenbaum quoted in Kopelson, *The Queer Afterlife of Vaslav Nijinsky*, p. 214.

240 'a sign ... extremely modest': quoted in Hanna Jarvinen in K. Kallioniemi et al. (ed.), *History of Stardom Reconsidered* (Turku, 2007).

241 'although he was showman enough': Stravinsky and Craft, *Memories and Commentaries*, p. 41.

241 'there is nothing uglier': Haskell, *Balletomania,*p. 70.

241 'the risk, and': Drummond (ed.), *Speaking of Diaghilev*, p. 61.

241 'this most homosexual': Buckle, *Nijinsky*, p. 96.

242 'To make Sergey Pavlovich happy': Romola Nijinsky, *Nijinsky; and The last years of Nijinsky*, p. 109.

242 'predominantly homosexual': Buckle, *Nijinsky* (1980 edn), p. xxxii.

242 'Never, never, have I seen': Romola Nijinsky, *Nijinsky; and The last years of Nijinsky*, p. 295.

243 'in the normal man–woman': Buckle, *Nijinsky*, p. 144.

243 'of a race apart': Beaumont, *Nijinsky*, p. 25.

243 'made the relation': Arlene Croce quoted in J. L. Hanna, *Dance, Sex and Gender: Signs of Identity, Dominance, Defiance and Despair* (Chicago, IL, 1988), p. 185.

243 'Freud's chart of man's': L. Kirstein, *Movement and Metaphor: Four Centuries of Ballet* (London, 1970), p. 199.

243 'If the trilogy of *Faune*': A. Croce in Hanna, *Dance, Sex and Gender*,
    p. 185.

244 'very much akin to sex': Kavanagh, *Rudolf Nureyev: The Life*, p. 190.

244 'creative imagination': Stravinsky and Craft, *Memories and Commentaries*,
    p. 37.

244 '*sylphide étrange*': Astruc, *Le Pavillon des fantômes*, p. 138.

244 'potty. His soul': J. Mackrell, *Bloomsbury Ballerina: Lydia Lopokova,
    Imperial Dancer and Mrs Maynard Keynes* (London, 2008), p. 424.

245 'the hidden injuries of class': Richard Sennett and Jonathan Cobb, *The
    Hidden Injuries of Class* (New York, 1972).

245 'mind broke because': Kavanagh, *Rudolf Nureyev: The Life*, p. 413.

246 'Balanchine always said': E. Denby, *Dance Writings* (London, 1986),
    p. 492.

246 'At the moment': street dancer José Esteban Muñoz quoted in Stoneley,
    A Queer History of the Ballet, p. 20.

246 'a dancer can leave nothing': Mackrell, *Bloomsbury Ballerina*, p. xix.

246 'know how the great Taglioni': Haskell, *Balletomania*, p. 4.

247 'spiritual activity in physical form': Gottlieb (ed.), *Reading Dance*, p. 338
    (from Susan Sontag, French *Vogue*, December 1986).

247 'his technique': *Spectator*, 14 April 1950.

247 'incorporeal lightness': Drummond (ed.), *Speaking of Diaghilev*, p. 93;
    see also Karsavina in the *Dancing Times*, 1950.

247 'Never has any other dancer': Bourman, *The Tragedy of Nijinsky*, p. 8.

247 'the nature of the Dance': Nijinska, *Early Memoirs*, p. 517.

247 'the highest form': Massine, *My Life in Ballet*, pp. 86–7.

247 'two Nijinskys': Tamara Nijinsky, *Nijinsky and Romola*, p. 379.

247 'Where the essential Nijinsky existed': Romola Nijinsky, *Nijinsky; and
    The last years of Nijinsky*, p. 114.

247 'wrapped up … take place': Tamara Nijinsky, *Nijinsky and Romola*, p. 77.

248 'Nijinsky alone … merriment below': Draper, *Music at Midnight*, p. 187.

248 'You could never believe': Cocteau, *Journals*, p. 53.

248 'Too familiar': Cocteau, *The Cock and the Harlequin*, p. 46.

249 'I do not like': Nijinsky, *Nijinsky's Diary*, p. 128.

249 'What kind of beauty': Buckle, *Nijinsky*, p. 298.

249 'I could not agree': Nijinsky, *Nijinsky's Diary*, p. 103.

249 'I want to prove': ibid., p. 42.

249 'Now that … one else': N. Wright, *Rattigan's Nijinsky* (London, 2011),
    p. 42.

250 'Absolutely everything he invented': Drummond (ed.), *Speaking of Diaghilev*, p. 114.

250 'I would not hesitate': Rambert, *Quicksilver: The Autobiography of Marie Rambert*, p. 60.

250 Ninette de Valois: Parker, *Nijinsky*, p. 10.

250 'Had Niijinsky tried': Karsavina, *Theatre Street*, p. 151.

251 Come, come now: a very loose paraphrase of Haskell, *Balletmania*, p. 47.

251 'Ah! What poet': Francis de Moimandre's Introduction to G. Barbier, *Designs on the Dances of Vaslav Nijinsky* (London, 1913).

251 'the greatest of stage artists': C. Van Vechten, *Music After the Great War* (New York, 1915), p. 77.

251 'his dancing has the unbroken quality': Magriel, *Nijinsky, Pavlova, Duncan: Three Lives in Dance*, p. 7.

252 'I have never seen': ibid., p. 65.

252 'tiny, almost unnoticeable movements': L. M. Newman (ed.), *The Correspondence of Edward Gordon Craig and Count Harry Kessler* (London, 1995), p. 78.

252 'Looking at him': Denby in Magriel, *Nijinsky, Pavlova, Duncan: Three Lives in Dance*, p. 20.

252 'It was not only … melting tenderness': Beaumont, 'Garland for Nijinsky' in *Ballet Annual 1950*, pp. 189–90.

253 'He looks as if the body': Magriel, *Nijinsky, Pavlova, Duncan: Three Lives in Dance*, p. 21.

253 'I do not see anything … on stage': ibid., pp. 20–21.

253 'probably … some photographs': Nijinsky, *Nijinsky's Diary*, p. xliv.

254 'can be interpreted': A. Croce, *New Yorker* review of Buckle's *Diaghilev*, 12 May 1980.

Bibliography

After the hardback edition of this book came out I discovered three invaluable sources to which I wish I had had access during my research and which anyone with an interest in Nijinsky would find fascinating. The first is an app, 'Nijinsky: God of Dance' containing the entire Roger Dodge collection of Nijinsky photographs. The second is the unedited translation of Count Harry Kessler's diaries, which includes the best single description of the first night of *Sacre*: L.E. Easton, ed., *Journey to the Abyss* (New York, 2011). The third is A.R. Foster, *Tamara Karsavina: Diaghilev's Ballerina* (London, 2010).

Acton, H., *Memoirs of an Aesthete* (London, 1948)

Afanasiev, A. (ed.), *The Three Kingdoms: Russian Fairy Tales* (Moscow, 1997)

Aschengreen, E., *Jean Cocteau and the Dance* (Gyldendal, 1986)

Astruc, G., *Le Pavillon des fantômes* (Paris, 1929)

Barbier, G., *Designs on the Dances of Vaslav Nijinsky* (London, 1913)

Beaton, C., *The Glass of Fashion* (London, 1954)

Beaumont, C. W., *Enrico Cecchetti. A Memoir* (London, 1929)

—, *Vaslav Nijinsky* (London, 1932)

—, *Michel Fokine and his Ballets* (London, 1935)

—, *The Diaghilev Ballet in London* (London, 1940)

—, *Ballet Design Past and Present* (London, 1946)

—, 'Garland for Nijinsky' and 'Nijinsky's Funeral' in *Ballet Annual 1950*

—, *Bookseller at the Ballet: Memoirs 1891 to 1929* (London, 1975)

Beecham, T., *A Mingled Chime* (London, 1973)

Benois, A. S., *Reminiscences of the Russian Ballet in London* (London, 1941)

Berg, S. C., *Le Sacre du printemps: Seven Productions from Nijinsky to Martha Graham* (Ann Arbor, MI, 1988)

Blom, P., *The Vertigo Years* (London, 2008)

Bourman, A., *The Tragedy of Nijinsky* (London, 1937)

Bowlt, J., Z. Tregulova and N. R. Giordano (eds), *Feast of Wonders: Sergei Diaghilev and the Ballets Russes* (Milan, 2009)

Bruce, H. J., *Silken Dalliance* (London, 1946)

Buckle, R., *Nijinsky* (London, 1971; see the 1980 edition for the revised introduction)

—, (ed.), *Sotheby's catalogues for the Ballets Russes sales of 1968 and 1969* (London, 1972)

—, *Diaghilev* (London, 1979)

Bull, D., *The Everyday Dancer* (London, 2011)

Burns, E. (ed.), *Gertrude Stein on Picasso* (New York, NY, 1970)

Burt, R., *The Male Dancer: Bodies, Spectacle, Sexualities* (London, 1995)

Calvocoressi, M., *Music and Ballet: Recollections of M.D. Calvocoressi* (New York, NY, 1978)

Cecchetti, E. with O. Racster, *The Master of the Russian Ballet* (London, 1922)

Chagall, M., *My Life* (London, 1965)

Chaplin, C., *My Autobiography* (London, 1964)

Christiansen, R., *The Visitors: Culture Shock in Nineteenth Century Britain* (London, 2000)

Cocteau, J., *The Cock and the Harlequin (Le Coq et l'Arlequin)* trans. R. H. Myers (London, 1921)

—, *Paris Album 1900–1914* (London, 1956)

—, *Journals* (London, 1957)

—, *My Contemporaries* (London, 1967)

Code, D. J., *Claude Debussy* (London, 2010)

Cossart, M. de, *Ida Rubinstein* (Liverpool, 1987)

Croce, A., *Writing in the Dark: Dancing in the New Yorker* (Gainesville, FL, 2005)

Davenport-Hine, R., *A Night at the Majestic* (London, 2006)

Davis., M. E., *Ballets Russes Style: Diaghilev's Dancers and Paris Fashion* (London, 2010)

Debussy, C., *Letters*, trans. R. Nichols (London, 1987)

Decter, J., *Nicholas Roerich* (London, 1989)

Denby, E., *Dance Writings* (London, 1986)

Dolin, A., *Autobiography* (London, 1960)

—, *The Sleeping Ballerina* (London, 1966)

Draper, M., *Music at Midnight* (Kingswood, Surrey, 1929)

Drummond, J. (ed.), *Speaking of Diaghilev* (London, 1997)

Duncan, I., *My Life* (New York, NY, 1995)

Easton, L. M., *The Red Count* (Berkeley, CA, 2002)

Eksteins, M., *Rites of Spring: The Great War and the Birth of the Modern Age* (London, 1989)

Fitzgerald, Z., *Save Me the Waltz* (New York, NY, 1968)

Flanner, J., *Paris was Yesterday* (London, 2003)

Fokine, M., *Memoirs of a Ballet Master* (London, 1961)

Garafola, L., *Diaghilev's Ballets Russes* (New York, NY, 1989)

—, *Legacies of Twentieth Century Dance* (Middletown, CT, 2005)

Garafola, L., and N. V. N. Baer (eds), *The Ballets Russes and its World* (New Haven, CT, 1999)

Gathorne-Hardy, R. (ed.), *Ottoline: the Early Memoirs of Lady Ottoline Morrell* (London, 1964)

Gold, A. and R. Fizdale, *Misia: The Life of Misia Sert* (New York, 1980)

Gottlieb, R. (ed.), *Reading Dance* (New York, NY, 2008)

Gramont, duchesse de, *Years of Plenty* (London, 1932)

Green, M., *Children of the Sun: A Narrative of 'Decadence' in England after 1918* (New York, NY, 1977)

Grigoriev, S., *The Diaghilev Ballet 1909–1929* (Harmondsworth, 1953)

Gross, V., *Nijinsky on Stage* (London, 1971)

Guest, A. H., 'Nijinsky's Own Faune' in *Dancing Times*, January and February 1992, pp. 976 and 977.

Guest, A. H. and C. Jeschke, *Nijinsky's Faune Restored* (Philadelphia, PA, 1991)

Hanna, J. L., *Dance, Sex and Gender: Signs of Identity, Dominance, Defiance and Despair* (Chicago, IL, 1988)

Haskell, A. L., *Ballet Russe: The Age of Diaghilev* (London, 1968)

—, *Balletomane at Large: an autobiography* (London, 1972)

—, *Balletomania: The Story of an Obsession* (London, 1977)

—, (ed.), *Ballet Decade* (London, 1956)

—, with W. Nouvel, *Diaghileff: His Artistic and Private Life* (London, 1935)

Healey, D., *Homosexual Desire in Revolutionary Russia: The Regulation of Sexual and Gender Dissent* (Chicago, IL, 2001)

Hill, P., *Stravinsky and the Rite of Spring* (Cambridge, 2000)

Hodson, M., *Nijinsky's Bloomsbury Ballet* (Hillsdale, NY, 2008)

Holroyd, M., *Lytton Strachey: A Critical Biography, Vol. 2 1910–1932* (London, 1968)

Homans, J., *Apollo's Angels: A History of Ballet* (London, 2010)

Ingram, S., *Zarathustra's Sisters: Women's Autobiography and the Shaping of Cultural History* (Toronto, Canada, 2003)

Kahan, S., *Music's Modern Muse* (Rochester, NY, 2003)

Kallioniemi, K. et al. (ed.), *History of Stardom Reconsidered* (Turku, 2007)

Karsavina, T., *Theatre Street* (London, 1948)

Kavanagh, J., *Rudolf Nureyev: The Life* (London, 2008)

Kelly, T. F., *First Nights* (New Haven, CT, 2000)

Kerensky, O., *Anna Pavlova* (London, 1973)

Keynes, M., ed., *Lydia Lopokova* (London, 1983)

Khan, A., *The Memoirs of the Aga Khan* (London, 1953)

Kirkland, G., *Dancing on my Grave* (London, 1988)

Kirstein, L., *Fokine* (London, 1934)

—, *Dance: A Short History of Classic Theatrical Dancing* (New York, NY, 1969)

—, *Movement and Metaphor: Four Centuries of Ballet* (London, 1970)

—, *Nijinsky Dancing* (London, 1975)

—, *By With To & From. A Lincoln Kirstein Reader* (New York, 1991)

Kochno, B., *Diaghilev and the Ballets Russes* (New York, 1970)

Kodichek, A. (ed.), *Diaghilev: Creator of the Ballets Russes* (London, 1996)

Kopelson, K., *The Queer Afterlife of Vaslav Nijinsky* (San Francisco, CA, 1997)

Kottler, J. A., *Divine Madness: Ten Stories of Creative Struggle* (San Francisco, CA, 2006)

Krasovskaya, V., *Nijinsky* (New York, NY, 1979)

Kshessinska, M., *Dancing in St Petersburg* (Alton, Hants, 2005)

Kurth, P., *Isadora: A Sensational Life* (Boston, MA, 2001)

Kuzmin, M., *Selected Writings* (Cranbury, NJ, 2005)

Lehrer, J., *Proust was a Neuroscientist* (Edinburgh, 2012)

Levinson, A., *Bakst: The Story of the Artist's Life* (New York, NY, 1971)

Lieven, P., *The Birth of the Ballets Russes* (Woking, 1936)

Lifar, S., *Serge Diaghilev: His Life, His Work, His Legend* (London, 1940)

—, trans. J. H. Morgan, *Ma Vie: From Kiev to Kiev* (London, 1970)

Macaulay, A., *Matthew Bourne and his Adventures in Dance* (London, 2000)

Macdonald, N., *Diaghilev Observed by Critics in England and the United States 1911–1929* (London, 1975)

Mackrell, J., *Bloomsbury Ballerina: Lydia Lopokova, Imperial Dancer and Mrs Maynard Keynes* (London, 2008)

Magriel, P., *Nijinsky, Pavlova, Duncan: Three Lives in Dance* (New York, 1977)

Mallon, T., *A Book of One's Own: People and their Diaries* (London, 1985)

Massine, L., *My Life in Ballet* (London, 1928)

Masters, B., *Great Hostesses* (London, 1982)

Mellow, J. R., *Charmed Circle: Gertrude Stein & Company* (New York, NY, 1974)

Melville, J., *Diaghilev and Friends* (London, 2009)

Meyer, Baron Adolf de, *L'Après-midi d'un faune: Vaslav Nijinsky. Photographs by Baron Adolf de Meyer, with an essay by Jennifer Dunning and contributions by Richard Buckle and Ann Hutchinson Guest* (New York, 1983)

Milhaud, D., *Notes without Music* (London, 1952)

Montenegro, R., *Vaslav Nijinsky: An Artistic Interpretation of his Work* (London, 1913)

Monteux, D., *It's All in the Music: The Life and Work of Pierre Monteux* (London, 1966)

Newman, L. M. (ed.), *The Correspondence of Edward Gordon Craig and Count Harry Kessler* (London, 1995)

Nicholson, J., *The Perfect Summer* (London, 2006)

Nijinska, B., *Early Memoirs* (Durham, NC, 1981)

Nijinsky, R., *Nijinsky* (London, 1933)

—, *The Last Years of Nijinsky* (London, 1952)

—, *Nijinsky; and, The Last Years of Nijinsky* (London, 1980)

Nijinsky, R. (ed.), *The Diary of Vaslav Nijinsky* (London, 1936)

Nijinsky, T., *Nijinsky and Romola* (London, 1991)

Nijinsky, V., translated by K. FitzLyon, with an introduction by J. Accocella, *Nijinsky's Diary* (New York, 1999)

Oliveroff, A., *Flight of the Swan: A Memory of Anna Pavlova* (New York, NY, 1935)

Ostwald, P., *Vaslav Nijinsky: A Leap into Madness* (London, 1991)

Parker, D., *Nijinsky* (London, 1988)

Pavlova, A., *Pages of My Life* (New York, NY, 1947)

Peters, A. K., *Jean Cocteau and his World* (London, 1987)

Picardie, J., *Chanel: The Legend and the Life* (London, 2011)

Pritchard, J. (ed.), *Diaghilev and the Golden Age of the Ballets Russes 1909–1929* (London, 2009)

Radiguet, R., *Count Orgel's Ball* (New York, NY, 1989)

Rambert, M., *Quicksilver: The Autobiography of Marie Rambert* (London, 1991)

Reiss, F., *Nijinsky: A Biography* (London, 1960)

Richardson, J., *A Life of Picasso*, vol. 2, *1907–1917: The Painter of Modern Life* (London, 1996); vol. 3, *The Triumphant Years, 1917–1932* (New York, NY, 2007)

Rose, F., *Saying Life* (London, 1961)

Ross, A., *The Rest is Noise* (New York, NY, 2007)

Rubinstein, A., *My Many Years* (London, 1980)

—, *My Young Years* (London, 1973)

Sandoz, M., *The Crystal Salt Cellar* (Guildford, 1954)

Scheijen, S., *Diaghilev* (London, 2009)

— (ed.), *Working for Diaghilev* (Amsterdam, 2004)

Scholl, T., *From Petipa to Balanchine: Classical Revival and the Modernisation of Ballet* (London, 1993)

Sennett, R. and J. Cobb, *The Hidden Injuries of Class* (New York, 1972)

Sert, M., *Two or Three Muses* (London, 1953)

Seymour, M., *Ottoline Morrell: Life on a Grand Scale* (London, 1998)

Shapcott, T., *White Stags of Exile* (London, 1984)

Schouvaloff, A., *The Art of Ballets Russes* (New Haven, CT, 1997)

Siegel, M. B., *Mirrors and Scrims: The Life and Afterlife of Ballet* (Middletown, CT, 2010)

Sitwell, O., *Great Morning* (London, 1948)

Sokolova, L., *Dancing for Diaghilev* (London, 1960)

Sorley, K. W., *Cyril W. Beaumont* (Alton, 2006)

Spencer, C., *Léon Bakst* (London, 1978)

Steegmuller, F., *Cocteau: A Biography* (London, 1970)

Stein, G., *Selected Writings*, edited by Carl van Vechten (New York, NY, 1962)

Stoneley, P., *A Queer History of the Ballet* (London, 2007)

Storr, A., *The Dynamics of Creation* (Harmondsworth, 1976)

Stravinsky, I., *Stravinsky in Conversation with Robert Craft* (Harmondsworth, 1960)

—, *The Rite of Spring: Sketches 1911–1913* (London, 1969)

—, *An Autobiography* (New York, NY, 1998)

Stravinsky, I. and R. Craft, *Memories and Commentaries* (London, 1960)

Stravinsky, V., and R. Craft, *Stravinsky in Pictures and Documents* (London, 1979)

Tarushkin, R., *Stravinsky and the Russian Tradition* (Oxford, 1996)

Tuchman, B., *The Proud Tower* (London, 1997)

Vaill, A., *Everybody was so Young* (Boston, MA, 1998)

van den Toorn, P. C., *Stravinsky and the Rite of Spring* (Oxford, 1987)

Van Vechten, C., *Music after the Great War* (New York, NY, 1915)

Wilson, C., *The Outsider* (London, 1990)

Wolkonsky, S., *My Reminiscences*, vol. 2 (London, 1925)

Wright, N., *Rattigan's Nijinsky* (London, 2011)

Acknowledgements

This book began with an article about the Ballets Russes that I hoped to write but never did, so the first people I want to thank won't have any idea why: Charlotte Sinclair of *Vogue*; Elinor Hughes and Tim Morley, who, promoting the Diaghilev exhibition at the Victoria and Albert Museum in 2010, encouraged my growing interest in Nijinsky even though I couldn't find anyone to commission me to write about him; and Deirdre Fernand, who unwittingly gave me the final push when she suggested that despite my being neither a dance critic nor a dancer, writing a book about ballet need not be an impossible dream.

Many people helped and advised me while I worked on the book. I am grateful to the staffs of the British Library; the library of the Victoria and Albert Museum and its Theatre Collection at Blythe House; Bob Kosovsky and Amy Schwegel of the New York Public Library, music and dance divisions respectively; Tom Clark; Fiona Porter; Pieter Symonds and Arike Oke of the Rambert Ballet Company and Ann Stewart, whom I met through them, as well as Marc Farah, for putting me in touch with Pieter in the first place. Nuala Herbert gave me a valuable insight into the *Rite of Spring* and Pell Mountain lent me Russian books that I could not have seen elsewhere. Roger Gibbs kindly discussed which house in St Moritz Nijinsky and Romola had lived in and which toboggan run they might have used. My father, John Moore, stepfather, Josh Miller, and Lady Bateman read the book in draft and supplied me with important corrections.

Living in Simon and Lucy Harrison's house while I wrote the book gave me the gift of a study with a door I could close behind me. And Haydee Dullas ensured that I never worried about my children when I was thinking about Nijinsky. Most of all, though, I am indebted to my husband, whose unfailing love and support make everything possible; work is the least of it.

Grateful thanks are due to Andrew Franklin, Daniel Crewe, Penny Daniel, Valentina Zanca and everyone at else Profile Books as well as Jane Robertson, who negotiated my typescript, and with all of whom it has been a delight to work at every stage. Pryor Dodge of the Dodge Collection, and Dr Hans-Michael Shäfer of the Neumeier Foundation provided most of the exquisite photographs and drawings which illuminate the book. Andrew Kidd has been (as expected) the best of agents: I hope there will be many more projects like this in our future together.

One of the greatest pleasures of this book was working again with the late Peter Carson, who commissioned it and continued to edit and support it even after retiring. I count myself immensely privileged to have been one of his writers.

List of Illustrations

INTERIOR ILLUSTRATIONS

Frontispiece: Nijinsky in *Le Spectre de la Rose* by Valentine Hugo (Paris, 1912). Sketch: Stiftung John Neumeier – Dance Collection.

p. 77 Nijinsky and Karsavina in *Le Carnaval* by Ernst Oppler (Berlin, *c.* 1910, printed 1921). Sketch: Stiftung John Neumeier – Dance Collection

p. 88 Nijinsky backstage after a performance of *Le Spectre de la Rose*, by Jean Cocteau (Paris, 1913). Sketch: Stiftung John Neumeier – Dance Collection

p. 107 Pen-and-ink drawing by Emile Antoine Bourdelle, Nijinski in *Le Carnaval*, (Paris, *c.* 1910), located in Musee Bourdelle Sketch: © Roger-Viollet/TopFoto

p. 114 Nijinsky and the Nymphs in *Afternoon of a Faun*, by Ernest Oppler (Berlin, 1912). Sketch: Stiftung John Neumeier – Dance Collection

PLATES

1. Nijinsky in the dress uniform of the Imperial Theatre School, *c.* 1900. Photo: Roger Pryor Dodge Collection
2. Nijinsky and Anna Pavlova in the first version of *La Pavillion d'Armide*, 1907. Photo: Roger Pryor Dodge Collection
3. Nijinsky in Paris, 1909. Photo: Roger Pryor Dodge Collection
4. Publicity stills for the 'Danse Siamoise', by Druet, Paris, 1910. Photo: Roger Pryor Dodge Collection

While every effort has been made to contact copyright-holders of illustrations, the author and publishers would be grateful for information about any illustrations where they have been unable to trace them, and would be glad to make amendments in further editions.

Index